CHILDREN'S PHANTASIES

O. Weininger

CHILDREN'S PHANTASIES

The Shaping of Relationships

O. Weininger

Karnac Books
London 1989

First published in 1989 by
H. Karnac (Books) Ltd.
58 Gloucester Road
London SW7 4QY

Copyright © 1989
by Otto Weininger

British Library Cataloguing in Publication Data

Weininger, Otto
    Children's phantasies: the shaping of relationships.
    1. Children. Development. Role of fantasies.
    I. Title
    155.4'18

ISBN 0-946439-54-0

Printed in Great Britain by A. Wheaton & Co., Ltd., Exeter

CONTENTS

FOREWORD

Hanna Segal

The concept of unconscious phantasy is one of the earliest and most fundamental concepts in psychoanalysis.

Freud first refers to phantasy in a letter to Fliess, and throughout his letters to Fliess and drafts for his papers on hysteria he ponders on the relation between phantasy, memory, dreams and symptom formation. Originally he considers phantasy as a defence against memory. Gradually his view extends to phantasy being a defence against reality as well as against memory. He also mentions that sometimes phantasy is promoted by impulses. He comes to see it as underlying and being embodied in hysterical symptoms and also as playing a fundamental role in the aetiology of all neuroses. But, unlike later workers, he sees unconscious phantasy as appearing fairly late in mental development. For instance, in the 'Formulations on the Two Principles of Mental Functioning' (1911b) he says:

With the introduction of the reality principle one mode of thought activity was split off; it was kept free from

reality-testing and remained subordinated to the pleasure principle. This activity is phantasizing.

He also sees that unconscious phantasy plays a part in
artistic creativity, but it is unclear in his writing to what
extent he considered phantasy as a fundamental part of
development, active and evolving throughout life. For instance, when he speaks of auto-eroticism as an outcome of
secondary narcissism, a turning to an introjected breast, he
does not actually spell out that this introjected breast is an
unconscious phantasy. And when he speaks of children's
sexual theories, he does not describe them as fantasies, nor
does he relate them to unconscious phantasies.

Freud's discovery of the unconscious processes was also
the discovery of unconscious phantasy and symbolism
because he reached unconscious conflicts and impulses
through understanding the symbolic language of symptoms
embodying unconscious phantasies. But he himself did not
seem to give to this function quite the weight that was given
to it by subsequent workers. Melanie Klein, working with
small children, was impressed by the dynamic power and
the ubiquity of unconscious phantasy underlying all the
child's activities, play, work and relationships. Moreover,
the younger the child, the more dominated his relationships
and activities seemed to be by unconscious phantasies,
whilst the older the child, at least in the case of children not
too grossly disturbed, the more they could relate to reality.
That, one could say, is obvious; gradually the reality
principle is getting established. However, unconscious
phantasy could be seen to be active before this, rather than
a reaction to the reality principle having been established.
She found on investigation both of children and adults that
whilst they were more and more related to reality, the
unconscious phantasy did not stop or was not necessarily
split off from reality. It underwent a change in content and
in its relation to reality. I have put forward the view that
reality testing is in essence a testing of unconscious
phantasy with the reality experience. Mental health is in a

large measure related to the individual's capacity to tolerate discrepancies between the unconscious phantasies and the reality experience and learning from that experience, a theme also developed by W. Bion.

Otto Weininger, who is Professor of Applied Psychology at the Ontario Institute for Studies in Education, illustrates in this book the manifestations of unconscious phantasy in children, normal, neurotic or psychotic, in various settings such as playgroups, ordinary schools or special schools for disturbed children, the family milieu or play therapy. He uses Melanie Klein's developmental theory and shows the evolution of phantasies in their content, in the way they are symbolized and their functioning in terms of the child's evolution from the paranoid–schizoid position to the depressive position and the Oedipus complex. To facilitate the reading of this book by those not familiar with Melanie Klein's work, it may be worth while to describe briefly the theory that she uses. In Klein's view, from the beginning the infant is capable of forming relationships predominantly in phantasy but also in reality. From the moment of birth he/she is exposed to a welter of perceptions, pleasant and unpleasant, and impulses, loving and hating. He/she deals with this situation of chaos by the mechanism of splitting—a kind of primitive sorting out of what is good and what is bad. Impulses are linked with the phantasy of objects. The infant's hungers and desires lead him to phantasizing an ideal object that will satisfy all desires, and he tries to expel from his inside all pain and hatred and attributes them to a bad external object—the bad breast. The good external experiences are attributed to the ideal breast that he/she wishes to incorporate and identify with, whereas the bad experiences are attributed to the bad one. From the beginning therefore there is an interplay of projection and introjection. The infant's projections create ideal and persecutory figures that colour his experience of reality. Those figures also get introjected. Not only the ideal breast, as in original desire, but, for various reasons, the persecutory one also gets introjected. In that way the infant builds, to begin with, an internal world peopled with phantastic objects with extreme characteristics. But there is also an interplay between phantasy and reality, since from the beginning some reality sense operates and whilst phantasy colours and distorts the external experience, at the same time reality corrects and modulates the phantasy.

The earliest stage of development, which Klein called the paranoid–schizoid position, is characterized by the split of both the ego and the object and a prevalence of omnipotence and of projective processes. But if the infant is able to tolerate the discrepancies between phantasy and reality, the split gradually diminishes. The good and bad objects and the good and bad parts come closer together. The infant or child becomes more aware of his ambivalence to a mother who is both good and bad. Still under the dominance of a largely omnipotent phantasy, he becomes concerned about the damage he is doing to his object and therefore conscious of guilt and fear of loss. And since this object is introjected, he also has an experience of a destroyed internal world and self. This change of the state of integration and the change in the content of phantasies that go with it have far-reaching consequences. Idealization and dread of persecution give way to the capacity of love for a more real object, a capacity for and awareness of one's aggression and the creative wish to make reparation. And as it is an important part of reparation to free the object from control and distortion by projections, the reality sense increases and a differentiation is gradually established between the external and the internal reality. As a result of those changes, not only does the content of phantasy change, but it also loses its omnipotent character and can become a source of sublimation and creativity. This fundamental transition between the paranoid–schizoid and depressive mode of functioning is a nodal point in development.

Professor Weininger has a wide experience of children in all settings. Among his many activities he was involved in setting up and directing a school for seriously emotionally disturbed children alongside a clinic that he also directed.

He also developed a family court clinic. He worked a great deal with babies, children and adolescents and did research on cognitive and emotional processes. Most of this book was written while he was on sabbatical leave at the University of British Columbia where he was attached to the Child Study Center and had the opportunity of being with young children many hours a day. His book is an outcome of an exceptionally wide and rich experience. He observes very sensitively and shows how his understanding of unconscious phantasy can throw light on most diverse activities and relationships.

In the last section of the book Otto Weininger gives an account of a psychoanalytic psychotherapy done under his supervision. The therapist's technique is eclectic; but Professor Weininger's understanding of the material is wholly psychoanalytic and informed by a deep understanding of Klein's work. He shows the evolution of the child's phantasies about his family and himself in his play involving an imaginary family of snakes. This material is very moving and convincing.

W hat do young children imagine? How do these thoughts influence what they do and say? And how do their actions and speech affect their relationships with other children, with parents and adults? Children think all the time: sometimes they show their thoughts through play, at other times they play and describe what they are doing, or they may sit beside us and tell us about their very private thoughts and imaginations. It is only when they trust and recognize that adults are willing and interested to discuss their thoughts that children begin to show the complexity, both frightening and satisfying, of their thinking—even at two years of age.

In this book I describe my conversations with young children and the thoughts, imaginations and phantasies[1]

---

[1]Phantasy refers to the content of the unconscious mental processes present in all individuals and is primarily concerned about objects. Very early phantasies, the 'earliest impulses of desire and aggressiveness, are expressed in and dealt with by mental processes far removed from words and conscious relational thinking, and determined by the logic of emotion' (Isaacs, 1948, p. 84).

they slowly revealed to me after I had played with them for several months. Some of the children are normal young boys and girls, some of them are emotionally upset, but all have desirable as well as frightening thoughts. The difference between these two groups of children is that the healthy young children are flexible and adaptable enough to play out and understand these frightening phantasies and also continue to feel good about themselves by experiencing satisfying feelings. Emotionally disturbed children, on the other hand, rarely understand their frightening feelings, and they cannot always put aside feelings by playing out what they want. Only play psychotherapy helps these children to change their rigid defenses and allows them to understand their fears. They also have difficulty experiencing feelings of satisfaction and the resultant feelings related to good self-esteem. If these children do something that suggests that they are capable, then they often panic, imagining that whatever *goodness*[2] they have gained will be quickly taken from them. They cannot accept goodness, not because they do not want to 'feel good', but because they unconsciously believe that they have stolen or robbed someone to gain this and that some form of retaliation will follow as a consequence. This unconsciously affects their relationships to others, and they either fight or withdraw, usually in terror. Healthy children may, of course, also withdraw or attack; but they do not show this as a constant pattern. Their flexibility and adaptable control allow them to perceive others as non-threatening and loving.

I describe the way children react to their imaginations and phantasies in light of several major Kleinian constructs and thus demonstrate the continued vitality and viability of Melanie Klein's way of understanding children's play, thoughts and relationships. Over the many years that I

---

[2]Goodness is a quality that I think children feel they have—a quality that keeps away badness or evil.

have worked with children and adults, I have found that Kleinian constructs have been invaluable in providing an understanding of unconscious motivation and in helping me to develop my own ideas about human nature.

O. Weininger

ACKNOWLEDGEMENTS

I am continually impressed with how much young children have to teach us about their world. There have been times when I have felt somewhat smug and thought—well, surely, now, after more than 25 years of working with little children and their parents, I know a great deal about their thinking, their emotions and their imagination. But then along comes another child to let me know that her feelings, her ideas, her spoken words and her gestures contain so much we 'child-watchers' still have to understand.

However, for what they have already helped me to understand about their lives, I am truly and deeply grateful. So many children have told me about their private thoughts, their pleasures and pains, their likes and dislikes, their despair and hopes, their fears and bravery, their hates and their loves. I want to thank all of these children who talked so earnestly, often with such passion and with what seemed to me a great desire that I really understand what they were telling me. I feel very fortunate for having met these children and for having the opportunity to be with them for many hours.

There are so many other people who have helped me. My students have listened to me as I narrated some of the children's thoughts and ideas, they have helped me by questioning my understanding of the children's thoughts, and in doing so they have brought many things into clearer focus.

Elizabeth Church and Mary Morris helped me with the editing and re-editing of my manuscript, and I want to thank them for the hours they spent reading our words, both the children's and my own. They encouraged and supported my work, and they were kind even when they criticized me.

I find that when I am about to write something, I 'write' it in my head first and then put my thoughts to paper. I often realize that this must be very hard on those who are closest to me, because at that time I do not respond very well. I must seem distant, if not aloof—but the 'head-writing' takes precedence over all my other feelings. I think that Sylvia, my wife, must feel lonely at such times, and I thank her for being patient and caring about me and my work. I am sure that Mary Macri and Johanna Cutcher, my long-time friends, felt my preoccupation—and they continued to help me with my work. I want to thank them very much for the 'space' they gave me.

Teeya Scholten, whose psychotherapy with a ten-year-old boy is contained in this book, was kind enough to allow me to report upon our work. I think this takes courage and trust; I hope I have reported our work effectively, and I am grateful for the time we talked and worked together.

I am sure there are many, many others who have helped me in writing this book—and while I will not name them all, I want them to know how appreciative I am of all their support.

CHILDREN'S PHANTASIES

INTRODUCTION

Everything, good or bad, that we have gone through from our earliest days onwards, all that we have received from the external world and all that we have felt in our inner world, happy and unhappy experiences, relationships to people, activities, interests and thoughts of all kinds—that is to say, everything we have lived through—makes part of our selves and goes to build up our personalities. If some of our past relationships, with all the associated memories, with the wealth of feelings they called forth, could suddenly be wiped out of our lives, how impoverished and empty we should feel! How much love, trust, gratification, comfort and gratitude, which we experienced and returned, would be lost! Many of us would not even want to have missed some of our painful experiences, for they have also contributed to the enrichment of our personalities. [Klein & Riviere, 1953, p. 111]

In her pioneering explorations of the relevance of Freudian theory to the earliest stages of psychic development, Melanie Klein created not only a new system of analysis, but also a new form of treatment

1

particularly suited to the needs of children: play psychotherapy. She not only enormously enhanced our understanding of the family drama that shapes each life, but
also grasped the crucial importance of play as a key to this
understanding. Play is 'not only a way of exploring and
mastering the external world but also, through expressing
and working through phantasies, a means of exploring and
mastering anxieties. In play the child dramatizes his
phantasies, and in doing so elaborates and works through
his conflicts' (Segal, 1979, p. 30). The primary aim of this
book is to explore the relevance of Klein's analytic theory
(for a review of Klein's theory, see Weininger, 1984) to our
experiences as parents, teachers and clinicians. In the
chapters that follow I outline the ways in which Klein's
insights can illuminate our understanding of a whole
spectrum of children's experience, ranging from the inevitable and productive crises of normal development to its
most profound disturbances. As Klein points out:

> No child's mind is free from fears and suspicions, but if
> the relation to our parents is built predominantly upon
> trust and love, we can establish them firmly in our minds
> as guiding and helpful figures, which are a source of
> comfort and harmony and the prototype for all friendly
> relationships in later life. [Klein & Riviere, 1953, p. 113]

Let me illustrate this with an example of a normal little
boy's relationship with his mother during a crisis. Tim was
three years old. His mother had recently suffered a
miscarriage, and she told me that she had been very upset
for quite a while afterwards. This baby had been very much
wanted and anxiously awaited, and with the miscarriage
both she and her husband felt very sad for about three
months. Tim responded to their sadness at times by
withdrawing, and at times with anger. He was easily
frustrated, and, whereas before he would stay with a task,
now he not only gave up quickly, but he also protested
loudly. His behaviour changed one morning when he

announced to his mother that he wanted to have a uterus. His mother was surprised and somewhat shocked and told him that boys have penises. Nevertheless, Tim stated that he didn't want a penis, he wanted a uterus. When his mother said that he was like his father and he had a penis and that all boys have penises and that all girls and mummies have uteruses, Tim persisted, answering that he didn't want a penis, he wanted to have a uterus. Finally, when his mother asked him why he wanted to have a uterus, Tim stated that he would then be able to have a baby.

I had the opportunity to observe Tim as he played with a fire-engine at his play-school; the fire-engine had a long projectile ladder, which he erected and pushed into the space on the lower shelf, thereby knocking off the crayons, toys, blocks and paper. Tim said that his fire-engine ladder was big and that it could 'push off the toys'. I asked Tim if fire-engine ladders could also save people if there was a fire. His answer was startling: 'It always hurts'. I suggested that it could also rescue and make others feel better, and he answered, 'Maybe, but this one doesn't', and proceeded to knock the objects off the shelf. Tim continued to say that he wanted to change his penis for a uterus and to have a baby. Tim knew that 'ladies have babies', and he 'wanted to have a baby'. Tim's play demonstrated that his penis was a dangerous object and by its erectile nature could penetrate in harmful ways. Tim also phantasized that his penis penetrated mother and caused her to lose the baby. Tim's baby was to be offered as reparation[1] for his mother's miscarriage, which Tim considered he had caused.

In conversation with his mother I said that Tim needed to do something 'nice' for his mother and that he felt responsible for her miscarriage. I suggested that she have Tim help her with the housework, and have him do the special work of cleaning rugs with the vacuum-cleaner. I expected that by doing the vacuuming Tim would phantasize that he was offering to repair the love object, the mother, and that he would no longer need to give his mother the desired baby. His mother was surprised at my remarks but agreed to let him help her.

Tim took to cleaning the rugs with great vigour; he enjoyed the movement of the vacuum-cleaner, the long hose, and the way the dirt 'just was gone'. Tim helped his mother every day for the next three weeks, and gradually his relationship to her changed. He no longer talked about wanting a uterus, and he was no longer angry and impulsive; he became the 'easy-going', friendly, interested little boy his parents had known a few months earlier.

Tim's anxiety about the phantasized damage and subsequent miscarriage created a potentially serious threat to the relationship between son and mother. The opportunity to do something 'good' and clean up 'dirt' re-established their trusting and loving relationship. The relationship between Tim and mother went back on-track. They once again enjoyed each other, were no longer anxious and tense when they were together, and they had effectively worked through a crisis. Tim is a young boy who is developing normally, and so he and his mother could work through the crisis fairly easily. If Tim had been an emotionally disturbed child, this crisis would not have been worked through so easily or so well without the appropriate intervention of play psychotherapy and parental guidance.

Throughout this book I have attempted to link the shapes of normal development with their pathological distortions by detailed reference to examples drawn from my own experiences—as a delighted visitor in playgroups and preprimary classrooms, as a practising psychotherapist and as the director for several years of a special school for severely emotionally disturbed children. The first parts of the book follow the basic Kleinian theory of psychic growth through the paranoid–schizoid, depressive and Oedipal 'positions'.[2] The remaining parts apply Klein's basic concepts to a variety of practical and professional problems. Thus, for example, the concept of 'reparation'—as reflected in Tim's 'helping' his mother—is dealt with in relation to the earliest normal expressions of aggression and the Oedipal drama (chapters three, five, six) and as a crucial element in cognitive development (chapters four, seven), which must be taken into account in educational planning (chapter nine). Similarly, the more specifically clinical problem of 'transference' is addressed directly in a chapter on the basic techniques of play psychotherapy. Transference is also tacitly reflected throughout the book in my own—sometimes uneasy—position as observer–participant in classroom or social settings and then dramatized at some length in the 'snake family' case (chapter eleven).

This book moves from general observations of children's behaviour to theoretical and specifically professional—that is, pedagogical or clinical—concerns, and in conclusion focusses on a direct detailed report of certain selected aspects of a supervised case of play psychotherapy with a ten-year-old boy, whose vivid presence will, I hope, stay with the reader as long as it has with me.

NOTES

1. Tim offers a *gift* to his mother. Reparation is an ego function directed at the wish to restore. 'What the infant wants to do is to recreate mother and maintain her as a good internal object' (Weininger, 1984, p. 37) and to make sure she is not hurt, damaged or injured by any of his phantasies.
2. Position is a 'mental configuration' characterized by a specific aspect of object relations (Weininger, 1984, p. X), where object relations indicate the relation of a person to his or her object.

PART ONE

Good, bad and enough:
some basic processes
in the paranoid–schizoid position

CHAPTER ONE

Splitting and idealization

Jane, aged four years and four months, was normally a pleasant member of a playgroup in which I recently participated. One day she came up to me and called me 'a very bad person'. In mock attack, she began to wave her fists, while at the same time opening and closing her mouth as if to devour me. While this episode was precipitated by her frustration at play, its psychic origins may be traced back to the earliest moments of life—to the 'splitting'[1] between good and bad and the complex projection and introjection of these qualities. These defensive mechanisms characterize the child's first responses to existence. (For an elaboration of the paranoid–schizoid position see Segal, 1973; Weininger, 1984.)

The incident started in the 'grocery store' centre of the playroom, an area where a pretend store had been set up with a real cash-register on a counter and shelves of tins, boxes of biscuits and baby foods. Jane wanted to take over James's job as cashier and was very angry with me because I would not allow her to push him away and physically prevented her from doing so by placing myself between the two children. After her 'attack' on me she went off to another centre in the room, where one of the teachers was playing with some other children. She dropped herself down on the teacher and told her that she hated 'him', pointing to me across the room. Then she whispered in the teacher's ear that she liked some of me and that some of me was good, but 'right now he has a lot of bad'.

Jane remained with the teacher for a short time and then wandered back, this time trying not to look at me. When I asked her why she wasn't looking at me, she replied, 'Because I don't want to see the bad', and I think she meant 'the bad in you'. Jane continued to skirt the area and then said that maybe there 'was not more bad' because she would wait her turn. Jane did wait for a few minutes, and then she was able to have her turn as cashier.

This playgroup outburst with its resolution shows some of the basic characteristics of the splitting process, one of the earliest mechanisms the infant uses to cope with and defend against anxiety, here acted-out by a four-year-old whose capacity to handle her feelings was still limited. When Jane felt something, she needed to have the feelings acknowledged and satisfied. If this did not happen, she became angry, but she was not able to be angry at herself, because she was too young to understand that she had to wait her turn. She projected onto me her angry impatience and the anxious feelings of persecution associated with it—that is, the feeling that someone was going to make her do something. Was I not, after all, the bad object who was literally blocking her way? As I was now the bad object, she went elsewhere to complain. However, Jane had played with me several times before and had obviously enjoyed herself; thus, even when confronted with a clear instance where I was frustrating her, Jane could not see me as entirely bad. Her reaction to this difficult and frustrating situation was to have the bad part of me stop her from doing what she wanted. But as her splitting was normal and had not led to rigidity of thought and action, she was able to preserve the earlier pleasure we had shared and to acknowledge some good in me.

By projecting her *badness* onto me but by also being able to recognize some good in me, Jane could then wander around the centre awaiting her turn, and, as she said shortly afterwards, there was 'no more bad'—no more projected attacks and no anticipated retaliation. The anxiety of this persecution could diminish because while she was splitting, she could still see sufficient good within me to make me not only attractive, but also not so damaged or destroyed that I would seek revenge. Time, reflection and her essential health were combined with the calm 'containing' by the teacher to bring this episode to a satisfying resolution. Here, as so often happens, the easy, though by no means crisis-free, atmosphere of the playgroup allowed the processes of learning about the self and the world to reveal their essential psychic shapes.

The process of splitting is the infant's way of dealing with the formless anxiety that originates with the very meaning of life itself, a life vulnerable to annihilation. In phantasy the infant splits the primal object, the breast, which is the source of all of his or her experiences of satisfaction and frustration, into 'good' and 'bad' in order to maintain the breast's good, nurturing, satisfying qualities. The breast has been gratifying, and this gratification is expressed as love towards the object, but the breast is also frustrating because it is not always present, nor does it flow as freely as the infant may wish. Sometimes the flow of milk is too slow, at other times too fast; at times the nipple slips out of the infant's mouth, or it may make the baby feel as if he or she is suffocating because it closes the baby's nostrils. The unconscious phantasies attached to such temporary frustrations within this oral phase are that the breast is 'ungiving', or trying to 'smother'. In part because of the infant's projected anger towards the breast, in part because of his or her fear of retaliation, the breast is phantasized as attacking. It thus becomes persecutory as well as gratifying as it becomes associated with both 'good' and 'bad' feelings. However, the infant's ego is not sufficiently stable or coherent to accept such conflicting attributes. The infant deals with such conflict by splitting the breast. As a result, there is now in the infant psyche a distinction between love and hate, which persists because of the symbolic splitting of the breast into good and bad part-objects.

As we have seen, the demand for continual gratification is the source of the infant's anger. At first this anger is expressed as oral hostility—impulses to attack, devour, destroy and break up the breast into fragments. At times the infant will *take in* a bad breast—one experienced as damaging his or her insides, from which he or she needs some protection. The bad fragments make up the bad part-object breast, whereas the loving, gratifying part remains as the good part-object breast. The good part-object maintains an integration of the immature coherence of the developing ego. It is this good part-object that is introjected into the ego and maintained safe by a continuing splitting and projection process.

The infant's ego, which is fragile at best, needs the containing capacity of the mother or the person caring for the infant. It is exceptionally important for the mothering person to be an active presence. The mother provides both psychological and physical support. She continues to reappear after leaving the infant's presence. She interprets her infant's crying not just as attention-seeking but as a signal that the baby needs nurturing. Rather than creating extra frustration by letting the baby 'cry it out', she recognizes that something is bothering him or her. I do not think that a parent will 'spoil' the baby with this sort of continuous care; rather, it is the lack of continuity of care that will damage the baby by creating a premature 'independence' (Weininger, 1982), in which infants quickly learn that they cannot count on their parents and that they have to make use of their own resources, which are, at this point, largely persecutory. Thus they begin to insulate themselves from others in an effort to avoid persecution and so reduce their dependency (Bick, 1968). In other words, 'they try to go it alone'—and, of course, in so doing they continuously feel frustrated. The residual phantasy of being attacked simultaneously reinforces the need to be independent and adds to the sense of persecution. At best, a vicious cycle of difficult interactional behaviour will ensue; at worst, an autistic closing-down occurs.

However, at all times, and probably with all infants, feelings of frustration threaten the quality of the internal good part-object. If the mothering person is not able to be 'continually present' in phantasy, the good part-object may lose its strength, and the infant will feel as if everything is 'bad' inside. The result may be continued crying, fretfulness, difficulty in feeding, gagging and spitting up—generally 'colicky' behaviour. Accompanying sleeping difficulties seem to reflect the phantasies of utter vulnerability to an attacking bad breast, which surface in nightmares. Parents describe children at about two or three months waking up with a start, crying even before they are awake, looking 'wild-eyed', thrashing about in their cribs and even hitting their heads on the quilted bars. When I question the parents, they say that feeding was often difficult. The infants would not want to eat, were fussy, and when the parents did get some food into them, would usually spit it out quickly and angrily. Distraction sometimes worked, but generally feeding times were very difficult, and the more distraught the parents became—because they thought that the infant was not getting enough food—the more upset the infant became. I think that these infants felt persecuted by the food—that is, food had become the symbolic equivalent of the attacking bad breast.

As splitting of the object occurs in an effort to try and maintain some freedom from attack, a corresponding split occurs within the ego:

> Therefore the phantasies and feelings about the state of the internal object influence vitally the structure of the ego. The more sadism prevails in the process of incorporating the object, and the more the object is felt to be in

bits, the more the ego is in danger of being split in relation to the internalized object bits. [Klein, 1946, p. 101]

This process of distortion may be reflected in children's behaviour, but its effects may also persist into adulthood. The following two cases—one of a two-year-old with a relatively easily isolatable physical 'flap', the other a 30-year-old with a complex pattern of neurotic symptoms—suggest the range of problems that can emerge.

When I first met the two-year-old girl whom I had been asked to see because of her strange behaviour, I was immediately aware of her symptom: the unusual, apparently defensive waving of her hands, which began as soon as she came into the examining room. As she toddled about, seemingly unaware of the furniture in the room and bumping into it, she waved her hands in front of her face in a side-to-side motion, almost as if she were brushing away some invisible things. The action made me think of a car's windscreen wipers as they clean the glass. I asked the mother when this motion had started, and she told me that she thought it had begun when her daughter was three months old and had accidentally been scalded by some hot milk. No physical scars remained, but since that time the girl had gradually developed this compulsive waving of her hands in front of her face, usually when she was in the presence of other people. Her mother felt that the waving increased when the little girl was tired, upset, angry, hungry or uncomfortable in some way.

The girl's play revealed other characteristics of this apparently self-protective behavioural symptom. At first it seemed dissociated from her other movements. When she started to play, moving a doll and baby carriage, she had to stop the hand-waving, but as soon as she had moved the toys, she made a few waves across her face, went back to the play, put the doll in the doll carriage, made a pass across her face, and then went back to the toys. The movements across her face were fleeting; they probably took only a second, and play was resumed quickly. She seemed unaware of the abrupt discontinuity in her actions. At the same time, her play with the dolls and the baby carriage reflected some of the anxiety from which this symbolic defence seemed to spring. She seemed worried about the strength of the doll carriage. She pushed and poked at it, turned it over, examined it carefully, gingerly placed the doll into it and immediately took it out again. I said that it seemed to me that she was afraid that the baby would be hurt. With that she stood in front of me waving her hands and saying, 'No, no, no, no.' She returned to the carriage and again examined it and repeated the action.

This child was trying simultaneously to maintain and defend against split-off hostile bits that had been physically experienced in the past as persecutory, hot, attacking milk. She was unable to experience reality fully. She bumped into furniture, thereby feeling attacked; she tried either to clear away the bad or to protect herself from it by the hand-waving. At the same time she attempted to carry on play or other behaviours, which only added to her difficulties. It seemed that she continually frustrated herself, found the world dangerous, and then needed to defend herself by not acknowledging outer reality as a part of her own reality. In this process the object and the ego became split and feelings of anger, frustration and persecution were cut off from reparative interactions[2] and normal interpersonal relationships.

In this child the necessary splitting by which the infant normally deals with the basic fear of annihilation had been arrested and distorted in development. The child's persecutory fear, perhaps derived from or reinforced by the hot milk, was an expression of the annihilation anxiety. The world was experienced as overwhelming and extremely powerful and dangerous, and her fear of being destroyed was prominent. Splitting off the bad parts became necessary as the fragile ego attempted to reduce danger in order to maintain some wholeness. The defensive hand movements represented an effort to ward off any threat—to separate

herself from the bad and maintain some goodness. Awareness of reality was sacrificed to a pathetically misdirected
attempt to preserve safety and internal stability. The
emotional energy necessary to maintain this state of
defensiveness reduced the child's capacity to play effectively
and also engendered a lack of interpersonal warmth in
order to guard against further frustration and the resulting
painful feelings. A great deal of the child's emotional energy
was compulsively directed to maintaining the splitting both
of the object and the ego, and in turn less energy was
available for relationships.

An example of a more complex manifestation of splitting
occurred in the context of an adult's relationship to the
therapist. A young woman of 30 in treatment with me
became very angry at me and accused me of not really being
interested in her. She complained that I was callously
ignoring her painful physical symptoms, which she had
been experiencing for many months. She noted that I did
not suggest that she visit her physician and she said that I
did not really know whether she was suffering from a
neurological problem; she was experiencing numbness in
her hand and in her arm and pain that travelled up her left
arm into her neck, culminating in a tightness in her jaw,
which gave her headaches. She added that her stomach felt
as if it was on fire and that I didn't seem 'the least bit
worried that it might be a serious ulcer.' I responded to her
that my concern was to determine why she was experiencing all this pain. When asked whether she should go to see
her physician, I told her that that was a decision she had to
make, but that our work was to understand her pain. I then
interpreted her pain as the pain she wished to direct against
me in order to make me less of an envied object. Her
response to this was tearful. She said that she did not want
to hurt me and that I was the only one left who could help
her. She asked 'Why would I then want to hurt you?'

I understood her symptoms as a result of the splitting off
of hostility towards me and redirecting it towards herself.
Her capacity to understand that this split-off hostility was

being expressed through pain was severely limited. She could not understand anything other than her pain, although her capacity to comprehend was usually considerably above average. By splitting off her hostility as well as some ego functions, she prevented herself from feeling and understanding her hostility and from becoming overwhelmed by her unconscious anxiety. She had stopped part of her ego from being effective, even though she said, 'Whenever this happens [i.e., when she feels the physical pain and I interpret it as symbolic hostility] I feel dizzy, as if I am going to faint, and you still don't seem to care.' This was another indication of how the split-off function reduced her awareness. Certainly there was also an unconscious expression of a desire to be taken care of, to be examined and touched and to be nurtured. These were all feelings she said she had missed in her very early childhood, when her mother was too busy with other people, or too busy 'doing things to herself, to make her look [physically] better.'

This woman desired care and nurturing and was very angry and felt persecuted that she had not received it in childhood. Her painful physical experiences were unconscious expressions of 'please touch me and take care of me.' At the same time she was almost saying, 'I don't want to know how angry I am with the object because it is not caring for me. If this pain is introjected then I will not be aware of anything other than physical pain because knowing and understanding will be erased. My thinking will be disorganized and so I will be unaware of the intensity of my anger and the object's potential revenge and retaliation.' As no retaliation was anticipated, no useful therapeutic regression could take place. The physical aches and real pains substituted for a genuine confrontation with her painful past. They not only reduced the expression of anger, but also diminished the possibility of knowing offered by the potentially threatening work of treatment.

The anguished distortions of cases such as these should not make us forget that, under normal circumstances, splitting is the natural beginning of a potentially rich and healthy psychic life. The process is a necessary response to the anxiety of existence in that earliest stage of experience that Klein defines as the 'paranoid–schizoid position'. It allows the ego to 'come through' the terror of annihilation with a feeling that there is some order both to internal and to external reality.

By returning to the playgroup, we can trace the process of splitting through some of its more complex normal developments as the child confronts the necessary opportunities and setbacks of a life of relationships with others, in a freer form than that of the patient–therapist transference.

Both the following examples illustrate the process of 'idealization' by which the ego projects its good and bad aspects into an object and then identifies part of that object with the self. Idealization is where the good experiences of the infant are associated with an ideal object, which is phantasized as being very valuable, desired and well identified with. The split-off bad object contains the hostility that is feared as destructive and damaging. The infant then fears retaliation by this bad object and defends against it. As defense against these fears even stronger idealization of the good object will be felt, and then the object can be perceived as protecting the child from any danger, especially the danger of annihilation.

Three-year-old Kate was very fond of me and would sit on my lap telling me to read her a story. She would choose the book and present it to me. I was to do what she wanted, and usually this was possible. When I walked into her group activity room where she was with the other children, she would come over to me, put her hand into mine, look at me, and smile, sometimes saying nothing, at other times telling me we should paint. She usually stayed by my side for the morning. On one particular occasion, she told me, 'We are going to paint.' We both went over to the paint table, and she became very occupied putting thin lines of glue onto her paper. She dribbled the glue from above the paper and let it 'wiggle' onto the paper. She talked as she worked, telling me that she was making 'wiggly lines' that were 'thin' or 'small' or 'big' or 'fat'. She made pools of glue on the paper and then said she wanted to put a 'yellow circle' on the glue pool. Later she added a 'purple square', a 'yellow' piece of cellophane and a 'pink triangle' of paper. These small pieces of paper covered the pools of glue, but Kate then went on to dribble glue on these pieces. She smiled a lot, told me what she was doing, and sometimes held my hand when she was not busy putting the shapes on her glue pools. Generally she seemed very happy and busy. She worked for about 25 minutes and then remarked, 'I'm finished this and it's for you.' I thanked her and told her I liked her painting. She then said we were going to have a tea party. We went to the doll centre. Kate set about looking for plastic fruit, which she wanted to pretend-cut into pieces to give me. At that moment I was called out of the room, and I said to Kate that I was happy we had the time to be together, but now I had to go to a meeting. Kate smiled, and I said goodbye and left. However, after I had left, the teacher said, Kate threw the plastic apple and banana fruit on the floor, was angry and 'stomped' out of the doll centre. She did not want to play any more and would not talk for the rest of the morning—about 40 minutes. Kate was obviously angry with me.

Initially, the painting that she had made and given to me was a way of reducing her anxieties relating to her unconscious phantasy that she was 'taking' too much from me and thereby damaging me so that I would seek, in her phantasy, revenge and retaliation, by becoming angry with her and taking her good internal objects. This gift to me allowed her to construct a phantasy of reparation, which prevented her destructive impulses from creating excessive anxiety that might cause her to withdraw and become rigid. She then did not have to phantasize that I would attack her, and her internal and external worlds remained safe and secure. No splitting-off was necessary, and she did not fear retaliation. Her reparation was successful perhaps because it symbolized a broader relationship. As she wiggled the glue onto the paper and put the pieces of paper into the glue, symbolically and in phantasy she was using the semen she obtained from me to feel successful in creating babies. (The pieces of paper were always put into the glue pools—that is, babies were always coming from the glue pools made by the glue on the paper; sometimes they were covered over by the glue, but, as Kate said, 'the circles are inside the paper'.) Integration rather than splitting-off was characteristic of her play, and successful working-through of destructive feelings appeared possible.

But when I had to leave, her persecutory and depressive feelings became too strong for her to handle alone. Her reaction was a form of splitting: the fruit became split-off objects that were thrown away; the feeling of safety and security derived from the assurance of having an internal idealized good object rapidly left her, and she became very upset, angry and disappointed. At least two phantasies were too frightening to allow Kate to continue her play. First, the phantasy of having robbed me, which she perceived as causing me to leave her, created persecutory fears. This phantasy was a recreation of oral-sadistic impulses directed at the mother's body, robbing her of her good objects, particularly babies and penises. A second phantasy was that of having controlled me, which is the original phantasy of having controlled the mother. Thus, Kate phantasized that I left her because I was angry with her for what she had done to me and that I could not tolerate being used up any more. In throwing the fruit away, Kate phantasized that it was bad, or at least not good enough to keep me with her. Her own internal objects no longer seemed good enough, and throwing away the plastic fruit and stopping playing were her ways of splitting off any further bad feelings coming from her phantasy. Her feeling of persecution and despair was so strong at that moment that she had to do nothing in order not to disturb her 'equilibrium–safety'. Neither anger nor depression were evident. Kate just walked about or sat looking 'blank' and would not play with the others. Her failure to control me led to regression, which reinforced anxieties and further emphasized the need to split off these feelings.

Kate is a 'normal' little girl, but my desertion created too much anxiety for her. Kate had created me as an ideal object to protect her own internal good. When this ideal object deserted her, this left her feeling empty. She could only handle her anxieties by splitting them off and denying them, because she could not tolerate the blow to her self-esteem and confidence in herself. She was able to manage her angry feelings by doing very little. After I left, an observer in the playroom said that when a fight broke out between two boys, because they both wanted the same toy, Kate walked over to the kicking and punching boys and watched them with a blank expression on her face. When one boy said to the other, 'A fire will come and burn you up and you'll be sad and the wind'll blow you away', Kate wandered slowly back to the paint table. Kate asked for a piece of paper, chose a red oil pastel and made a careful, firm red mark up and down the paper. She then showed the observer the 'hurt' on her hand. She replaced the oil pastel, and some other pastels popped up as she tried to fit the one back in. Kate then said, 'See. Two hurts.'

In another instance, a child of four said that he was going to put a plastic monkey into the box and close the box tightly with tape. He said that the monkey was stopping him from doing all the things he wanted to do, like 'take all the books off the shelf, and put all the blocks into the water tray.' He was splitting off the aspect of the internal objects, which he phantasized as preventing him from doing what he wanted. Based on this play and on what I understood about this child, I interpreted to him that as I did not seem to be the kind, playing monkey he wanted, he did not want me to be with him because he was angry with me and I might be dangerous. This boy had said that when he played with his father, his father was always 'too rough' and hurt him. The boy had added that he wanted a playfather who would do just what he wanted and 'never hurt' him. In our relationship, the child felt that he controlled me, that he had control over his internal objects and they would not be dangerous or hurtful. However, just that week, in a 'play-fight' with his father, he had been bruised, and he had felt the pain for several hours. He had not been able to say anything to his father, because his father also said, 'Men don't complain, and if you want to be a man, don't complain.' The child had interpreted 'complain' to mean cry, and so he had neither cried nor said anything about his pain. By taping up the play monkey in the box, he was trying to split off the persecutory aspects of the internal object and make it less painful for him, and at the same time allow him to feel in charge of what he was going to do, say or feel.

The symbolic themes of adult sexuality and 'manliness' in these examples indicate some of the ways the process of splitting is complicated by relationships to real parents or parent-substitutes. The relationship of this process to the later Oedipal conflict is observable at a very early age. Often a three- to five-month-old baby will seem to develop an exceptional preference for one parent—usually the mother—towards whom the baby is very solicitous and protective. Many of us have noticed how some babies try to push their father away when the father approaches their mother, and try to separate the mother from her husband by leaning outwards as if to pull her away. Aspects of Oedipal conflict as well as reparation are present, but splitting the parents is the dominant observable behaviour. One parent becomes the good parent, while the other one becomes bad. The good one can seem to do no wrong or harm and becomes idealized. This parent is the one who can feed, wash, dress, and put the baby to bed, while the other parent is met with howls of protest should he or she try to take over. The other parent seems to have become the persecutor. At times, as is often the case with such extremes of behaviour, a shift can occur, and suddenly the mother is the bad one; the father now becomes the good idealized one. Perhaps anxiety about not sufficiently protecting the mother, or not making adequate reparation, leads to this change in experienced feeling; or perhaps the bad object is phantasized for a short time as good in order to master the badness and not feel persecuted. It seems important to preserve the feeling that the object remains good and will not attack the child. I think we see this in situations where people refuse to recognize the danger they might be in, or where a child does not perceive parental aggression directed toward the child and returns again and again, only to be slapped or hit or even kicked time after time.

One final example will leave us with a clearer image of the normal development of these feelings of the paranoid–schizoid period. This describes how a little boy worked through his anxious feelings about his father by splitting which involved phantasy and idealization of the penis.

A small boy of three told me that he needed to have a fishing rod that was just like the father's. He said it had to be very strong and very fat. When I asked him how he thought he would get this fishing rod, he told me quite simply that I was going to give it to him! I suggested to him that he saw me as having everything that was good and that he wanted to have this good thing for himself so he could be strong and big as Daddy. The child replied, 'Yes', and handed me a piece of paper, indicating as he pulled at his penis through his trousers, that I was to roll the paper into a cylinder. I said that he felt good and strong when he could touch himself and he looked at me and smiled, obviously not at all anxious about his penis. He perceived me as the good object, not threatening but powerful, who could be intro-jected without anxiety. He talked about his Dad fishing and how he could catch such big fish. I asked the boy if his own fishing rod would catch big fish. He answered 'Yes' and wondered how he was going to catch the fish. The child then told me to cut out a big fish from another sheet of red paper and attach it to the fishing rod by means of a string. I followed his directions and created a fishing rod with a red fish attached to it by a short string. The child went away to another part of the room waving his rod and saying that he was going fishing. He wandered about as if casting his rod and then returned to me smiling and obviously pleased to show me what a big fish he had caught. He did this several times, always bringing the fish over to me to show me what a good fisherman he was, adding that he could catch as many fish as his father and that he was going to grow up to be a big fisherman.

Whenever the boy felt upset because he had not been successful at a job, or because he felt he was being ignored, he would take his fishing rod and go 'fishing' for a few minutes; he would then return with the attached fish and announce, 'Here, I've caught a fish and you are to eat it.' I proceeded to pretend-eat the fish. He was pleased and went to catch another fish for me to eat. When he seemed to feel better, the fishing and feeding stopped, and he returned to his play.

This child was able to maintain a good penis in spite of periodic feelings of anxiety by presenting a fish to eat and thereby offering reparation for unconscious phantasies of aggression towards the introjected father–penis object. He pacified his oral–aggressive phantasies of having taken his father's penis by feeding the potentially destroying penis, and he felt comfortable and in control. Gradually the fishing rod and fish became less and less needed. He spoke about the 'strong things' he could do on the climbing frame and trampoline. The strength of the good penis was introjected, and because it was not spoiled during the times of crisis or frustration, the introject became and remained part of the ego and served to further the functions of the ego. The boy's capacity to recognize reality and yet handle his anxieties was supported, at first by the splitting and later by the idealization that was initially transferred to me and later returned to his father. This was particularly evident when he said that his father was the best fisherman who could catch a fish any time he wanted to. He and his father were to go on fishing trips, he said, and he wouldn't be afraid of falling into the water because he could swim, because 'My Dad said that he would buy me a special jacket and I would never drown.' He would also catch a fish for his mother, and she 'would like his fish to be a good [eating] fish.' He added, 'My mother said she has two fishermans.'

This normal little boy was able to play out his anxieties of aggression, envy, guilt, and reparation and strengthen the functions of his ego. His identification with his father was strengthened, and he looked upon his mother, who brought him to the preschool group, as someone who needed to 'feel good'. He said, 'I can make my Mum nice by giving her a kiss and she says she feels good.' He did not view himself just as a rival to his father, but, like him, able to please his mother, yet not having to try 'to have her for himself'—that is, his relationship to his mother did not produce anxiety, he saw his father's sexuality as beneficial to his mother and saw himself as 'helping out' his mother.

NOTES

1. Splitting refers to the separation of the good and the bad object. Idealization is bound up with splitting in which parts of an object are projected into another and then idealized. Projection is the process whereby parts of the self are *put into* an external object, whereas introjection is the process of taking in parts or all of an object. The objects are entities, mostly people, or representations of people which are symbolically introjected into the ego. These people are part-objects at first (within the paranoid–schizoid position), as for example, the breast, or the penis, and later in development are whole objects, like the mother or the father.

2. These reparative interactions are with others in reality or in phantasy, which permit the child to feel as if goodness has been restored to the damaged person and that the internal object, destroyed or damaged in phantasy, has been re-created or restored.

CHAPTER TWO

Feeling good, having enough and not fearing the other

P arents often talk about their young children's excessive demands for toys and materials. They describe how their children will try to take other children's toys and become very angry or cry if they are not allowed to take what they want. Whether one or four years old, children share the overpowering desire to have whatever anyone else is playing with, particularly if another child is playing with it nearby. These children are usually easy-going and friendly, and they become involved with play materials without any great effort on the part of the parents. They are usually eager to try out new toys, as long as they can use the materials and toys 'their way' and not in some prescribed style.

Often, however, they do not seem to be able to sit alongside another child and allow the other child to play with toys. They insist that the toys are theirs, and they noisily gather up everything for themselves. We have all observed a tug-of-war over a toy, with both children holding onto the toy tightly, unwilling to let go; when one child finally does let go, the child with the toy usually tumbles to the ground from the force of his or her pull. Crying and screaming often accompany this, but no one thinks that the behaviour is abnormal. The children may be described as immature, selfish, egocentric, demanding—perhaps, in a word, as greedy. Such children want as large a collection of things as they can gather; they may have a great number of stuffed toys, dolls, cars and trucks of their own, but they always seem to want another. There is a . seemingly ceaseless demand to be surrounded by things.

We can understand the meaning of such behaviour if we consider that the toys and materials that the child demands are the conscious representations of unconscious internal phantasy objects. The child has gradually built up an internal representation of the objects he or she has obtained through the relationship with his or her mother (Klein, 1932). This relationship, which operates primarily at an unconscious level, allows the child to sense that he or she has enough good internal objects, or has bad objects or an inadequate supply of good objects and needs more. In taking more from the mother, the child believes he or she is in danger of retaliation for having stolen objects from the mother and usually attemps to protect him or herself from the phantasized onslaught of the feared yet desired mother (Klein, 1975; Klein & Riviere, 1953; Weininger, 1984). The phantasized attacks may be handled by defensive reactions such as splitting, projection, denial and repression, all of which are at the service of maintaining the integrity of the fragile ego.

The greed the child experiences—the need to have, the demand for more—is not necessarily pathological. Children need to go through the normal developmental process of discovering what they need, what they can obtain, and what they cannot have. The frustration occasioned by these experiences, coupled with the good-enough mothering provided by most parents, enables the ego to be sustained through potentially damaging episodes. In such situations occurring throughout development children recognize that the phantasized retaliatory attacks are not happening, and that the demands made upon the parent are not hurtful or damaging to them. Therefore, they gradually move through persecutory and depressive anxieties to positions of maturity, where they can recognize not only their own needs, but also the needs of others. As Klein says,

If we have become able, deep in our unconscious minds, to clear our feelings to some extent towards our parents of grievances, and have forgiven them for the frustrations we had to bear, then we can be at peace with ourselves and are able to love others in the true sense of the word. [Klein & Riviere, 1953, p. 119]

Greed creates demands that we have things for ourselves and involves an outward expression of aggression. It is accompanied by the anxiety that others may have more than we do and occurs because we believe that we have not been given as much as we need. The child phantasizes that the mother has an internal goodness that she is keeping for herself, or sharing with the father and others. She or he feels deprived of this goodness, and anxiety arises due to the phantasy that he or she will not be given enough to counter the badness within. Greed originates not only from the perception that there is more available and he or she has not obtained 'it', but also from the need for 'more' in order not to be overwhelmed by bad internal objects (Klein, 1957; Segal, 1973). There is also another process that is involved in increasing greed. Bad objects must be projected to another, and then controlled so that there will be less danger that the 'bad' will, in turn, attack. The mother thus becomes the recipient of the projected 'bad', and if this occurs, the child must try to control the mother. One way to control the mother is to have enough good objects for him or herself. This means that the child has had to take them, which in turn might mean, in phantasy, that the mother might attack the child for having robbed her. The father might also be phantasized as angry because these good objects are being denied to him. Young couples often describe how their seven- to nine-month-old baby tries to push the father away when being held by the mother. The child phantasizes that the father will take what is the child's and might 'gang up' with the mother to retaliate for the child's taking and 'robbing'.

In the above process the child uses aggressive energy to rob, and this is phantasized as destructive, or at least damaging. The destructive aspect is that the mother will be left with, or given, only bad objects by the baby, and the damaging aspect is that the baby will empty the mother of her internal goodness. Retaliation is anticipated by the baby, and defensive manoeuvres result.

These developmental concepts about the child's internal phantasy world help us to understand that when playing, the child needs to have everything, not simply as a measure of love and support but at an unconscious level as a bulwark in case some of the internal objects go bad or are overcome by retaliation. Then the child, having acquired other objects, is able to phantasize that an ever-present and ever-giving breast is available. And so this child needs to collect enough materials around him as he plays. The ever-giving breast (materials) will not only make up for what may become lost, but will also protect should there be an attack.

Let us look at an example. Three young children were playing, and one of the three-year-olds demanded all the toys. This child said that he needed to have everything; he put all the toys between his legs as he sat on the floor and then leaned over them and effectively hid them. He then said that no one could 'smash' him because he had 'everything'. This child felt that he was protected by having everything that the phantasized breast could provide. As in most cases of greed, what he had became insufficient—he needed more, particularly when he saw one child pick up another small truck. He wanted this truck as well and cried loudly that he wanted 'that'. When the child did not give the truck to him, he yelled as if he were in pain, and a staff member, not knowing the circumstances but concerned about his crying, came over to comfort him. However, the child cried even louder, as if he phantasized an attack from her. No amount of talking seemed to help him—he 'needed' the truck. In a sense, the child phantasized that the truck had been stolen from him, and that now, being diminished, he would be vulnerable to outside attacks. This loss was so very painful partly due to the phantasy that he did not have enough good objects to protect him and partly because he imagined himself as bad because he had taken the mother's objects and was, therefore, unworthy of good things. The internal breast had turned bad, and he therefore needed to obtain more supplies to try to circumvent this experience.

If a child has many play materials, he or she interprets this as meaning that he or she is good and must have been a good child in order to have been given a lot. The circularity of this thought process is not atypical of children—if I have a lot, I must be good—I must be good because I have a lot. In this way the phantasized process of acquisition—the greedy way the large amount came—is repressed or denied or ambiguously remembered. Thus the collection allows the child to avoid the aggressive content of impulses and phantasies. Whereas aggression means that the child must have damaged the breast, having such a large collection, with repression of the aggression, reassures the child that no damage was done. In this way, the guilt and retaliation can be avoided, at least for a little while.

Some parents seem to need to give their children large numbers of dolls, cars, games or other toys. Perhaps they are trying to help their children not to phantasize retaliation—that is, they may have a very strong desire to be seen as 'good parents' who never frustrate their children. Unfortunately, greed is never satisfied and needs to be worked through within the relationship between children and parents. Giving too much may also be the parents' unconscious way of relieving their own phantasy of retaliation; by giving their children many toys, they may be unconsciously placing themselves in the position of their children in an effort to assure themselves that they do not have to take or rob from their own parents. They are able to avoid aggression and believe that they do not or never did have any dangerous impulse to do harm to the breast. By providing so generously for their children, they also attempt to avoid their children's (and their own) feelings of dissatisfaction about the relationship between child and parent.

I have often observed young children of five to seven call another child 'greedy'. In one instance, four children were playing, and one boy insisted that he had to give out the blocks. He managed to keep the majority of the blocks for himself, and when all the blocks had been sorted, another boy said, 'You're very greedy—I don't play with greedy kids.' In another instance, two young girls were playing house; one girl said that she was going shopping and would buy all the groceries. The other girl said that she wanted to do some of the shopping, but the first repeated she would do it. On hearing this, the second girl stated that she would never play with such a 'greedy' girl. In another situation, where children of three and four were colouring with magic markers, one child controlled the markers, would only give them out when asked for a specific colour, and insisted on having the markers returned to him. The other children allowed this to go on for several minutes, and then one of them said, 'You shouldn't keep all the magic markers for yourself. You should have them in the middle of the table.' The boy refused to do this, and all the children left the colouring table, saying that he was a 'very greedy' boy and they would not play with him any longer.

Children project their own greed onto the child who is being greedy, and then, in order to cope with their own feelings of dissatisfaction at not having enough, they leave. By isolating and rejecting the insatiable child, the other children avoid their own greed and yet are still able to express the aggression attached to this impulse. Should a child remain with the unappeasable person, unable to leave because of the adult authority or unable to express contempt for this child, as for example in a classroom, then the aggressive feelings are internalized. These children are often sad children, behaving as if they do not deserve to have objects for themselves. In play psychotherapy, one such child of nine, a depressed boy, expressed this as, 'I don't deserve to have anything for myself; I took too much when I was a baby, and I should not take anything now.' He had a recurrent nightmare in which he was chased by a large gorilla who kept appearing from nowhere. The gorilla chased him into a very small house and would not let him get out. The boy talked about this dream in a very sad way, saying that he had 'bad feelings'. When we talked about his bad feelings, the boy said that he did not want to feel bad but he did not know how to feel good. He sensed that as he was bad, he did not deserve any good things, and he continued to play with a child whom he called 'greedy'. Staying in such a situation may be regarded as a form of reparation, punishing oneself for having harmed the breast in phantasy. The child is asking for forgiveness, but as he or she is not given anything by the greedy child, the unconscious assumption is that the reparation has been insufficient.

Children are concerned that sometimes they may 'suck their parents dry'—an expression that is heard every now and then from parents: 'You want so much, you'll suck me dry!' ... 'I give you everything, and I get nothing back.' ... 'I work my fingers to the bone to give you everything.' Children may respond to these remarks by feeling that they have to be independent because they believe that they take too much from their parents when they are dependent. Indeed, the expected retaliation for this aggression may force too early an independence (Weininger, 1982). This premature independence is observed in children who play several games at the same time, or try to do everything at once and are unable to concentrate on one event. They appear dissatisfied, and they are attempting to discover the goodness they feel they lack. In order to find some goodness, and to reassure themselves that the good breast has not disappeared or been destroyed, they flit from one experience to another. This does not allow them to gain the needed satisfaction, however, and their activity may become more frantic at times. They do not find satisfaction, because they do not stay with any activity or event long enough for it to become satisfying, and they continue to feel dissatisfied. This dissatisfaction is expressed as aggression towards others who are unconsciously equated with the phantasized ungiving breast. Some such hyperactive children unconsciously feel that they have 'sucked' their mothers dry and that therefore no good or satisfying object exists.

Greed is a sense of insufficiency, a desperate wanting what another has, a fear that someone might get more than you have, and it threatens the child's sense of safety and security. Children develop many ways—some healthy and some not—of coping with this pressure. They may say that they do not want an object and even express contempt for it in an effort to avoid disappointment. For example, a young child said he did not want to play with the blocks because 'they always fell down' when he built something. In reality, there was no room for him in the block centre. He usually enjoyed playing with the blocks, but by expressing contempt he was avoiding feelings that he might not be able to control. He made the blocks unattractive and 'spoiled' them, and he no longer wanted them. As Klein and Riviere (1953) point out, this 'is a simpler method, less complicated and more immediately pleasurable', as the child does not have to imagine that he will be punished for breaking the rules and playing in a block centre that holds only three children. Another thing that children may do to cope with their phantasized greed and its destructive power is to negate themselves. An extreme example can be seen in two 12-year-old children who said that they had been such a burden to their parents that their parents would be better off without them. In an effort to make sure that no more of the goodness of the breast was harmed, they contemplated suicide. Such children have little internal goodness to fall back on and few resources that tell them that they are good.

Some children have large collections of toys or many friends as a way of coping with their greed. Then they can take such a 'little bit' from each object that none of the objects will realize that some of their 'goodness' has been taken, and there should be no retaliation. In one way, collections can be a way of avoiding confronting aggression and greed, and the familiar collections of baseball cards, matchbook covers, marbles, coins, small stones, bottle caps, and so forth that clutter many children's rooms provide a normal outlet for these feelings. The collection represents an inexhaustible reservoir of affection and dependency, and at the same time provides a symbol of the child's own internal goodness. The toys, games and stuffed animals that parents give help children to allay phantasized fears of taking too much from parents, especially from their mothers, and to maintain the needed phantasy of the ever-giving breast, so that children gradually come to feel that they have enough of their own and can even give some goodness back to their parents. Their reparation for phantasized destructive impulses against the breast allows them to gain a more mature relationship with their parents. They no longer fear that they will be emptied, nor that they will 'suck dry' the breast. They develop confidence in themselves and pleasure in relationships with other people.

PART TWO

Aggression, expression and love: development through the depressive position

CHAPTER THREE

Aggression and regression

Adrian, a three-year-old boy, was very angry one morning. He wanted whatever anyone had, and when he saw another child riding on a tricycle, painting or building a block tower, he would snatch the child's play materials. At first he was satisfied with having other children's toys, but soon this was not enough. He knocked over one child's block tower, snatched another's paint brush and smeared his own design on the painting, and took parts of a third child's puzzle and hid them. He then slapped a child riding on a tricycle and kicked a boy who was building a tower. Although he did not really hurt the other children, when they hit him back he moved away, and the expression on his face became frightening: he glared, bared his teeth and screamed at them to go away.

I must emphasize that usually Adrian was a pleasant, happy, normal little boy who enjoyed his time with the other children. Sometimes he played cooperatively, but more frequently he played alongside another child, talking to him or her while usually remaining quite interested in his own activity. This particular morning was Adrian's first day back at the playgroup after eight days, and he seemed angry and destructive. When I said, 'You are angry a lot this morning,' Adrian answered, 'I'm mad.' I asked him if he knew why he was mad, and he replied that he did, but he would not tell me because he was 'so mad'.

Adrian's behaviour continued to escalate to hitting other children. It appeared that because Adrian could not become involved in play himself, perhaps because he had been away for eight days, greed and envy forced him to try to destroy the other children. He might have been saying to himself that if he did not or could not make something, then no one else was allowed to do so because this only highlighted his own difficulties. Since stopping other children's play was not sufficient, he tried to destroy them. In this way the other child would have no 'goodness' left, and Adrian would no longer experience greed and envy. Since he could not play, he had to spoil and destroy the goodness of the other children's play and so remove his own envious desires.

When another child, a boy of the same age and build, hit him back, Adrian withdrew a few feet and, with no one around, hit himself three times in the face. He continued to stand there with a very sorrowful expression and remained alone for about five minutes, after which he slowly walked away towards the door of the room as if to leave. He was momentarily stopped when his attention was diverted to a toy car, which he pushed about on the floor, but he eventually gave that up and stood against the door looking very dejected. I approached him and said that he was trying to stop himself from being so mad, but he denied this. When I added, 'I don't think you feel like you can make good things for Mummy this morning,' Adrian told me to be quiet and added, 'Don't say those things.' However, he moved over to the sand table and, alone, began constructing tunnels. Slapping himself seemed to be an expression of his unconscious phantasy of persecution—that is, he felt persecuted by his own spoiling and expected retaliation. When he did start to play with the toy car and 'make it go on the road', he was attempting reparation, but that was not effective, and he was left feeling anxious. By standing at the door, he was hoping that something would happen; he was not able to help himself but needed someone to contain him.

Adrian's eight-day absence created sufficient anxiety that this ordinarily happy child regressed and expressed this by physically destructive attacks on others, as if in phantasy these attacks were on the mother's body. His anxiety could not be overcome by reparative symbolic play, and he could not tolerate the frustration of seeing others play while he was not able to, and so he regressed to sadistic attacks on the primary object that created the original envy. He attempted to destroy another child whose creative play symbolized the mother's capacity to have other babies. Adrian could do nothing; he could not play nor could he talk with others. He was alone with his anxiety and frustrations and could make no reparation. The attacks were a symptomatic expression of regression. Only with some adult containment and interpretive comments could Adrian move to the sand tables. In this regressive medium he could dig tunnels, as if he were looking for the goodness that he phantasized he had destroyed.

If the child's anxiety and guilt because of phantasized danger and/or lack of adequate reparation is contained by an adult, regression and further attacks need not occur. Aggression and subsequent anxiety and guilt can be expected to happen quite normally, but it is the extent and degree of anxiety that determine whether progression or regression of ego will ensue. Anxiety, mastered by nurturing and good experiences provided by adults, leads to more effective reparation and eventually to sublimation. By contrast, anxiety that is too great or poorly contained by an adult results in regression. The emotional energies are mobilized to protect the child at the level of his or her regression, and, therefore, little is available for interaction with others. Patience, tolerance and recognition of the child's pain will help and will add to the store of good experiences that will enable the child to emerge from regression.

Let us transpose the above situation into early infancy and consider the result. If too much of the young infant's emotional energy has been used to counter the phantasy of retaliation by the attacked object, then less energy will be available for future retaliating phantasies and their vicissitudes. Such a child will be more susceptible to regression because he or she will have less energy to withstand anxiety and frustration.

I worked with a five-year-old child who was in this situation. Sam was described by his young parents as a 'holy terror'. He was 'always angry, always fighting and always trying to wreck everything in the house, his things as well as ours.' The parents had stripped the child's room of everything except a bed because he 'destroyed everything', but that did not work because he pulled the bed apart. They finally gave him just a mattress to sleep on. He was unable to play with other children; he would hurt and bite them, and none of the neighbourhood children would come close to him. Whenever the parents found a toy Sam liked, the toy would last for about '30 minutes at the longest' before being destroyed. At meals, he would spit out part of his food. It was unpredictable when he would wet and soil himself. He might hug his parents but would then scream at them, trying to bite them. As the parents put it, 'We've tried everything, we've been easy with him, we've been firm with him. We have punished him and even given him spankings; we tried to punish him by not feeding him, we've tried to get him things—you might say we have been inconsistent, but we have stuck to one approach for a time, and nothing has worked. He is just a very angry kid, and we don't know what to do with him.'

It seemed that Sam could not master any degree of anxiety; whenever he felt any anxiety brought on by internal or external factors, he lashed out and tried to destroy, as if he were trying to destroy the source of the anxiety. Although he had developed normally and had well-developed speech and motor controls, his indiscriminate sadism indicated that he could not control the phantasy of early retaliatory revengeful objects. Sam looked on everything and everyone as potential attackers, and he retaliated as soon as his anxiety became too great to tolerate. He could not handle frustration, and if he felt that he was being stopped by someone or something, he would scream and lash out in anger. However, his parents said that they often could not pinpoint what was frustrating him. As there were no external events causing frustration, it would seem then that it was his unconscious phantasized revenge for what was damaging him that motivated the aggressive outbursts. Sam was unable to effect reparation, and this led to further anxiety of persecution and consequent regression to an earlier phase where emotional energies were fixated. A child regresses to where the greatest amount of emotional energy is available, which is also where aggression is the strongest.

Sam had been separated from his parents when he was two months old: they had had to go to another country to work and felt that it would be too dangerous to take Sam with them. They left him with an aunt for nine months, and when they returned and again set up their family household they noticed that whereas Sam had been a 'fairly easy-going baby, he had now turned into a monster'. The parents stated, 'He wouldn't let us hold him, he was very difficult to feed, and he had a hard time sleeping and would scream for hours at a time.' The parents felt that his behaviour had changed very little over the past four years: he still was a very angry child.

Sam's separation from his parents at such an early age could easily have led to the phantasy of having destroyed the mother because she did not come back or reappear undamaged. This meant to him that his anger had been so great that he caused her destruction. As she did not return, his attempts at reparation were ineffective. By the time Sam's parents did come back, his aggression and anger were so strong that his emotional energy was fixated at two to nine months. Good-parenting, by way of parents returning unharmed, was lacking, and Sam phantasized that the lack of parents was because of the damage he did to the object. This could only result in retaliation, and so ego development was arrested.

Thus, although his language and motor ability were at a four- to five-year-old level, Sam's social and emotional skills, his ability to play and his creativity were seriously underdeveloped. Destructive feelings towards his mother were projected and perceived as now being within her and, therefore, potentially capable of being turned onto him in a phantasized destructive attack. As he grew older, he attributed these destructive projected phantasies to everything around him. Indeed, Sam's aggression was projected indiscriminately. He was fighting his own projections, expecting that they would come back and harm him, and so he attempted to destroy in an effort to survive such a phantasized onslaught.

The above example illustrates how children's behaviour does not necessarily mirror their real environment but illustrates how they think about reality and how they interpret events and other people. Perception of reality is influenced by unconscious phantasies that interact with children's moods and feelings. For example, if a baby is very hungry, the prevailing feeling is one of discomfort, disappointment, perhaps even pain, but the expression is anger, which is shown by fierce screaming. When the breast or bottle is offered, the baby does not accept it but turns away or pushes it away, refusing milk even though hungry. The breast has become bad, because in phantasy the baby has attacked the breast and it will now return the attack. Consequently he or she refuses food because the breast is not experienced as good any more. By pushing away and screaming, the baby expresses hostility towards the breast but also towards his or her own projected badness in the breast.

Children experience unconscious phantasies as if they are actually happening in reality: the phantasy alters reality, and the child then attacks. Further fear of retaliation results, and the child phantasizes that there are more attackers. This seemed the case in a boy two and a half years old who was tired and hungry but would scream when offered food. When his parents did not offer food but talked to him, he screamed as well. Actually, when anyone in the room talked, he screamed. It appeared as if he perceived 'words' as attackers and responded by screaming at them. Only when everyone became silent and sat still for several minutes did the child calm down and eat the food that was placed close to him.

Another example is of a boy of eight who was playing ball with an adult; when the adult inadvertently stepped on the boy's foot, the boy fell and slid in the sand. There were no visible cuts or scrapes, yet the boy clutched his groin and cried loudly, refusing any comfort or attention from anyone. If anyone came close to him, he responded with loud screams and kicked his feet at the person while still clutching his groin. He sat apart from the group, cursed at offers of help and became sullen and silent. When the ball came his way, he grabbed it and then kicked it away from those who were playing with it. This happened several times, and at one point he picked up the ball and doused it in a mud puddle. He finally took the ball and refused to return it, making motions as if he were going to throw it out of the park and into the oncoming traffic, but instead of throwing the ball he hid it beside a bush, but inside the fence. He refused to be part of the group and went back to class uncommunicative, glowering and very angry. Once inside the school, he continued to sulk, and he made his anger apparent by crashing plates against the table and walls at lunchtime. Initially the boy had seemed to enjoy the ball game. He was actively kicking and throwing the ball; he appeared in control of the ball, which was possibly a symbolic equivalent of the phantasized breast. However, this pleasure soon changed to disappointment and pain, because the satisfying 'object' was not sufficiently protecting. It became persecuting. By throwing the ball away, he was attempting to destroy the source of danger. He also deprived the other children of pleasure, as if to say that if he could not get satisfaction, then no one would. Then he tried to spoil the ball by dousing it in muddy water, symbolic of faeces and urine. The damaged and destroyed breast could now be thrown away, into the street traffic. Because he hid the ball instead, he was indicating that he hoped the 'good' ball would return.

The unexpected accident when the adult stepped on the child's foot, causing him to fall, stopped and spoiled an exciting, enjoyable game of ball with others. However, judging from the extreme reaction, this event seems to have had a deeper symbolic meaning for this boy. It may have evoked the unconscious phantasy of his pleasure with mother occasioning genital attacks by the father, as shown by grabbing his groin and refusing any comfort. His phantasy that he would be attacked for pleasure with mother was so strong that he could not play the game again. He behaved as though everyone was attacking and he had to defend himself continually. This phantasy continued even at lunchtime, when he 'destroyed' plates and food also representing mother. Thus taking more from her was phantasized as once again occasioning attacks from the revengeful father.

I created, and for eight years directed, a school for emotionally disturbed and educationally underachieving children. Many children in this school were violently aggressive. Indeed, they were so physically powerful in their anger that only with considerable difficulty could four adults hold them. There were many day-to-day expressions of extreme aggression. For example, when ten-year-old Jamie was in a rage, he would kick the furniture and throw anything he could get his hands on against walls or at people who were trying to help him. Terry, an 11-year-old girl, would physically attack her teacher by punching and scratching her, giving the reason that she wanted to bruise her and make her bleed. In one instance a 14-year-old threatened the class with a knife. Other children expressed their anger by trying to trip people, or, as one ten-year-old boy did, by sneezing and coughing on people. For many of these children their phantasies altered reality to such an extent that they perceived everything as constantly attacking. Their world had turned persecutory, and when they first came to the school they showed the staff by their defiant angry behaviour how painful it was to allow anyone in this persecutory world to influence them. If they did, they would have to recognize how the external world (parents) had been bad to them and to understand their own feelings of badness and hostile phantasies.

We can see from the preceding examples that powerful aggressive feelings exist in children; children's thoughts are often dominated by phantasies of terrifying monsters, and when these attack, children phantasize some sort of retaliation. However, there are also idealized saviour figures as well, constructed to offer protection from the 'monsters'. These phantasies become attached to the nurturing and caring people in the child's world, and it is these people who can, through their actions, perpetuate or alleviate the terror of the child's phantasy. If children continue to have good experiences, the fears diminish, and the children can use emotional energy more positively for developing relationships. If the fears are reinforced by bad experience, then the children's capacity to relate to others and see goodness in them is reduced, so that some children may have to withdraw from the outside world, or become suspicious and attacking.

These bad experiences are not so difficult to imagine—we only have to think of the great number of children who are abused, both physically and sexually, by their parents. As Sheleff points out, parenthood does not in itself provide an 'instinctive capacity to love one's offspring' (Sheleff, 1981, p. 42). Indeed, there seems to be some truth in a further statement that 'the harshness of parental behaviour is the source of the child's problems and that the child's fear of prior parental hostility is a relevant factor in child–parent relations' (Sheleff, 1981, p. 330). However, this is not the whole story; the truth is somewhat more complicated. The unconscious phantasies of children, as well as parents' actual treatment, colour their perceptions of their parents. If a child fears that he or she has been bad and is not met with hostility from the parents, then the frightening phantasy is calmed because it is not confirmed by reality. However, a child who phantasizes that he or she is bad and deserves punishment and who is often beaten by the parents lives in an entirely persecutory universe, with no help from the external environment to minimize the frightening phantasy. We need to increase our understanding of the reality recognized by both children and parents.

In truth, most parent–child relationships are characterized at best by an

> . . . underlying ambivalence. Mixed with the love that a child may show his parents is the frustration they engender in him as he seeks his own independent way of life, his growing awareness of a distaste for various aspects of their behaviour, his resentment over the controls they impose upon him. Mixed with the love of a parent for his offspring is the burden that their upbringing will place on him, the anxiety that each stage of their development arouses in him, the fear that they will reject his guidance and abandon him in old age. [Sheleff, 1981, p. 42]

One of the most difficult things for us to do is to recognize the anger and hostility inherent in human behaviour. It is often difficult for parents to accept the ordinary amount of aggressive drive and energy that the young child needs to have available in order to ask questions. For a young child of three to seven years, asking questions requires considerable self-assertion. Some aggression is necessary just to get through to the parents; they may be talking to each other and admonish the child, 'Can't you see we are talking; you have to wait your turn.' Rather than teaching children that their questions are important, parents may fail to recognize the immediacy of young children's thoughts and actions, their egocentricism, and may squash the aggressive energy children need to explore their world (Sheleff, 1981). While this may sound harsh, all one needs to do is observe many parents with their young children. Parents rarely stop their conversations with other adults to answer children's questions, and when they do, other adults may say that the parents are 'spoiling' their children. By 'spoiling', the adults mean that the child will grow up into a demanding 'brat' who will never be able to acknowledge the presence of others. But egocentric behaviour and thinking cannot be eliminated by force or through rules imposed on children by adults; these processes gradually give way to social cooperation as children become more capable of exploring outer reality and become less dominated by internal phantasy. If the outside world continuously threatens or punishes, children lose the desire to alter their internal world and to explore reality. They become afraid of doing so precisely because reality is *not* satisfying or gratifying and is furthermore even seen as too threatening.

Adults who ignore children's questions may have difficulty recognizing that they are being aggressive to children. They may say they want to teach their children how to communicate or to take turns in conversation. Yet they do not see the immediacy of their children's needs and so interpret the behaviour only as too aggressive and unacceptable. Increased tolerance for children's aggression might come if they understood more of their own aggression.

An aspect of this became somewhat clearer to me as I was working with a group of adults who were planning to go to a foreign country as missionaries. I was asked if I would help these men and women achieve better relationships with the native people. My work with them involved a series of marathon group psychotherapy sessions, each lasting five hours, in which they started out talking about their feelings about the native people. They all said that they knew they would enjoy being with them, that they liked them, admired them and looked forward to being with them. Gradually this perception changed. At first some of them said, 'I think it will be hard to live in such a hot climate.' Later this became,

'I don't know whether I can bring the word of the Lord to that country'; then, 'I wonder if these people carry contagious diseases'; then, 'I have often thought of them as bad because of their colour—they look so different from me'; then, 'I think of them as just emerging from the jungle.' Unconscious phantasies gradually became consciously expressed: 'They might rob me; I should leave anything valuable at home,' 'They could spoil me if I let them get too close to me,' or even, 'They might murder me because they might hate what I have to say.'

The feelings of *their* internal goodness gave way to feelings of aggression and then to seeing destructive tendencies in the other. It was very difficult for these potential missionaries to recognize their own aggressiveness and how it could prevent them from forming working relationships with the natives of the country. An interpretation of this led them to judge their own aggressiveness more clearly and to explore why it was so hard for them to recognize this feeling in themselves. What emerged from these sessions was the feeling that they needed to become more tolerant, less impatient, and more aware of how their imagination influenced the way they judged and conducted the business of relationships.

'Phantasy is ... a constant and unavoidable accompaniment of real experiences, constantly interacting with them' (Segal, 1964, p. 3). There is an interaction between our unconscious phantasies and the real external world, yet even if the real world were fully positive and giving, it would not prevent or eradicate aggressive phantasies. Segal states:

> ... aggressive and persecutory phantasies and anxieties would exist. ... When the infant has been under the sway of angry phantasies, attacking the breast, [then] an actual bad experience becomes all the more important, as it confirms not only his feeling that the external world is bad, but also the sense of his own badness and the omnipotence of his malevolent phantasies. Good experiences, on the other hand, tend to lessen the anger, modify

the persecutory experiences and mobilize the baby's love
and gratitude and his belief in a good object. [Segal, 1964,
p. 4]

Parents need to provide young children with good
experiences, but they also need to accept that aggression
serves a useful purpose, at one level by providing the
necessary drive to grow and exhibit curiosity about the
world, and at another level to counter phantasized or real
dangers. If aggression is constantly thwarted, then growth
is limited or 'lopsided', and emotional energies become
fixated at the level of development where the aggressive
content of the phantasy creates the greatest persecutory
anxieties. In such a case, because emotional energy is
needed to counter these anxieties, there are very few
resources left with which to explore the world. While the
expectation would be that as the child develops, the world
around should expand and become more exciting, this will
not be able to happen if the child's resources are depleted in
the service of containing anxiety caused by aggressive
phantasies.

CHAPTER FOUR

Symbol formation, symbolic equation and the development of interests

A s two-year-old Jeremy sat at the table listening to adults talking, he suddenly said, loudly and clearly and with an impish grin, 'I love you Mummy.' When his mother answered, 'I love you too, Jeremy,' he replied, 'I love you two, I love you four, I love you eight, I love you eight and two,' to which his mother responded, 'I love you eighty-two; that's a great big love.' Jeremy looked at his food and then back at her and said, 'This is lots of love food.' He smiled, stopped talking and once again became occupied with eating his food. Then he suddenly stopped eating, looked up and announced, 'I love you too Daddy, eight two.' His father answered, 'I love you Jeremy.' Jeremy looked very pleased, gazed around the table and continued eating his food.

It is important to try to understand Jeremy's unconscious symbolism here, for in expressing his love for his mother, symbolically this little boy is also associating his energies with other things and extending his experience of the world. Obviously Jeremy's interests and desires are mainly directed towards his mother. However, in addition, the 'good internal object' of his unconscious is also being linked to the actual person at the table through a process of symbolization that both reflects and gives rise to other interests. In expressing his desire for his mother, he professes his great love for her in terms of numbers and tries to increase the size of numbers as an indication of the magnitude of his love. In a certain sense he is expressing an erotic desire for the mother's body, to have this for himself, not to share with anyone else and yet not to have to endure the experience of retaliation from a phantasized vengeful father. For Jeremy the numbers are symbolic of the intensity of his love and yet, because he is only two years old, he cannot handle either the feelings that his desire may provoke, or the boldness of his desire. Consequently Jeremy shifts the focus to the 'lots of love food', and the food, then, becomes his mother's love, something that he can take into himself and yet not anticipate danger for his greed. However, even having made such a connection he apparently does not feel safe, and so he announces, almost as an after-thought, that he loves his father as well. Having satisfied himself that father will not retaliate, he can eat his love-food. He has endowed an object, food, with symbolic meaning, love, and then transformed his interest to it.

As Segal says,

> Through symbolization the ego is attempting to deal with the anxieties stirred by its relation to the object. This is primarily the fear of bad objects and the fear of the loss or inaccessibility of good objects. Disturbances in the ego's relation to objects are reflected in disturbances of symbol formation. In particular, disturbances in differentiation between ego and object lead to disturbances in differentiation between the symbol and the object and therefore to concrete thinking characteristic of psychoses.
> [Segal, 1957, pp. 392–393]

If this crucial process of symbolization does not occur, then ego development is arrested (Klein, 1930a, p. 26).

Jeremy has reached the point where he is able to

differentiate the symbol or the substitute—the numbers—from the original object itself, the mother. Jeremy uses numbers to communicate; he is a secure and resilient child who seems in control of the symbolic expressions of his unconscious phantasies. Thus we see how Jeremy communicates the symbolization process going on within himself by using words. 'Not all internal communication is verbal thinking, but all verbalizing is an internal communication by means of symbols—words' (Segal, 1957, p. 396).

At about this same time, Jeremy was also able to communicate in words his understanding of the function of his mother's brassière. He said, 'Here is your two-nipple-holder thing.' Jeremy is bright, verbal and interested in his world, and he is able to formulate symbols for sublimation of unconscious impulses. As long as these symbols continue to represent those urgent desires, then his capacity for symbol formation will grow and develop. The symbols are then used in ways that are in keeping with the nature of the symbol rather than the original desire they represented. Jeremy uses numbers to express the magnitude of his love for his mother, but he also counts—whether it is puzzle pieces while making a puzzle, or his fingers. Jeremy now becomes aware of the meaning of numbers themselves, and gradually this symbolic event will no longer be an unconscious process in his life but will become functionally autonomous. Numbers will no longer be attached to his love for his mother but will be observed as a love of numbers. Jeremy will begin to exhibit prowess in numbers and numbering activities.

Thus, the way in which Jeremy uses numbers represents a sublimation process that fosters ego growth. Numbers, the symbols, represent the mother, and Jeremy uses numbers successfully and at times with an awareness of how this competency influences and pleases his mother. This process can occur when the paranoid–schizoid anxieties have been mostly overcome and the child is within the depressive position. The child has experienced the loss and return of the mother, is able to tolerate frustration and the anxiety of retaliation for greed and can now use symbols as a way of maintaining the internal object. 'The symbol is used not to deny but overcome loss' (Segal, 1957, p. 395). We will have more to say about the different mechanisms facilitating and preventing/altering/distorting symbol formation in the paranoid–schizoid and depressive positions.

Klein points out how the anxieties of the paranoid–schizoid position are resolved through the direction of sadistic impulses towards objects other than mother and that 'with the libidinal interest, it is the anxiety in the phase that I have described (sadism expressed as phantasized attacks on the object by urethral, anal, oral and muscular sadism) which sets going the mechanism of identification' (Klein, 1930a). This identification is the forerunner of symbolism. The sadism that the baby phantasizes about the loved object is potentially dangerous because not only will the sadistic impulse destroy the nurturing object, but it will also destroy himself or herself through the mother's phantasized retaliation. The resultant anxiety forces the baby to search for other means of expressing his unconscious impulses. 'This anxiety contributes to make him equate the organs in question with other things; owing to his equation these in their turn become objects of anxiety' (Klein, 1930a, p. 26). The baby thus equates the dangerous object with other things in the world, and these things take on the anxiety instead of the original object, the mother. Jeremy's interest in numbers did not seem accidental; one of his father's main interests is mathematics and statistical analysis, and his son had watched him work at various mathematical computations. Jeremy had also heard his mother express her delight in and admiration for his father's number skills. Jeremy's use of numbers serves three functions: identification with father, sublimation of sadism, and an effective means to overcome loss.

Projective identification[1] also plays an important role in symbol formation, particularly in the earliest stages (Segal, 1964). As Jeremy projects his sadistic desires onto his mother, he identifies with parts of the object and anticipates retaliation for his sadism. In an effort to control his projection, Jeremy forms a symbolic equation. Numbers, important to him because of his father's interest, become a substitute that has the potential to become as satisfying as the original object without the dangers inherent in hating and loving such an object. Numbers become the original object in the symbolic equation as described by Segal (1957), but also become a sublimation and protection, for as numbers gradually represent the original object, they can be treated aggressively. Jeremy illustrates his aggressiveness with numbers by throwing down the numbered parts of a puzzle, by feigning an inability to recognize numbers when presented by his parents, or by squishing rubber numbers under his bottom. The numbers can also be handled very carefully and smiling at the same time, patting them softly and kissing them. Jeremy also expands his use of numbers. For example, he looks at the calendar for the number of the month; he collects things, which he counts; he presses number buttons on the television to obtain different channels. In this way numbers become a basis for the development of new interests as well as for the elaboration of symbolic skills.

By contrast, three-year-old Patrick provides an example of the distortion of the normal development of symbol formation by a 'symbolic equation'. This 'symbolic equation' involves the complete identification of the feared internal object with outer reality, and this substitutes for the normal development of symbol formation. We were attaching plastic pieces that contained magnets to a metal board. Patrick wanted to put all the plastic pieces—squares, semicircles, circles, triangles and other shapes, along with butterflies, various small plastic fruits and birds—on the board. As he placed them, he talked, but because he had a lisp and was mumbling, it was very difficult to understand him. He laid out the pieces in a straight line without any reference to their size, shape or design and apparently in a random fashion. When he finished, I asked what he had made. He looked at me with a sad smile and said, 'A big thing.' I asked him if the big thing was inside of him and made him feel very bad. Patrick's response was again, 'Yes,' but this time he said that 'the spider' was bad and was in him. He pointed to a picture of a spider on the wall and said that it was in his 'tummy'. I said, 'You also have bad pictures in your head.' Patrick said, 'Yes, and hurt.' I responded by saying that he was afraid that the bad things would make him very sick. Patrick immediately responded, saying the word 'ghost'. When I asked him to tell me about his ghost, all he could or would say was that it was 'big' and 'bad', and he then raised his arms as if to indicate a huge thing descending on him. When I mentioned this impression, Patrick smiled and moved close to me, allowing his body to touch mine. Then he went back to the metal board and pieces. This time he tried to make a picture. He took a semicircle, put it at the top of the board and said, 'Moon'; he tried to arrange the other pieces as some sort of picture, but he was not successful. The pieces seemed to be in a jumble and did not make any sense to me. Patrick moved away and once again looked withdrawn.

In general, Patrick did not play with toys; he usually sat quietly looking around him, but he did not appear to see—he just looked vacant. Other children teased him or hurt him. Occasionally, when a child came to play with him, Patrick turned away, and the child moved on, but usually not before he had hurt or pushed Patrick, to which Patrick did not respond. He did not talk very much, and when he did, it was usually to the classroom teacher or to her assistant. Patrick was physically adept, could ride a tricycle, could use scissors, and was able to pick up small things carefully; he did not use paper and pencil— apparently because he did not want to, not because he was not able to. When one little girl tried to give him a piece of paper with some marks on it that she had made, Patrick simply let the paper slide out of his hand. He did not seem to be able to take things from others. In general, Patrick would not play with the other children in the class, nor would he try to become involved in the activities the teacher suggested. The activities that he did attempt were holding a block in his hand, placing the magnetic pieces on the board or pushing a truck around on the floor, but only within a very restricted space. Patrick's father was described as an alcoholic who had been hospitalized on several occasions; his mother worked to support the family and had little time for Patrick. On more than one occasion Patrick's father was overheard talking to his son in a violent and hostile manner; for example, once, when his son got off the tricycle and came over to him, he said, 'You get back on that bike you little bastard and if you don't I'll smash that bike on your head.' Patrick seemed to live in a loveless, hostile world. It is perhaps not so surprising that he showed very little interest in the playgroup and could only become involved in such a limited range of activities. It was as if he had virtually given up attempting to establish effective contact with his world. Little is known of this child's very early life experiences, except that he has had this harsh home environment from birth.

Patrick has not formed an effective basis for sublimation. Play and toys—themselves the objects with which he should have been able to begin the process of sublimation—seemed not only to represent an unsatisfying object, but were often completely identified with it. All the fears, anxieties and retaliation phantasies of the original internal object were still attached to the toys, and everything Patrick did with them was fraught with dangers. Thus, for example, the paper that the little girl gave him could become the dreaded penis that would attack him for the phantasy of his own attack upon his mother's insides. In order to stave off destruction, Patrick imposed rigid restrictions on his relationships to things and to people, and I suspect that this was his way of attempting to relieve himself of the enormous anxiety that he must constantly have felt. It may have seemed to him that if he could isolate himself and not have to relate to anyone, he would be safe. Perhaps he could make some contact with me and allow himself to touch me, because he felt I understood him. As I made no demands upon him and did not force him to do anything, it was safe for him to experiment. However, his touch was fleeting and not repeated. He could not as yet turn to new activities.

Patrick reduced his anxiety by limiting his contact with reality and by retaining as much as possible the original defenses against sadism. He could neither project his sadistic impulses nor identify parts of them with outer reality so that symbolic sublimation would be able to take place. Patrick was unable to make use of symbols because he could not substitute. When I attempted to become involved in his play by introducing a new thing such as a plastic magnetic orange or banana, he recoiled, moved away and looked at me vacantly. This vacant stare remained for several seconds, and then Patrick went back to placing the pieces on the board, ignoring my pieces and not looking at me. I had become another threatening object that seemed to raise phantasies in him. Only after such phantasies were quelled did he seem able to recover and to go back to placing his pieces on the board.

In speaking of the 'symbolic equation', Segal notes:

> The symbolic equation between the original object and the symbol in the external world is, I think, the basis of the schizophrenic's concrete thinking where substitutes for the original object, or part of the self, can be used quite freely, but ... they are hardly different from the original object: They are felt and treated as though they were identical with it. This nondifferentiation between the thing symbolized and the symbol is part of a disturbance in the relation between the ego and the object. [Segal, 1957, p. 93]

Thus, for Patrick the symbol was the object and stimulated just as much anxiety as the original persecutory object; in fact, the symbol stimulated part of the dreaded harsh superego and prevented any further interaction between inner phantasies and the external world, because of the ego's low capacity to experience anxiety without the fear of annihilation (Weininger, 1984). The early projective identification of the paranoid position of 'fearing another' forced Patrick to stop further development of symbols in his attempt to prevent further destructive impulses from getting at him (Klein, 1946; Weininger, 1984). That is, if he projected his sadism and identified with the object, he would not be able to control the object and then he would be depleted. His thinking was omnipotent: 'What I phantasize in my inner world will occur in the outer world, and so in order to prevent this I have to stop thinking and doing.' As the external world was experienced as bad, he wanted to destroy it, but he feared that if he did, there would be retaliation. Thus, growth was inhibited and the emotional energies were directed solely towards preserving inhibition of impulses and inhibitions of learning.

For a child such as Patrick, symbolic equation makes everything dangerous because sublimation of aggression cannot occur. Instead, the aggression was projected, the projection could not be adequately controlled and anxieties increased. Trapped in this situation, Patrick had insufficient emotional energies to allow healthy symbol formation to take place, even if the rigid superego had permitted it. There was no energy left to initiate or sustain social interactions or pleasures. He could neither develop new symbols nor alter original ones. Patrick was thus held prisoner in his limited and dangerous world and could not escape. Therefore, he compulsively used his few symbols, and even these were symbolic equations of the paranoid–schizoid position. Change was too threatening, and survival was maintained only by imposing tragic limitations on development.

An even more extreme example of the rigidity of the symbolic equation, with apparently none of the devious justification provided by the deprived and hostile early environment of Patrick's home, is Carl, a three-year-old boy, who was referred to me for play psychotherapy because of his refusal to 'talk'. When I first saw Carl, he was standing beside his mother and father looking at a wall; he neither moved nor talked but seemed absorbed by the blank wall. When I said that the four of us would meet in the room next-door, Carl gave no sign that he had heard me. His father took Carl's hand and led him to the interview room. Carl came along with no fuss or talk. Once in the room, he resumed his standing position staring at a wall. He remained standing beside his seated father for 20 minutes, and neither mother nor father could interest him in sitting or playing with the toys in the room. Carl's parents were concerned about his lack of language. They reported, 'He said three or four words when he was 23 months old, and he used these words for about five months, and now he doesn't say anything. It is hard for us to know what he wants; he grunts and points but we never seem to get him the right thing. He cries and screams a lot, and his original words, like "go", "dog", "bye", are not in his vocabulary any longer.' The parents indicated that he crawled, stood, and walked 'early', that he was toilet-trained at about two years six months and had remained bowel- and bladder-trained except for 'occasional accidents'. The parents could give no further information about their son's lack of speech. When I asked about his way of relating to other people, they said, 'Now that you mention it, he does seem peculiar. We thought that it was just that he wasn't ready to play with other children.' Carl's response to other people was one of complete indifference. It was as if the others were not there, and he did not respond or speak to them. When I invited him to play with me, he did not move and looked at me as if I did not exist.

When I asked the parents how he responded to affection, they said he had never been a cuddly baby, but for the past several months he did not want to be held, and if he was held, he seemed to try to 'slip out of our arms'. I asked his mother to pick him up and place him on her lap. She did this, and Carl sat on her lap as if he were sitting on a chair: he neither gave her any recognition, nor did he adjust his body to her lap. He just sat upright and gave me the impression that he did not acknowledge his mother. When she tried to be affectionate and cuddly, Carl slipped off her lap and stood beside her, whereupon her feelings of despair and frustration gave way to tears. Rather than interpret the situation at this point, I said that I would play with Carl while his parents remained in the room. I offered him a teddy-bear, a truck, a stick and a ball. I placed these at his feet and then spoke about each toy. Carl did not look at the toys but stared away, and when I placed the ball in his hand, he held it for a moment and then let it slip out of his opened hand. Indeed, he did not respond to any of these toys. When I asked the parents whether he had any favourite toy, they replied that he liked a yellow plastic vegetable grater. This was a circular kitchen utensil comprised of two pieces, a round top and a circular bottom piece, which fitted together. When the top knob was turned, vegetable pieces emerged out of the bottom cylinder. I asked what he did with this grater, and they said, 'He turns the top knob round and round for hours at a time.' When I asked whether they placed vegetables in the container, they said, 'No, because he would make a mess.'

At this point I asked the parents to leave. Carl seemed not to notice their departure. He stood beside the chair, staring at the wall, did not seem to be anxious and continued to evince no interest in the room. When I presented him with a small cylinder on a stick, he began to spin the cylinder. I could only interest him in this kind of motion, and he seemed to need to make the movement by himself. He did not want to draw, scribble or use any other materials. He continued to spin the cylinder on the stick, seemingly oblivious to my presence. However, after 15 minutes of spinning he glanced at me. I remained seated beside him, not touching him, and I had the feeling that he could continue the spinning forever without allowing me to enter his world.

Carl's phantasy life was severely limited; he showed practically no symbol formation other than an attraction to spinning objects. His total lack of interest in the world was because he had not been able to give outer reality symbolic meaning. Therapeutic work with Carl indicated that he had experienced extreme sadism towards the loved primal object and fear of annihilation because of phantasized revenge and retaliation. As a result of this Carl developed and maintained very powerful splitting, which was a defense to keep badness away from the object and thereby preventing himself from becoming annihilated. Rigid behaviour sustained by constant vigilance ensued. The more Carl could control and limit his interest, the less chance there would be of sadistic impulses being experienced along with anxiety about his own destruction. He initiated very little behaviour; he moved only when led or carried, he did not feed himself, and even sleeping was a problem. He lay on his bed with his eyes open for 'most of the night', and his parents indicated that 'whenever we go in at night to see him, he is lying there with his eyes wide open. We wonder if he ever sleeps.' Essentially he could not formulate early symbols because all symbols became the original object. I think that Carl could evince no interest in anyone or anything because of the symbolic equation—everything became the dreaded object. His method of control was to keep the persecutory object from being attacked by him and from attacking him by not giving symbolic meaning to his outer world. The outer world then remained powerless, totally lacking interest; as long as he maintained this 'benign' state, he would not be destroyed—that is, his sadism would not evoke retaliation. His ego therefore could not develop.

As these examples indicate, the symbolic equation involves a regression to, and/or entrapment within, the paranoid–schizoid position. In normal development in the early paranoid–schizoid position, when the rudimentary creation of symbols through splitting[2] is accompanied by effective mothering, the symbolic equation can be transcended and changed to the symbol formation characteristic of the next stage of development, which Klein calls the 'depressive position'. With 'good enough' mothering children reach this position and have the kinds of experiences within it that permit them to cope with anxieties related to damage and loss arising from destructive phantasies. They are able to be confident in the return of the loved object in a non-damaged state. Their expressed aggression has been tolerated and contained, and they have survived the phantasized persecutory and retaliatory attacks associated with the 'bad' internal object. The object can now be perceived as whole: both good and bad are perceived to flow from the same object, and ambivalent feelings can begin to be recognized and resolved.

'Good-enough' mothering allows for the kind of early reparation and creativity we saw in Jeremy's language and activities. This is accomplished in part through the process of introjection, which keeps the internal object safe by 'borrowing' from the external object or parts of it. Originally the mother or parent 'lends' the infant parts of him- or herself, so that the child is able to tolerate anxiety. The parent contains the child's anxieties, in a sense 'holding' them until the child can handle them himself. This holding of feelings by another[3] allows the child to develop the capacity to further the distinction between inner and outer reality and to see symbols as the way in which objects can be guarded from any further hostility and destructiveness. The object is saved, the ego can differentiate inner from outer reality, and symbols, which act to prevent hostile impulses and reduce super-ego guilt, intensify the child's interest in the outer world. Curiosity, exploration and an adventurous spirit increasingly predominate over inhibitions and fearfulness.

The symbol formations that emerge with the passage into the depressive position not only permit the child to become more interested in outer reality because of the need to repair the damaged object through sublimation, but also permit abstract thought processes to occur. The child begins to consider the complexities and interrelatedness of symbols and combines two symbols to create a new one. A five-year-old took one symbol—a lollypop, which he said represented 'something good to have inside you' (symbol for the loved nurturing mother)—and some water (perhaps representing milk) and stirred the candy into the water to make a sweet pink liquid. He then said, 'If I put this good stuff into the freezer, I will have another kind of lollypop, a pink ice cube.' In this 'making new' in the real world he provided a vivid micro-enactment of the transformations and integrations taking place within his internal world. In effect, this represents creative transformation of the psychic past that Segal describes as 'a new achievement belonging to the depressive position'. As she points out:

> . . . The capacity to symbolize and in that way lessen anxiety and resolve conflict, is used in order to deal with the *earlier* unresolved conflicts by symbolizing them. Anxieties, which could not be dealt with earlier on, because of the extreme concreteness of the experience with the object and the object-substitutes in symbolic equation, can gradually be dealt with by the more integrated ego by symbolization, and in that way be integrated. [Segal, 1957, p. 396]

This symbolization and integration continue on throughout life.

NOTES

1. In projection, the individual projects aspects of oneself into another person. These aspects, primarily impulses, are then experienced as being contained by the other person. This person may then be feared as a persecutor or loved as an ideal. This person may also be viewed as being 'like' the projector. The projector may identify with this person, who now contains these projected impulses and is the earliest form of empathy. Fears of retaliation and persecution may arise from the projection of hate onto the other person and not necessarily from actual experiences of being hated.

2. Very early splitting occurs when the primal object—the breast—is divided into good and bad in order for the ego to maintain its integrity. 'It is splitting which allows the ego to emerge out of chaos and to order its experiences' (Segal, 1973, p. 35). The split-off parts may be projected into another object (person) and 'identifying parts of the object with

parts of the self, the ego forms its first most primitive symbols' (Segal, 1973, p. 36).

3. As Winnicott (1975) explains, 'the baby is being held by a mother who adapts to ego needs. ... The mother holds the situation, and does so over and over again, and at a critical point in the baby's life. The consequence is that something can be done about something. The mother's technique enables the infant's co-existing love and hate to become sorted out and interrelated and gradually brought under control from within in a way that is healthy' (p. 236).

CHAPTER FIVE

Reparation and restoration

W hen three-year-old Peter came into the playgroup classroom, he looked around the room and then came over to me, took my hand and said that he wanted to 'make a painting'. He had known me for three months, and we often had friendly, spontaneous conversations, sometimes from across the room and at other times close to me. He did not seem concerned that the other 11 children in the room, all about the same age, watched him as he continued to go about his play in a very business-like manner. This day he led me by the hand to the painting easel. He took a large brush and streaked yellow paint across a big sheet of paper. He then made large streaks with red and black paint. He went on to do two more paintings, using a wide range of colours, sometimes streaked on with his right hand, at other times with his left. In his second painting he wiped the painting with his hands and announced that this was an 'Octopus sleeping'. The third painting became 'Dinner-time'. He said to me that when the paintings were dry, he wanted to give them to his Mummy. The paintings were put to dry, and Peter began to play with a toy set of small *Brio* trains, which occupied him for the next 40 minutes. During that time he talked about how fast the train was going, whether it was going over a bridge or under a bridge and what kind of 'stuff' the train was carrying. Sometimes he directed the conversation to me, at other times he spoke to himself. Children may do the latter in order to clarify their thoughts by hearing themselves talk. Peter enjoyed his play, and when snacktime came he was pleased and ate heartily.

Peter had not shown such enthusiasm for his play, for materials or for his snack for quite a while; when his mother came to pick him up, I showed her the paintings, and she remarked, 'Isn't that marvellous. He hasn't painted for months, and now he has made three paintings. I'm so happy that he has gone back to painting. He used to enjoy it, and I don't know why he stopped.' She said that she was particularly pleased because one of his paintings was a picture of 'Mummy and me' and represented for her a closeness between them, something that she felt had been missing for the past while.

Peter's paintings appeared to be a reparative act and seemed to have freed him so that he could go on and play with the trains as well as eat his snack. The paintings looked like an interplay of lines and colours, with much crossing over of lines, particularly the 'Mummy and me' painting, and I think that this represented the unconscious phantasy of early attacks on the breast and mother's body being repaired by a painting of himself and his mother. Giving the paintings to his mother represented giving part of himself back to her, the part that he phantasized he had stolen from her. By making the reparation, he could continue to play. His play with the trains appeared symbolic of 'good intercourse' when he was pushing the train in and out of the bridge (tunnel) and up and down the hill, representing the reparative wish expressed in genital coitus. Peter often laughed as he pushed his train, and when I asked what he was doing he said that 'it was fun' and 'felt good'. When I asked if he was pushing his train into the

Mummy bridge, Peter said, 'Of course!' I asked if his train was doing good things for the Mummy, and Peter simply looked at me and with an expression of complete acknowledgement said, 'Yes!'

Peter was able to offer reparation, which was pleasing to his mother and which unconsciously repaired his phantasized image of his mother. At snacktime he was no longer tentative about eating. Furthermore, his relationship with me was such that I became the good father who was not going to castrate him for 'fixing up' the mother. Our relationship assisted him with his reparation and reinforced his identification with the good penis.

Peter's mother indicated that he had recently been overly aggressive and was difficult to control at times. Anxiety and guilt resulting from aggression can be seen as normal aspects of his development and may have reflected his desires for further independence and development of self-control. The aggression that was expressed acted as a trigger to develop further superego control of such aggression, but not before reparative phantasies took place. That is, reparation was spurred on by aggression, which led to superego guilt. In this child the degree of anxiety was not great enough to lead to fixation or regression to an earlier state, but, rather, he could endure the onslaught of anxiety and reduce it by reparations. This was possible perhaps because of the transference to myself and sufficient early gratification.

Children who either do not have the opportunity for effective relationships when they are about three to five, or who have not had adequate early gratification, may not be able to overcome regression and aggression with the ease with which Peter had done. Their reparative phantasies are not able to develop into effective reparations because their aggression feels out of control. They unconsciously fear that they have done so many dangerous things that they will never be forgiven, and so they do not have the feeling of hopefulness necessary for reparation. Their sadistic, devouring phantasies have damaged or destroyed so much in their mothers that they cannot proceed with reparation. Their emotional energy becomes then immobilized at earlier pre-genital levels in order to stem the rise of impending doom brought about by increasing anxiety due to the aggressive phantasies.

Another little boy of four was quite unable to make any kind of reparation. When his playgroup teacher suggested that he make something to take home, he did not want to. This situation persisted for several months, and if anyone invited him to make something, he flew into a temper tantrum. Jack was the youngest of three children born to very poor and, it seemed to me, very deprived parents. They had little money and few resources to call upon. Neither parent could maintain a job, and they were continuously on welfare—the 'dole', as they called it. They often left Jack alone, even when he was three months old. They said that they had no alternative but to put him in his crib in order to go out to look for work or to line up for the dole. As a result, Jack was left unattended for hours at a time. They reported that Jack was so quiet when they returned that this proved to them that he could 'get on alone', and so they continued to leave him without a babysitter. His brother and sister remained with him after school hours, and the three became 'latch-key' children.

At the age of four, Jack was very difficult. He refused to do anything he was asked. At times he could not eat, often for two days or so, he slept where he wished, and he continued to wet and to soil his clothes. He would swear and have frequent temper outbursts, particularly if someone asked him to do something, and he would not talk to others unless he decided that he wanted to. Jack would remain silent for days at a time, except for swearing. He also would not go to the toilet or clean himself, and he would not go to sleep when asked to. His parents said that they wanted 'help for him because he won't go to school, and school won't take him like that.' How right they were! They had tried to enrol him in school, and Jack had lasted one day in a pre-school classroom. The teacher had not been able to cope with him, and he had had to be removed.

Jack's refusal to make anything to take home was his expression of his inability to make reparation to his mother and father. He felt that he had so little for himself that he could not tolerate the idea of giving anything away, particularly to those who already had so thoroughly ignored and deprived him. In order to make something, he felt he had to take it from himself. This was experienced as a further loss of internal objects, something that I felt Jack just could not suffer. His feeling of being persecuted was expressed in his refusal to do anything that he was asked and in his lack of communication, except when he wanted to. Everything and everyone was seen as attacking or demanding, and no doubt Jack felt that he would never be capable of anything that would bring him enough from another. Thus, when he was three months old, he remained quiet when his parents came home, and this proved to his parents that he was 'fine' without them. Actually, I think Jack was trying to be 'so good' in order to get his parents to stay at home with him. His attempts to be good for them, not to cause any stir, met with failure, and the hopelessness of that situation transferred itself to all situations. He could never do enough or be enough for anyone, and any attempt to do so would only be met with failure—a failure that was experienced by Jack as a further persecutory attack. Thus he did nothing, would have little to do with others and utterly refused to make anything to take home.

Jack also would not allow others to do anything for him, because this would also be experienced as an attack; he avoided relationships because he did not know what the other person would want of him in return. He seemed to be feeling that nothing had worked before, why should it work now? He could not acknowledge his own helplessness, for that made him even more vulnerable. Thus he was forced to view his need for nurturing and dependency as a serious threat to his existence, and any reference to this by word or deed was met with a temper outburst. Essentially, Jack could not trust another person, nor could he have any hope that he could make things better.

During the time that I worked with Jack, I made no demands of him except to tell him that we would meet in a special room once a day for a little while and that there were things in the room that we could use if we wanted to. Jack did not say that he would enter the room, but, surprisingly, he did come into the room with me. However, he insisted that the door remain open and that the toys I had brought for him remain outside the room. The room was, therefore, bare, except for two chairs, a table, and a sink. During the first month, we came into this empty room, and I interpreted to him that I thought that he experienced everything as persecutory, saying, 'a lot of things have been very scary and bad for you.' When I said he wanted everything empty like he felt it was when he was a baby, he looked at me and said, 'Shut up, I don't want you to talk like that.' In the next session, I again connected the emptiness with the persecutory anxiety, saying, 'getting things from Mum and Dad always made you feel scared.' Jack responded that he 'didn't mind being alone', and anyway it was none of my business. Jack seemed to understand that his feelings were frightening him and that he had to keep them out (represented by keeping all the toys out of the room), and that these feelings were usually aggressive and destructive. Therefore, he had to keep everyone and everything away from him, otherwise he might kill them. These projections of his phantasy allowed him to maintain some degree of stability—by avoiding others, he was avoiding his feelings. The consistency of his session, his freedom to control the room (his internal objects) and his perception of me as unchanging and non-demanding helped Jack to feel that he could gradually control his feelings. The projections gradually diminished. He showed this by initiating conversations with me about how people got sick and needed help. I interpreted that if a child got sick then he had to be taken care of and that then it was not the child's fault. This interpretation acknowledged that dependency could be gratified without acknowledging the donor, and therefore independent feelings would not be unconsciously threatened. Surprisingly, Jack agreed. This seemed to be a turning-point, because at the next session he brought the box of toys into the room. I asked if I could put his name on this box so that it would remain his for all the time we were together. Jack agreed.

This change seemed to be in the direction of hopefulness. However, Jack did not want to use the crayons, paper, glue or string in his box. He played with two trucks—a small one, the 'baby truck' and a big one, the 'mummy truck'; he usually had the big truck being carted about by the small truck, which I interpreted as his attempts at reparation— that is, he was not asking for help, he was giving help to the big 'mummy truck'. Periodically he would throw the 'baby truck' against the wall, saying, 'It isn't big enough, it isn't strong enough, it's too small.' I interpreted these remarks as his difficulty in trusting his reparation, but also in trusting the transference-treatment process, saying that he had been so disappointed so often that he was finding it difficult to allow himself to trust.

As the mummy truck was carted about, Jack said that he should put some stuff into the truck, and he put crayons into it. I said that he was trying to give the mummy truck back her insides so that she might feel like a strong truck and maybe help the baby truck. Jack did not say anything, but he went on stuffing crayons into the truck. When he could not get them all in, he became very angry and threw the baby truck against the wall. I interpreted this as his fear that he was giving all his things away; he was experiencing his own jealousy and was afraid that he would be empty and then destroyed because he had no more good things left in him. I then said that I thought that he was afraid that he would lose his 'wiener' (penis) because the mummy truck wanted everything from him. He became quiet and pensive, looked at me curiously and said, 'Why do you say wiener? I'm not supposed to talk about that, but I think about my wiener a lot.' I said that I thought that he was afraid that someone would take it away from him—and he replied that his Dad had said that if he didn't 'pee properly he would cut if off and give it to someone who could use it properly.'

Jack's attempts at reparation had stopped because he had phantasized that he was not giving the mother truck the proper things in the proper way. Whereas reparation might be achieved by a good penis, his penis was not proper and, therefore, bad. So he had to punish the baby truck for inadequate reparation by throwing it at the wall. Once again his feeling of hopelessness came back to him. Such feelings implied that he questioned the hopefulness of the transference and that he also questioned whether he could be good enough that his parents would stay with him. His phantasy was that he had driven them away because he was bad and had damaged them by stealing his mother's internal penises and babies. Thus, the child felt persecuted because of his phantasized damage to the parents, particularly to his mother but also to his father, who had already threatened to take away his 'wiener'. In the child's mind this meant that it would be taken from him and given back to his mother, from whom he phantasized that he had taken it. The reparation was to repair the damage, but the placing of the penis (crayons) into the mummy truck was to make restitution. By denying any need for dependency, and, therefore, any need to be with anyone, Jack's greed and jealousy could be controlled by him. In this way he was recreating for himself the goodness he felt he was giving to his parents when he was an infant and being 'good and quiet'. However, this denial did not work, and trust and hopefulness were lost. Reparation and restitution done in this restricting way were not sufficient and only evoked further paranoid persecutory anxiety. Jack remained alone in order to maintain the ego cohesiveness that he manifested at the beginning of treatment. Jack realized that he could not get his mother's comfort, and this prevented him from attempting any forms of reparation. Jack could not 'fix-up' his mummy truck by himself, and yet he could not let someone (me) help him with his reparations.

In his play with the trucks and the crayons Jack personified objects, having one object attempt to repair another; in other words, one unconscious phantasy was attempting to relieve the damage created by another phantasy. There does not appear to be a hierarchy of phantasies; rather, these phantasies exist within the deep recesses of the unconscious mind. These phantasies are controlled by the emotional energy that is available to the person. Such energy prevents their eruption into consciousness, as well as their development to less threatening phantasies, because events and situations continue to be viewed as threatening and persecutory. The stimulus for these hostile unconscious phantasies in the infant exists within the interactional dynamics between the infant and the mothering person. If an infant's phantasies are 'lived out' and confirmed in reality, as Jack's were, then the ego's survival is threatened. Thus Jack avoided events and situations by being quiet and doing little or nothing, protecting himself from persecutory attacks that he perceived would be brought on by his violent outbursts.

In his treatment Jack could not give his mother back the split-off penises that he phantasized he had taken, and this meant that the penises could not restore her. Reparation was therefore ineffective. Only when the mother is made good or whole again can the reparation process proceed. In my interpretation to Jack I pointed out that his 'wieners' did not seem to make the mummy truck full again. Jack went back to carrying the mummy truck on top of the baby truck and once again tried to push crayons into the mummy truck. This time he got a few more inside, perhaps because his patience seemed to be greater and he was taking more time. Thus we see Jack being able to integrate the split-off parts of aggression and the former ineffective reparation of 'doing nothing', which allowed him to begin the process of reparation through restoration.

Reparation is an unconscious process, and although a form of restoration can go on at a conscious level through play and through other processes, only within the unconscious can the internal objects become repaired. Only in this way can the phantasy be altered. Parents need to create an emotional climate where this can occur, but the sufficient condition seems to be that in which the unconscious phantasy creates the process of reparation and the split-off parts, which have been sadistically introjected and projected, become integrated. This process allows a change in the phantasy so that it is no longer so dangerous because it no longer contains the sadistic attacks and persecutory retaliation.

An interesting example of reparation and restoration of split-off parts was provided to me in an interview with a mother concerning the behaviour of her three-year-old son, Avi. The mother was upset because Avi behaved very aggressively and at times hostilely towards his 14-month-old sister. His last aggressive episode had been very disturbing to the parents: he was shopping with his mother and seemed calm and comfortable, but when he and his mother were in a dressing room while she was trying on a dress, a little boy peeked under the curtain. Avi followed the small child back to the child's mother and asked if the little boy was a baby. The mother replied that he was a baby because he was only 12 months old, and at that point Avi smacked the boy with his fist. Both mothers were very upset, and Avi's mother felt that the other woman was about to accuse her of not being an adequate mother. She left the store feeling very angry and upset and told Avi that he must not hurt other people.

Avi's mother went on to say that Avi was very aggressive with his sister and with his peers. He wanted his own way all the time and had no patience for other children's way of doing things. He demanded his mother's constant attention and became very fussy and cranky when he could not do things his way. However, when he was with a playgroup of three-year-olds, Avi was not at all aggressive, appearing quite different from the cranky, aggressive child pictured by his mother. In the playgroup he was quiet, wandered about looking at things, playing with toys, having snacks and painting, and he did not bother with the other children.

Avi's mother went on to describe their home life, telling me that she and her husband had a 15-minute talk with Avi every night. They usually did this separately. Avi's father was often away from home. Avi asked many questions about birth and death, brothers and sisters, and Avi's mother tried to give full anatomical details and behavioural descriptions, often using texts to illustrate. Avi was interested in bridges and bridge-building, and, as his mother was an engineer, she and Avi had long technical talks about bridges, so that Avi was able to discuss 'footings' and 'abutments', 'concrete' and 'wooden' bridges and the differences between them, and many other technical aspects of bridge-building. She felt that with these many efforts she had done so much for Avi, and now she felt slighted; she was disappointed in him because he was such an angry and demanding child. She described her disappointment as a 'feeling of being let down', and she said that her husband, who was usually impatient and volatile, was also angry with Avi because he had spent so much time talking with him about how he should do things 'properly'.

Avi's mother had approached Avi from a very logical point of view, expecting that he would respond readily to all her 'positive input'. I suggested that she might begin to think about Avi's behaviour from a very illogical point of view and about how illogical emotions usually are. She could understand this and said that she had tried to be very rational and to do things for Avi so that he, in turn, would do things for her. This approach to Avi seemed like a barter, as if he were an adult just like herself, rational and logical. She remarked that maybe she was trying too hard. I pointed out that she seemed to smother him with all her explanations and details, and in this way she was perhaps trying to smother his illogical anger. She could understand this and added that she had thought that she was stimulating him, as she wanted him to have a good teaching home atmosphere. I suggested that, because she was trying so hard, Avi was picking up her dissatisfaction and in fact her own irritation with him. She agreed that she felt angry but more frequently felt very tearful. She then added that maybe her tears were instead of anger and might be tears of disappointment. I agreed. She continued, as if now thinking aloud, wondering if Avi was feeling her despair at not being a good mother, or not thought of as a good mother, because no one would think of her as a good mother if her son hit babies. I suggested that Avi felt her feeling of not being good enough as a mother. He also felt that he had taken some of her away so that she was no longer as 'full' or as 'capable' (whole) as she would have been before. She noted that Avi did ask her why she was sad, why she got angry with him and why Daddy left so often, and she again wondered whether this was what he meant—that she wasn't a full person but a disappointed mother.

I suggested that perhaps Avi was trying to get rid of babies in order to save her from any further hurts and that he saw other babies as taking too much from her but that he did this in order to deny his own taking from her. I also reminded her of all that she gave, the amount of detail she gave about birth, bridges and other things. She responded by describing how exhausted she felt after one of her discussions with him. It was difficult for her to view Avi's irrational emotional side as one of feeling badly that he had taken so much from her, but her recognition of her exhaustion and her own anger with him seemed to convince her of this. She could now see how Avi had attacked other babies to save her. I added that he wished to save her for himself and was upset that she was exhausted and angry. I said that Avi needed to feel independent, as three-year-olds always do, and yet not have to feel that his independence was at her expense. This meant that she had to help him to do things successfully, yet carried out by himself. She said that he liked to clean the vegetables, peel the potatoes and carrots and 'even' mop the floor as well as wash the dishes. I pointed out that Avi could then see the accomplishment himself, he could see that the floor and the dishes that had been dirty were now clean, and so on. She accepted that this was a way he could help. I then suggested that perhaps he and his father help together. She said that his father liked to do the dishes, and she thought that this could be arranged. She agreed that she could see herself as over-protective and even 'over-demanding', but in a subtle way, and she could see that Avi needed 'more space and room to be himself'.

Within two weeks Avi's behaviour changed, and he was not the hostile little boy that he had been. The short interview with his mother provided the opportunity for her to help him with the process of reparation. Avi could clean up the angry 'mess' that he was making of his mother, and he could begin to do something that countered the phantasy of damaging and taking to much, leaving the mummy-object depleted, exhausted and tired. Avi's mother had also noted that he said, 'I don't want you to get old and die.' This remark suggests the presence in Avi of an overconcern about the effects of his taking too much.

Avi's aggressive behaviour was a way of preventing babies from taking too much from his mother, because he wanted her for himself (jealousy). It was also a way of trying to stave off revengeful attacks from his introjected objects, which had become sadistic and were experienced as attacking his own insides. As Klein points out, 'the Oedipus tendencies are followed by introjection of the object, which then becomes one from which punishment is to be expected' (Klein, 1928, p. 168).

The child attacks in order to fight off the expected punishment and hurt. The felt anxiety is a result, I think, of the escalating hostility in which the attacks were phanta-sized as bringing on an internal assault on himself, another attempt on his part to fend off the feeling of being attacked. To the child this would be a never-ending cycle of persecution—attack, damage and anxiety. Frustration would be more sharply felt, and most situations would be experienced as overwhelming. As his mother said, Avi could not even play any more, his play was 'perfectionistic' (as she said her own actions usually were); he was also impatient (as she noted his father was impatient with himself). She felt that Avi was not the happy little boy that he had been several months previously. Avi's introjective identification with his internal objects (parents) was exemplified by his outward behaviour. The conscious act of working with his father as a conscious companion (and, on an unconscious level, a good introject and positive identification) aided Avi's repairing and restoring of his mother. Since his father was helping him and was with him, he was no longer seen as the dangerous person that Avi had sent out of the house. Therefore, he could now gratify the mother and so help her become 'better'. His father was also at home more, which meant to Avi that he was not angry with Avi or hurt by Avi having taken the mother's penises. The anxiety resulting from the dread of father damaging him is experienced as another superego onslaught. Now the child phantasizes that he will be maimed and eaten up, ruined and consumed. The stronger the sadism, the stronger the jealousy. The more the child wants the internal object of the mother, the stronger is the desire to steal and rob from her, and the more inferior he feels.

With father not at home, Avi could not gain a 'real' basis for identification or overcome the phantasy of attacking father. Anxiety was too prominent for him to be able to do this. Avi could not see that his father could sustain his mother, and that his mother had the strength to repair any phantasized damage done by him to the father's penis. As the father's presence was felt more often, and as the child was not attacked in reality, this anxiety of the 'tyranny of a super-ego' (Klein, 1928) gradually lessened, and Avi's identification with father increased.

In one way, at least, as Avi and his father washed dishes and as his mother seemed to be less 'demanding', a kind of sublimation[1] came into effect. Avi was with his father, and his mother must have felt 'easier' to Avi. In such a way sublimation aids in the act of repairing the objects and alters the unconscious demands and their conscious representations.

Avi cleaned the house happily and successfully. He felt that his parents could help and heal each other, and his anxieties regarding attacks and revenge for damage could subside. Avi's feelings of hope and trust in himself were also restored,[2] enabling him to maintain love for his parents and to deal with reality more accurately.

Avi could now see his parents as being able to help him; his aggressive behaviour had diminished greatly, and he and his father made bridges together and washed dishes together, while he continued to help his mother clean up. His parents described his conversations with them as calmer, slightly less intense and less detailed, while they gave Avi more opportunity to express what he was thinking rather than overwhelming him with their detailed descriptions. Their relationships were restored.

When reparation is achieved, psychosexual growth and development continue, the Oedipal revengeful and destructive phantasies are worked through, and a successful resolution is achieved. This freeing of energies through reparative action persists throughout our lives. For example, let us think of the traditional practice of gift-giving. When adults give each other gifts about which both are pleased, their pleasure in each other may be enriched and intensified. It takes two, as it were, to create a successful reparation. The climate for successful reparation is created by the other's response of pleasure, which helps the unconscious phantasies become less threatening; perhaps a sadistic superego, an angry conscience, becomes less restrictive or harsh, allowing the ego functions, the doing part of the child, to emerge and be fulfilled. Thus a child like Avi may have spent his life either trying to repair or avoiding reparation if his parents had remained trapped in their own remote rigidities.

A happy postscript to our first example of three-year-old Peter, who made the 'Mummy and me' picture as a gift for his mother, vividly reminds us of the possibility of a creative resolution that is productive and forward-looking. Peter's mother had been delighted by the first picture and let him know how pleased she was. Peter's next picture consisted of a paper filled with small lines radiating from the centre. In a loud voice he called his creation 'Sunshine'. He actually squealed with delighted laughter as he looked at his finished picture. This picture was the sun shining—or perhaps the *son* shining. He was pleased with himself; he had been able to do something that pleased his mother, and now he symbolically created a pleased son representing his successful reparation. His mother, by responding so positively, had created a climate in which Peter could grow emotionally. He became happy with what he could do and demonstrated his growth by his inventive painting. However, perhaps of even greater significance was the assurance Peter felt, that he could give pleasure to his mother without the threat of retaliation from his phantasized father, who was now not perceived by Peter as jealous of whatever Peter could give to his wife. Peter saw his mother and father happy together. Peter's behaviour had also changed: he was friendly to the girls, he spoke more often to the female adults in the group and generally seemed less afraid of trying to do new things. Essentially, I think Peter has shown an increased integration of the penis-object, now phantasized as the good object that can be used in creative, fulfilling ways.

Avi's mother was able to create a reparative climate by engaging him as an active participant in the 'work of the house'. He cleaned vegetables, emptied waste-baskets and helped her to tidy rooms. Avi responded to her suggestions 'to help her' very positively and entered into this activity with great vigour and energy. Within about two weeks a dramatic change was observed in the playgroup. Avi came into the room, went to the painting table and remained with his 'mixed media' painting for about 20 minutes. He created a picture using paints, glue, bits of paper, wool, cloth and cellophane, and when he had completed it he announced that he wanted to take it home. He then went to a small group of children playing with musical toys, and instead of holding his hands over his ears as he usually did, he participated in the music-noise. He smiled a lot, talked to the children and adults, was pleased with what he did and obviously was exploring the toys. He became part of a small group of children who were very pleased with what they were playing and with themselves and expressed this pleasure by statements such as, 'Isn't this nice!' 'This is a good house,' 'I like this bridge,' 'I'm taking this box home.'

For Avi, successful reparation and some resolution of persecutory anxiety appeared to have been accomplished by the reparative atmosphere at home. Whereas before he had felt that his efforts were usually incomplete or lacking in sufficient detail because his mother asked for more and expressed her dissatisfaction (her continued phantasized attacks) by wanting Avi's productions to have greater detail, he now felt more confident in what he did. He felt more at ease with other children, no longer seeing them as attacking but as friends. It was important for Avi to make a successful painting first of all, something he had not yet done, before he could be with others. Once he had made the painting, the pleasure at his success was obvious in the way he subsequently approached the others. He took the painting home, and his mother later told me how pleased she was with it and that she had hung it up in her study. She also said that Avi was no longer aggressive towards other children, although sometimes he still hit his baby sister. She could now also see that sometimes his baby sister imitated him by wanting her attention when she was talking with Avi.

As the child is able to see that his or her reparations are successful, a belief in his or her own goodness grows. The goodness is in part the result of feeling less persecution and in part a reduction in the depressive guilt and anxiety about having taken too much, and done so much damage that successful reparation is not possible. Peter and Avi began to feel successful when their parents created a receptive climate. Their freedom from feelings of attack, guilt and despair permitted a blossoming of further development. This in turn pleased their parents, so that the parents were further motivated to help their children, and reciprocal interaction was set up between child and parent. Also, a dynamic transference evolved between the internal and outer worlds, so that the child's internal and external reality more closely matched the parents' expectations, which themselves had been altered because they had begun to understand the anxieties of their children.

The parents were pleased by their children's work, and the children saw and felt this, which helped them to overcome some of their anxieties. It was now possible to have a feeling of being good, a belief in oneself, and also to re-establish the parents as idealized objects. The idealized good object is internalized, and this good internal object helps to master frightening phantasies and supports further integration, adaptation and development. The original good object is reinstated in a more mature and developed form—that is, as a feeling of pride in oneself and one's accomplishments. This allows for a greater curiosity and exploration. Interventions at minor crisis points with children who have had good early parenting and who are for the most part emotionally healthy, as these two children were, can help to resolve issues that could develop into serious problems. Because of the adaptability of these parents and their acceptance of their children, this work could be carried out in single or several interviews. Specific guidance was offered to create 'climates' for emotional growth for the whole family; in some instances play psychotherapy was recommended.

The Oedipus complex triggers earlier persecutory and depressive anxieties. Excessive hostility, denial, impulsiveness, dissociation of unconscious phantasies and rigidity of defenses may prevent children from working through these anxieties. However, children can be prepared and helped to work through these anxieties. In this process reparation can strengthen and allow the child to have sufficient belief in himself or herself to be able to work through the Oedipal conflicts. These conflicts do not await resolution of persecutory or depressive feelings before emerging but originate within the anxieties of the paranoid–schizoid and depressive positions. (The Oedipal position is further elaborated in part three.)

NOTES

1. Klein points out that 'identification is a stage preliminary not only to symbol-formation but at the same time to the evolution of speech and sublimation' (Klein, 1975, p. 86).
2. We can be more effective when talking to parents if we avoid psychological terms connoting 'serious pathological' underlying emotional disturbance. It is better to talk about the 'illogical' aspects of emotions and to discuss unconscious processes in their conscious manifestations. Thus, I steer clear of terms such as 'reparation' and 'unconscious phantasy', and I talk instead of the child 'wanting to make you feel better', 'doing something for you', 'daydreaming' or 'using his or her imagination'.

PART THREE

Anxiety and independence: the Oedipal position and the emergence of the sufficient ego

CHAPTER SIX

An uneasy bedtime and two bad mornings: some anxieties of the early Oedipal

My wife and I often visited three-year-old Glen and his parents at their home. One evening we were having dinner together and the following incident took place: Glen was preparing for bed. He wanted to have three stories read to him by his mother, which she was quite willing to do. My wife was discussing some travel plans with Glen's father, and I was reading a book next-door to Glen's room, where his mother was reading to him. After a couple of stories, Glen's mother emerged and began talking to me. Glen complained, at first softly and then more loudly. His mother returned to him to find that Glen had filled his bed with his stuffed toys, leaving no room for her to sit down. She suggested that if he wanted her to sit down on the bed and continue to read to him, he would have to remove some of the toys. When Glen did not remove the toys, she returned to carry on her conversation with me. Glen was quiet at first but then began to cry loudly and plaintively. When his mother went back, he quietened down; she came out of his bedroom within five minutes, smiling, and announced, 'I found out what was wrong and why his crying was so persistent and baby-like.'

When she had gone back to Glen's room, he had asked, 'Where is Daddy? I want him to sleep with me.' His mother answered, 'He is talking with Sylvia.' Glen then asked, 'Why are you talking to Otto in that room?' Suddenly Glen's mother realized why he was crying so insistently. She told Glen that she loved him, that she and Daddy loved each other and that Daddy loved him very much, that everything was fine and that Mummy and Daddy were okay. She repeated this another time, and Glen smiled, and, as his mother told me, 'He fell asleep almost immediately.'

Glen was worried. He was distressed by the fact that his father was talking with another woman in one room and his mother was talking to another man in a different room. Glen seemed to be having the phantasy that his father and mother were separating and would no longer be his mother and father. He worried that he was not loved and that he had done something that might have stopped them from loving him. He saw himself as the centre, that it was his parents' love for him that kept them together. While he saw that they often kissed and hugged each other, he nevertheless saw himself as the reason for their reciprocal love. Glen phantasized that his love was so strong that it kept his parents together, loving and safe, but that he was keeping them together for himself.

He experienced great anxiety when he realized that his father was talking to another woman and that he could hear his mother talking to me in a different room. He removed all his stuffed toys from his bed, made room for his mother and cried for her to come to him. She was aware of his distress, from the quality of his crying and because he had made space for her, and she recognized that he needed to know that his mother and father still loved each other and him. She had been speaking softly to me, trying not to disturb Glen, but she probably spoke loudly enough for him to hear our voices but not the content. This led perhaps to his phantasy that something was wrong, even that he was the cause of the problem. She was sensitive to his feelings and to his need to know that he was not losing his parents and that they were not losing each other. With this knowledge, Glen fell asleep easily, assured that he was still a strong boy capable of holding his parents together and that he had done nothing to harm them. The unconscious phantasy of these early Oedipal stirrings was no doubt associated with hostility towards his loved, yet feared, father because of his desire for his mother. Glen anticipated some retaliation from his father for his attempts to have his mother sleep with him. He asked that his father come and sleep with him, perhaps as reparation, but perhaps also to control his desire for his mother.

This familiar episode of bedtime anxiety emerges from a complex web of feelings that links the child to his parents in the early Oedipal stage. As Klein points out, there is an intricate and often obscure connection between the early Oedipal turbulence and the child's whole experience in the family:

> The early stages of the Oedipus conflict are so largely dominated by pregenital phases of development that the genital phase, when it begins to be active, is at first heavily shrouded and only later, between the third and fifth year of life, becomes clearly recognizable. At this age the Oedipus complex and the formation of the superego reach their climax. But the fact that the Oedipus tendencies begin so much earlier than we supposed, the pressure of the sense of guilt that therefore falls upon the pregenital levels, the determining influence thus exercised so early upon the Oedipus development on the one hand and that of the superego on the other, and accordingly upon character formation, sexuality and the rest of the subject's development—all these things seem to me of great and hitherto unrecognized importance. [Klein, 1928, pp. 179–180]

Two 'bad mornings' of children in our playgroup reflect some of the basic ways in which these early Oedipal promptings begin to surface in the behaviour of both boys and girls. One day I was sitting beside the sand table when Catherine, two years and eleven months old, came over and began to dig in the damp sand. I watched her for a few moments not saying anything, and then she said, 'I'm making caves,' as she scooped out the sand with her shovel, digging deeper and deeper into the sand pile. Catherine continued this for about 20 minutes, telling me what she was doing and how the caves were progressing. She said at one point that she was making a 'big cave' and then looked at me with surprise as she put her hand into the sand, noting, 'There is nothing there.' I asked Catherine what she expected to find, but she stared at me and did not respond. At that moment she left the sand table, saying that she was going to 'do niceness to Lop' (the group's rabbit, which was free to roam around the classroom). Catherine went over to the rabbit, grabbed it by its neck and started to squeeze. When Lop managed to squirm out of her grip, Catherine looked back at me with a very sad expression. I said that Lop 'likes your niceness but I don't think he likes to be held.' Catherine returned to the sand table and continued to dig in the sand, but this time very half-heartedly, and after a few moments she wandered away from the table.

She drifted over to a female teacher who was about to read a story, sat close to her and seemed interested in the story. I was at that moment occupied in the doll centre, being served tea by a girl and a boy, both three. Before I was able to discuss Catherine's behaviour at the sand table, the teacher who had been reading to her came over to me to talk about her. I had not spoken with her about Catherine at all. The teacher said that at first Catherine was very interested in the story and sat quietly beside her. After a few minutes, however, she started to pick at her face with her fingers. She pinched both cheeks, and when the teacher asked her what she was doing, Catherine replied, 'I'm hurting my face.' When the teacher asked why she was doing this, Catherine responded, 'Because Mary [her mother] broke my face.' The teacher then remarked that she did not know what Catherine meant by saying that Mary broke her face, and Catherine said, 'She just broke my face, that's all.' The teacher tried to pursue this by asking why, and the child just reiterated, 'Mary hurt my face.' When the teacher asked whether she was sure of this, Catherine replied, 'Yes, she spanked me in my face on the street.' This short conversation upset the teacher because she wondered whether the child had been physically abused. I suggested another explanation—that we were listening to some of Catherine's phantasy and that I did not think that her mother had hit or spanked her. However, I did say that we had an excellent opportunity to check this out, because Catherine's mother was at the school that morning. I suggested to the teacher that she should talk to her about Catherine and try to discover whether something was bothering Catherine or whether something had happened that morning.

The teacher talked with the mother, who said that she could recall nothing particularly upsetting that had happened that morning. She and Catherine had had a usual morning and arrived at school in what mother described as 'good shape'. However, the mother reminded the teacher that four weeks ago her father had died, and that she had suddenly gone to her parents' hometown 3000 miles away and had been separated from Catherine for about two weeks. The mother added that her husband was out of town now and would be away from home for several days. She said that she found Catherine 'testing and clinging' and 'more so these past few days than usual'; she had told Catherine that her father would be away for a few days and would be home soon. She added that she had called in a babysitter for a short while, and Catherine was 'very unhappy about this'. There was no indication that the mother had slapped Catherine.

The teachers had noticed other changes in Catherine's behaviour. She had been very aware recently of 'getting dirty', she was making sure that 'things were as they should be' (in their proper place) and had insisted on showing off her new dress and new shoes for the past several mornings.

Catherine was worried about getting a stain on her dress, was often observed brushing herself or brushing her hands together to knock the sand off her fingers, and she often wanted to wash her hands when she had paint spots on them. Also, the dress she wore seemed particularly important, and she wore the same favourite smock-dress continuously. Her mother referred to this dress as Catherine's 'security dress', and this morning Catherine frequently smoothed its folds.

Catherine's behaviour reflected oral and anal anxieties in their early Oedipal form, arising at a period of unavoidable family strain (the successive enforced absences of mother and father). In her sand play Catherine seemed to have been making a 'receptive' female cave, which suggested that the original oral aim of gratification and taking from the mother was being transferred to genital development. Catherine noted that there was nothing in the cave, looked disappointed and sad and went over to give 'niceness' to the rabbit. This niceness was the oral gratification, which she still needed but which was being frustrated. When Catherine ate her snack, she held it in both hands, looked at it but ate very little. She wanted the food to be there, needed to look at it, but showed her oral frustration by not eating. The need for 'niceness' from mother and the growing feeling of not getting everything from mother led to feeling disappointed and angry with her. Her mother was naturally preoccupied with grief, and no doubt this exacerbated Catherine's feelings of disappointment. She wanted to find something in her cave, but when she found nothing, she felt disappointed. The disappointment in relation to mother led to a change in the identification pattern with her. In this way receptivity for the penis is induced in the girl, who then turns to the father as her love object (Klein, 1928, p. 167).

Early Oedipal desires are coupled with feelings of guilt and castration and, in the case of the little girl, are in part the result of an attempt to take the penis-object that the child phantasizes the mother contains within her body. This 'taking away' from mother adds to the sense of guilt already engendered by the pregenital superego, a product of early identification with her. Surely taking such valued objects will evoke retaliation and revenge. As oral sadism is very strong at this point in the young child's life, biting, devouring and cutting play a role in taking, orally, these valued objects, which, in turn, become attacking, and also result in an attacking persecutory parent. (In the housekeeping centre I have been very impressed by the three-year-olds' cutting activity. They all want to use the plastic knife to cut the pretend fruit. They scrape and saw, talking about how they are cutting it and will eat the pieces. They also often bite the pretend food, usually by 'cutting' off a piece and then biting it.) The phantasized or 'stolen' part-object becomes allied with the superego, and, as shown by the child's behaviour, the unconscious superego also becomes the cutting, biting and devouring sadistic superego.

Catherine's superego seemed to have taken on these first characteristics. She found nothing in her cave, symbolic of how she felt at her father's departure, but also at her mother's sudden leaving. She saw herself as bad for having done something to him, something that could in phantasy or in reality result in her mother being taken away from her again, as she had been when her grandfather had died. Perhaps she felt in some way responsible for his death, or, at least, perhaps she wished that her mother would leave the home so she could have her father all to herself. Whatever had happened in her mind, she had been with her father while her mother was away, and now her father had gone, and her mother had left her with a babysitter. She felt deserted, and this was experienced as guilt, an attack from her superego. She needed to defend herself from such a sadistic superego and did this by wearing her 'security dress' and by being neat and tidy and not having stains on her dress. The need to be clean counteracted the need for punishment. If she could stay clean—that is, if she did not take anything from her mother and make herself bad (dirty)—then she would not suffer punishment. This was difficult because the playroom was full of materials that could make her dirty. The equation of dirt and badness reflected her anal anxieties, and so she wandered about the room, touching some things but making sure that nothing touched her. It was, in fact, unusual for her to spend so long at the sand table; perhaps it was because her companion at the table was male, and because I did not ask her to do anything but was quiet and accepting and in this way, I think, less threatening to her. However, there was still some threat present, because she needed to go off and make 'niceness' to the rabbit.

The oral and anal anxieties that were added to the sadistic superego encouraged Catherine to seek a new love object and thus to look upon her father as a love object. She played out the receptive nature of her sexual organs (by making caves) and viewed it in phantasy as a potential source of gratification, which she did not receive from her mother. However, as a new source of gratification it was continuously in danger of being coupled with other frustrations because of her former identification with her mother. That is, previously the girl had experienced frustrations, both orally and anally. She tried to take in part-objects from the mother, but if and when she did, she experienced persecutory anxiety. Thus, her identification through introjection was 'shaky' and threatening, but what she seemed to require was a feeling (and phantasy) that she contained objects that were attractive. She viewed these attractive objects as being able to get her the same kind of satisfactions (or frustrations) as her mother. However, as she also experienced the harshness of her superego, she attempted other forms of gratification. This other form was vaginal satisfaction, and, as Klein points out, "Not only an unconscious awareness of the vagina, but also sensations in that organ and the rest of the genital apparatus, are aroused as soon as the Oedipus impulses make their appearance" (Klein, 1928, p. 174). Frustrations and maturation make for growing awareness as well as for the sense of possibly being able to achieve satisfaction within another area of the body even though frustration was felt so strongly in other areas (oral and anal). Most children have a sense of hope and possibility, and this helps them to move through hardship, to grow and develop. Continuous severe hardship will damage hope, but if a good enough early relationship existed between infant and mother (mothering person), then the child will be able to handle difficult times.

Catherine's play with caves in her sand-digging, a genital and also an anal activity, brought into focus a new source of potential gratification as well as the hostility towards the mother, whom she phantasized as having the father's penis. This is the beginning of the Oedipal phase in the young girl, which pushes her towards seeing her father as an attractive source, a potential source of genital gratification. Persecution by her phantasy mother for taking her internal objects reinforces her identification with her father. Castration anxiety is not present as it is with a boy, but anxiety at finding nothing in the caves and the sadistic aspects of the developing superego turn the girl towards her father. Her recognition that she does not have a penis—that is, that she might be damaged by an angry mother—adds to her feelings of hostility towards her mother, but also to her sense of guilt. In phantasy it was her mother who took her internal object from her and keeps it in her body. The girl experiences a phantasized retaliation as an attack on her insides, for having stolen from the mother. Thus, in the case of a small boy it is fear and anxiety that his penis will be taken from him, whereas in a young girl her recognition of not finding a good internal object is a consequence of having the phantasy that the mother damages the girl's insides.

Catherine's symbolic expression of her phantasy of being punished was to pinch her cheeks and say that her mother 'broke her face'. Having her mother 'break her face' also seemed to me to be a fairly straightforward way of expressing her phantasy that her mother had taken the penis—that is, had damaged her. Catherine's face was whole even though she said it was broken. I think that she looked to her father to repair her face and saw him as a love object. In order to do this she had to be identified with her mother. However, her identification with her mother was shaky because her mother had left her (which, Catherine phantasized, was because she had been bad). Her grandfather had died, and Catherine may have believed that this was because her mother had taken too much from him (as she felt she did from mother), and so Catherine's father might die because Catherine was taking too much from him. The coincidental occurrences of two losses—her father's absence on a business trip and her grandfather's death—was too great. Catherine's response was to punish herself by demonstrating that her face (her body) did not contain a penis. This was an attempt to placate her mother and, in consequence, her harsh superego. To gain gratification and to get the penis that she phantasized her mother had, Catherine had to be like (identify with) her mother. Essentially, in order not to be internally damaged, Catherine had to be like her mother.

After leaving the classroom, she went to a large room equipped as a gym (all the children usually went to this room). While her mother was watching her, Catherine climbed along a horizontal ladder with another girl. She then went to the trampoline, jumped about for several minutes and then crawled into a large net that had an opening to let the children climb in and move about inside. Catherine climbed around in the net for a while, looking pleased. Her mother looked pleased with Catherine's activity, and Catherine looked over to her several times. The tacit support from her mother lessened Catherine's superego sadism, and therefore she continued jumping and climbing. It also helped her to feel well and physically capable of vigorous activity, thus contributing to her sense of pride in being a girl. Unfortunately, too many parents tend to treat their daughters as 'fragile'. This leads to girls feeling frustrated and continuously concerned about their insides because they have not had the chance to find out what they can do with their bodies. Excessive concern by parents about their daughters' activity leads to the daughters having anxiety about bodily injury and deprives them of the potential joy and pride in their bodies. Without the opportunity to exercise their bodies, they continue to feel attacked and as though their bodies are broken, rather than strong and capable.

In the case of three-year-old Dan's 'bad morning', early Oedipal stirrings were also prompted by a normal crisis in family life—in this instance, his father's minor illness. The Oedipal expression was more complex because Dan transferred some of his troubled feelings to me and saw me as a symbol of both figures in the family drama. On this particular day (I had been a familiar person in the classroom for several weeks), Dan told me directly that he was my 'friend'. We were playing together in the doll-housekeeping centre. Dan was playing the role of father and telling me what to do: I was to put the baby to bed, cook the food and clean the clothes. He continued to order me about and then said that he had to go away. He went into the cupboard, put on a fedora hat and closed the door.

In the meantime another child, Cameron, three and a half years old, asked me to come over to the blocks with him to help him build a big tower. We started to build the tower; Cameron did most of the work, and I made sure that the blocks were resting on each other. Dan left the cupboard and saw me with Cameron at the blocks. He took off his hat, came over, and immediately tried to dismantle Cameron's tower of blocks. Cameron would not tolerate this and gave Dan a push that knocked him down. Dan got up and once again tried to take down the tower. When I suggested that he could add blocks to the structure, he said, 'No, I don't want to,' but when I suggested that he put 'these small people' into the tower, he immediately joined in. He placed the 'small people' (small blocks) onto various places of the tower, putting most of them on one block, which rapidly filled up. Dan continued to run around gathering up 'small people' and placing them on the block. At this point Cameron stopped building and sat down beside me to watch.

When Dan saw this he became more frantic in trying to find blocks and grabbed some from three-year-old Tanya, who was playing with them on the other side of the room. She started to scream and ran over to recapture her pieces. Dan put the small blocks on his block, then gestured as if he were going to knock down the whole tower. Cameron leapt up to protect his structure, and Dan stopped and came to sit down beside me, just where Cameron had been sitting. When Cameron saw this, he pushed Dan over and sat down. I had my arm extended so that I could touch both Cameron and Dan. Dan seemed upset; he was quiet and seemed not to be interested in doing anything except sitting beside me. He tried to get closer to me, but by now Cameron and Tanya kept him away from me. Tanya accused him of taking her people or blocks, and Cameron said he didn't want him to knock down his tower. I reached over to Dan, but my touch seemed not enough. Dan looked at me very sadly; he looked at the housekeeping centre; he looked back at me, but made no move to leave or say anything. He sat sufficiently close to me for me to be able to touch him with my hand. His behaviour was quite different from usual, as most of the time Dan was very talkative and active, and he would play with others cooperatively, asking lots of questions and wanting to demonstrate what he knew. But now he just sat there sadly. When his teacher came over I said that I thought Dan was upset, and I was not sure if he could 'hold on'—that is, maintain his composure—much longer.

Dan 'held on'. When it was time to get ready to leave school, he showed me how well he could put on his coat and boots, but he asked me to help him with his zip. The other children were also dressing, and everybody appeared happy. However, when Dan's mother arrived, he ran to her and immediately began to cry. His crying seemed uncontrollable, and his mother hugged him, saying she did not know why he was upset. She said Dan's father was very ill with the flu at home in bed and that Dan really had not wanted to come to school this morning. He had wanted to stay with his father, but both parents had decided that it would be better for Dan to be at school as his father felt so ill and would not have been able to care adequately for his son.

Dan cried a bit more but soon left happily with his mother. Usually Dan was very pleased to see his mother after school; he would talk to her and show her what he had done, and he never asked, to my knowledge, how his father was. Nor did he ask about his father even on that eventful day. However, this morning Dan was obviously distraught and not his usual self. He continued to come to school throughout the week, but his mother said that he was subdued and concerned at home until his father recovered.

Dan's behaviour and feelings are characteristic of the early stages of the Oedipal conflict. In reality Dan had to leave his ill father, but in phantasy Dan thought that his father might die, and that he would be responsible. Dan's activities at the doll-housekeeping centre were primarily oral and anal: having me buy food, put the baby to bed and clean the clothes. This was an attempt to defend himself against a sadistic superego. He felt threatened by frustrated oral and anal desires and phantasized that his mother either did not give enough to him or do enough for him. When he played the father, wearing his fedora hat and going into the cupboard, he was trying to satisfy his oral and anal needs and impulses. He cast me in the role of the all-giving mother, but he still had to hide in the cupboard because he phantasized that he had taken the penis from me. The hat represented the penis, which he phantasized that he had removed from mother's body and he was hiding from her phantasized retaliation. He stayed a long time in the cupboard, long enough for another child to come along and 'take me away'. When Cameron asked me to come with him, as I was not in the room for Dan exclusively and therefore could not remain in the doll centre, I said loudly enough for Dan to hear that I was going to play with Cameron at the blocks and would like Dan to come. I then told Cameron that I was playing with Dan, and Cameron accepted this in a logical way and said that Dan could come. I left the centre even though I felt, without really knowing why at that point, that it was important for Dan that I be with him.

When he finally emerged, Dan wandered over to the blocks and attempted to take down Cameron's tower. The tower represented the penis, which he wanted to pull down. Cameron's violent push prevented him, and the push and the fall then became symbolic retaliation for the penis that he had removed from his mother. His aggressive and sadistic action towards Cameron's tower was perhaps a result of hostility emanating from oral and anal frustration experienced in earlier relationships. This was re-experienced with me as the mother in the doll centre. I did not completely satisfy his needs, and so Dan hid with the penis—fedora hat. I felt now that I had 'lost' him. Perhaps the penis must now be sadistic, which would be represented in phantasy as a fear of castration by his father, an anxiety arising from within the Oedipal impulse.

As Dan was angry with his phantasy mother, enacted by me, for leaving him and depriving him, he could not allow me to be loving towards him. I could only touch him as a way of making contact with him. The hostility that he experienced towards me as the mother caused him to be demanding and threatening. This also made him feel very anxious, and he tried frantically to collect all the little people and place them back in the belly of the mother—which, interestingly, was the only open block in the tower—penis. In a sense, Dan was making the penis into the mother and thus returning to her not only the penis, but all her babies, too. He was so anxious to complete this task that he took over Tanya's blocks and made her, in turn, an attacker. She wanted her toys back, and Dan seemed to react to this as if she were a persecutor; he tried to avoid her by running around the tower, pushing the small toys into the open block. The interchange between the womb and the penis reflects here Klein's description of the feminine phase of the Oedipal phantasy. As she says:

> Here we can discern two aims which merge with one another. This one is directed by the desire for children,

the intention being to appropriate them, while the other aim is motivated by jealousy of the future brothers and sisters whose appearance is expected and by the wish to destroy them in the womb. A third object of the boy's oral-sadistic tendencies in the mother's womb is the father's penis. [Klein, 1928, p. 171]

In trying to work through some of his phantasies, Dan had me become the mother who would satisfy and not threaten if he took the penis. However, his anxiety was so great that he had to hide in the cupboard; perhaps he was putting the penis–fedora hat and himself back into the mother's body (the cupboard), or he was trying to find out what else existed inside her. When I left the scene, much of his anxiety, which had been contained by my being there, became experienced by him once again. I think that Dan was afraid that his body would be mutilated, that he would be castrated by an angry revengeful mother, and this was borne out by Tanya's attacks on him. The mother was feared, and this was associated with a fear of being castrated by his father.

When Dan tried to fill the mother–tower–penis by pushing in all the small baby blocks, which may also represent faeces, he was trying to stop anxiety from overwhelming him. However, there was also the penis to deal with. If he had taken it from the mother, then it must be replaced, or his superego would punish him, possibly by the phantasy that it might annihilate his ego. If it represented the penis that his father had given her, then he would be punished by his father for stealing it. Within this phase the primary fear and dread in the child is the phantasy of castration by the father, and this fear is directly and consciously located within the penis. Dan would then stop his energetic action and hold his penis and pants with both hands for several seconds at a time, obviously assuring himself of the presence and intactness of his penis, and attempting to exaggerate the size of the penis by pulling at it. The superego within this phase is sadistic and comprised of both the phantasized mother and father. The child phantasizes that the desirable objects, which have been taken from the parents, need to be returned, and this creates anxiety for the child in relation to his or her parents. The child wants to be independent, but in order to be so he needs sufficient good objects; however, if they are phantasized as having been robbed from his or her parents, then the child fears the parents' retaliation, which represents their revenge for having had their possessions stolen.

Dan's situation was complicated by his father being very ill. As I have suggested, Dan phantasized that his father was going to die, and he wanted to be at home to do something to prevent this from occurring. When I left him and disappeared from the doll-housekeeping centre, in a way I had died, and no doubt in phantasy Dan felt responsible for this. He was so sad and depressed that he could only allow me to touch him; when I talked to him, he looked down or away and did not answer me. The depth of his depressed feelings was only apparent when his mother arrived; he could contain his feelings no longer, her presence brought on the tears, and he began to cry loudly. I do not think that he was crying for her; rather, her presence seemed to trigger a substance to his phantasy at a reality level without providing the comfort and alleviation of fear that her presence ordinarily gave. At this point there was a phantasy operating: mother's not ill; I have taken a penis from mother–father, and my father is now suffering and dying because he has been mutilated by me. By staying home and taking care of his father, Dan would have been giving his father back his penis so that he would be well. His sense of guilt was too great. He had taken something from his parents and needed to return it. Therefore, he could not play with boys and men, because he needed to curb his rivalry (aggression) towards them.

Dan was trying to identify with his father, but he was obviously having a difficult time. Unfortunately, his father had become ill just at the wrong time! Dan blamed himself for his illness and wanted to repair the situation. However, it was not just the identification with his father that constituted the early Oedipal object phase, it was also his relationship with his mother. I had often observed Dan in the doll-housekeeping centre, where he played father and girls played mother. There were usually three or four mothers and one father, Dan. The other boys who played there were usually firemen, policemen or even babies, but Dan was the father with the 'harem'. In his play, he was trying to work through the lack of oral and anal gratification and his desire to identify with the father by having many opportunities to have many women. (Perhaps some of the male patients we see who have several girlfriends at the same time are in fact trying to work through their early Oedipal feminine phase.)

Had we known that Dan was upset that morning because he wanted to stay at home with his sick father, we could perhaps have helped him work through some of his anxiety. (This may be one very good reason why parents might let teachers of young children know how their students feel.) We could have provided Dan with the opportunity to create something to take home to his mother and father. This could have been a collage with pieces of paper built upon a solid piece of paper, which would have represented the penis once more within his mother's body. He could also have created other art, which would have been left at school in his special box with his name on it. He would have been returning the desired object, yet keeping some safe for himself in his box. The object in the box would be the penis in the mother, but the libidinal aim would now be changed to become 'epistemophilic' and become a way of 'doing' or 'creating' to reduce anxiety. This is essentially the process involved in learning. Dan would have retained and freed his original love object (mother) and freed her of sadistic persecution. He would also be like his father, who had a penis and produced 'work' (as he said his father did). This is what Klein describes as the 'amalgamation of the desire for a child with the epistemophilic impulse [which] enables a boy to effect a displacement on to the intellectual plane' (Klein, 1928, p. 172). This sublimation might have helped Dan deal with the trauma he was experiencing that morning, particularly if it had been presented as an act of creativity. Had it been put forward as an academic lesson, he would have felt attacked, because he, like all boys of three, already knew everything. Being taught would have created further aggressive activity as a way of disguising anxiety, for, as Klein notes,

> . . . the resistance to teaching at this point coincides with the boy's protest [in his fear of castration] against the feminine *role,* but it is rooted also in the dread of his mother, whom he intended to rob of the father's penis, her children, and female sexual organs. [Klein, 1928, p. 172]

We can use our understanding of young children to help them through the normal pain of emotional growth and development by providing opportunities and materials in the classroom to help them work through their phantasized danger in natural and productive ways. This link between phantasy and genuine creative or intellectual achievement is not artificial. These phantasies profoundly influence not only our feelings but also our opportunities for learning about the world. By displacement of aggression to situations within reality, the child has the opportunity not only of working through unconscious phantasies, but also of being able to create art, to begin to draw and to print, to do number work, and to read. These activities require and utilize a certain amount of energy and aggressiveness, which, when used in this way, provide the child with many opportunities to explore the situations that lie in front of him or her. Play-based classroom programs, therefore, provide the maximum opportunity for children to explore their phantasies and to do so in ways that I think of as learning about the real world (Weininger, 1979).

CHAPTER SEVEN

Achieving an independent self: some problems of adolescence

The profound connection between resolving the basic tensions of the family drama and learning about the self and the world is first revealed in the earliest Oedipal stirrings, as we have seen. Normally, however, it emerges most strikingly in adolescence. The long process of separating from the parents that reaches a crisis in the teenage years may often be associated with 'severe inhibitions in regard to learning ... combined with great general intractability and an attitude of knowing better'. [Klein, 1931, p. 216]

Michael was a troubled 14-year-old with whom I worked, who exhibited such severe learning problems in an extreme form. Michael presented me with the 'facts'—as he called them—about his school. He announced that school had nothing to teach him, that he could not learn the material that was presented in Social History classes and that he 'knew everything there was to be known about the things that are important to me.' Having made this pronouncement, he went on to state that he had always known more than anyone else, and now that he was big enough he would prove it 'by not listening in class and maybe even quitting school altogether.'

Michael had had school problems since the age of eight, when he was described as a learning-disabled student in reading and mathematics. He had been examined both physically and neurologically, and the primary recommendation was that he should be in a class for learning-disabled students. Michael had entered the class defiantly and had made very little progress. However, he was promoted every year because the school authorities felt that a grade failure would be too much of a blow to his self-esteem. Michael continued in a special class, and when he entered a junior high school at 12 years of age, he could read at a Grade-3 (8-year-old) level and perform mathematical skills at a Grade-4 (9-year-old) level. Neither of these skill levels allowed him to cope adequately with the work at junior high school. Michael was failing his grade, and, while he knew this, he seemed powerless to do anything constructive. He was described by his teachers as ineducable, and their recommendation was that he should be given an early school-leaving permit and encouraged to find an apprentice-work situation.

Michael was pleased when he was told this recommendation, but he also said that he 'would not quit school'. He decided that he would stay in class until he 'was thrown out or until I decide to quit myself.' He was not going to take advice from adults and was very suspicious of any interference in his life. As Klein describes it, Michael felt 'oppressed and paralysed'. He could not make a decision or accept a recommendation. His thinking was immobilized,

. . . on the one hand by the influences of the superego which it feels to be tyrannical and dangerous, and on the other hand by its distrust of accepting the influences of the real objects, often because they are felt to be in complete opposition to the demands of the superego, but more often because they are too closely identified with the dreaded internal ones. [Klein, 1931, p. 216]

Michael could not think, nor make decisions. His superego, identified with the internal persecuting parents, had to be avoided by projective identification, and in doing so Michael was forced to maintain an independence from adults who now contained his hostile and dreaded projections. In phantasy, these adults would destroy him. They would retaliate, because of his projected destructive phantasies, making him powerless and susceptible to dangerous adult impulses. These impulses were expressed as advice and recommendations or threats and demands and contained his hostile internal projections. Michael could, therefore, not accept help, direction or nurturing from adults. He was alone and felt he was the only one who could stop these hostile influences from destroying him.

Although most adolescents do not react with such force or determination against adults, they respond to adults in similar ways. Although they have some regard for adult advice and direction, they tend to be somewhat aloof, resentful and isolated and to feel that they know better than adults what is best for them. Many adolescents go through this process of rebellion or independence, which results from perceived superego demands following regression.

Regression is an inevitable consequence of the growing-up and becoming an adult process, and it is brought on in part by the significant physiological changes arising from sexual maturation. It occurs because adolescents wish to separate from their parents but also want to be dependent on them. Adolescents have to rework the original childhood separation from the mother and father, which involved relinquishing the omnipotent objects—breast and penis. While doing this, the child had to work through feelings of greed and envy. The successful resolution of these feelings was dependent upon whether the child could deal with the anxiety of phantasized retaliation. If this resolution occurred, the child's thinking became more oriented to the outside world. If it were not possible, because of insufficient nurturing experiences and incomplete internalization of a good superego, then the child became fixated at that point where aggression and anxiety were too great due to the effort to contain the excessive anxiety. Fixation is due to insufficient nurturing experiences and is not a cause of the anxiety (Segal, 1979).

Essentially, when the adolescent is faced with giving up dependency and becoming more independent, regression occurs and may indeed become a serious behavioural problem. This happens because of the demands of society, peers and internal pressure, and because there have not been sufficiently good experiences of early separation. The phantasy of depending upon others is mixed with persecutory fears of retaliation for early oral sadism, and the adolescent regresses to that developmental position. If the early separation has been worked through following good experiences, then the adolescent will still experience problems with adults, but not to the same extent.

For all adolescents independence creates anxiety as well as guilt—guilt for deserting the parents, being on one's own and not being closely interested in the workings of their families. If the ego is sufficiently coherent, then growth will occur, but first there is an adolescent rebellion, testing one's capacities in the face of adult knowledge and skills. Since adolescents necessarily find themselves to be somewhat lacking, their aggressiveness is triggered, as are subsequent phantasies of adult revenge, which in turn drives them farther away from adults and towards their adolescent society, a band of young people seeking ways of proving their independence from adults in dress, word, deed and action. Their striving to be independent, yet their inability to challenge adults on an adult level of knowledge forces adolescents to build their own values, style and manners. They are independent but feel alienated. This may be furthered by adults' mockery of, or hostility towards, their views. If adults begin to imitate their children, they deprive them of their sense of independence, and adolescents then need to find other ways, which may be even more bizarre. Nevertheless, with most adolescents, if fixation is not excessive and if adults acknowledge their children's

achievement (without copying it themselves), then reparative phantasies permit a reduction in sadism and anxiety,
which leads to further development in personality. The
adolescent will then be able to accept, with some criticism,
the influences of the adult world.

The change in cognitive functioning in adolescence,
formal operational thought replacing concrete operational
thought (Piaget, 1958), permits adolescents to work out a
conceptual separation from their families. To do this they
must achieve a feeling of successful reparation, sometimes
achieved by academic or athletic achievements, which are
acknowledged by the parents. If this occurs, the cognitive
advancement 'offers him both the power and responsibility
or task of conceptualizing his dilemma. Cognitively he is
developing the skill to be aware of and think about his
feelings' (Verburg, 1985, p. 7). Eventually, the interaction
between thinking about themselves and making effective
reparation enables adolescents to resolve their conflict
between independence and dependence. No longer do they
have to project and split off feelings; they are able to
integrate good and bad feelings. In one sense they rework
aspects of the depressive position, but this time they can use
their more developed cognitive operations as tools to aid in
achieving independence.

When Michael did make a decision to remain in school
following the school's recommendation that he be allowed to
leave early, he did so as an aggressive and independent act.
He had the opportunity of finding that there was no
retaliation from phantasized persecutory parents, and then
he was able to show more 'push for knowledge', as one of his
teachers said. Michael took on extra reading work and
asked for help in mathematics from his fellow classmates.
He did eventually leave the class, but he did so in a friendly
way, and he was able to find an apprentice position before
he left school.

When Jimmy, a 15-year-old, arrived for his first therapy
session, he looked at me very belligerently and angrily, but
when he was off-guard he looked sad and concerned. Jimmy

had come to therapy because he had been dressing in his mother's underwear and brassière, occasionally wearing her nightgowns to sleep in and sometimes putting on her swimsuit to go swimming in the family pool. His mother had begun locking her clothes' cupboards, but Jimmy was still able to find her garments and wear them.

He made sure that she saw him in her clothes, but when she asked him why he did this, he told her, 'It's none of your business.' The family tried to handle the situation by themselves for over a year, but Jimmy began to dress in his mother's clothes more frequently, to fail in school (he had always achieved very high marks) and to express hostile remarks and threats to his mother.

Jimmy talked about wearing his mother's clothes; he said that he felt comfortable in them and then added, 'Don't think I'm crazy. I don't go outside wearing that stuff.' I said to him that he wanted to be a big person, to do things his way and make his own decisions, yet at the same time he wanted to be a little boy. He said he could not understand that; 'I just like wearing the stuff.' I noted that he had decided to do this and no one was going to interfere. When he agreed, I went on to say that he was trying to have his mother in him or, rather, hold himself together by wearing her clothes. His first reaction to this was, 'That's crazy', but then he said, 'You mean when I wear that stuff, I'm a little boy wanting my mother to make sure I'm okay'. I agreed with this, and he went on to talk about how he had always done things on his own, how he had to be a loner, how he was always the biggest boy in the classroom and how he was always expected to do things even when he could not understand why he should. Jimmy said that he wanted to have friends, but most of the boys thought he was a freak because he was so large for his age, and so he was mostly on his own. Jimmy's parents also expected him to be independent, because they were usually too busy to be with him or even to listen to him. Jimmy was on his own most of the time and even more so lately, because his parents had been leaving the housekeeper in charge while they went on extended trips.

Jimmy resented being alone but tried to live up to his parents' expectations. He was seemingly independent, in charge of himself and doing well at school. However, when his parents had been away for two months, Jimmy reacted to their homecoming. He told them that they were not needed in the house, that he was getting along well without them; yet now on their return they resumed the role of parents and began to tell him their expectations of him. He responded by rebelling, being aloof and wearing his mother's garments.

Jimmy was expressing his desire to have his mother hold him together, but he was also expressing his aggression and destructive phantasies towards her by masturbating while he wore her clothes. He wanted to be dependent, yet he wanted to destroy the mother in the phantasized intercourse and take from her the penis, which he unconsciously felt would give him independence and freedom. Castration fears resulted in overt aggressiveness, which was viewed by his parents as 'another attempt on his part to be alone and have nothing to do with us.' In a way they were correct, for Jimmy did not want to have anything to do with his father, who he feared would castrate him for phantasized intercourse with his wife. Jimmy's attempts at independence and the stress of being prematurely independent by losing his parents created the phantasy of retaliation and subsequent regression.

He regressed to the sadistic level in the paranoid–schizoid position, which engendered suspiciousness and fear of oppressiveness along with fear of dependency and subsequent manipulation and phantasized rejection because of wanting too much from his parents. This resulted in increased dressing in his mother's garments, aggressiveness and intellectual (cognitive) deterioration. Jimmy believed unconsciously that he would no longer feel ambivalent, or have a harsh superego, or be controlled by the outside world, if he were separate and independent. Independence was achieved, but at the expense of ego function. Jimmy dealt with the adolescent crisis by regression and symptom formation, and this eventually led him into psychotherapy.

Because the adolescent's desire for independence entails a reworking of the original separation from the parents, the depressive position is reactivated. When depressive anxieties have been adequately resolved through reparative drives, then regression and loss of some ego functioning will not immobilize adolescents and create symptoms of pathology. With the loss experienced as a loss of dependency, depressive anxieties relating to goodness and belief in one's own internal objects are triggered. Adolescents may also fear that they have damaged their parents by taking too much from them and/or by making too many demands on them. If adolescents fear that they have made their parents upset by being too demanding or they have made them sick and old by taking too much from them, then they withdraw, and cognitive distortions take place. Adolescents then think they should be alone, and they give reasons for this and refuse to accept outside help because such help is identified with the internal persecutory objects. Adolescents separate from their families and sometimes from emotional support. They turn towards peers and peer-culture in an attempt to alleviate the aloneness and the persecutory anxiety brought about by depressive attacks and regression. When earlier depressive anxieties are resolved through reparation, a new resolution is possible, which involves cognitive interaction with reparative ego function. Adolescents will then evolve an independence built upon external influences and internal creative reparation and become ready and capable of accepting a role in adult society. They then begin to define their own role in society, find their own directions and their own courses and begin to formulate and realize their aspirations.

PART FOUR

Feeling, thought and creativity: the interdependence of phantasy and learning

CHAPTER EIGHT

Psychotic moments, thinking and reasoning

On this particular day Glen, the three-year-old boy described in chapter six, was tired and had not seen his mother, who had been away at a seminar for most of the day. At dinner he first said that he did not want anything, but when his mother offered him some food, he accepted it and began to eat. He ate heartily for about 20 minutes and then asked his mother to lift him out of his high-chair and put him on the floor. When someone else offered to do this, Glen made a sour face and grunted, 'No.' Only his mother was allowed to put him on the floor. As he went into another part of the kitchen, he noticed a spoon on the countertop and tried to get it. Finding it was out of his reach, he immediately began to scream and kick his feet on the floor. But it was the look on his face that struck me as the most arresting feature of Glen's tantrum. Whereas previously he had been smiling or looking attentively, his face was now distorted, his eyes became slits, his lips were stretched across his teeth, his nose was wrinkled up, and his forehead was taut. He looked wild, in keeping with the anger he was expressing. Anyone other than his mother

119

offering to help him was rejected with further exaggerations of his tantrum. If anyone, including his mother, spoke to him, he screamed loudly and put his hands to his ears as if the voices were hurting him.

At this moment I think Glen was psychotic. His behaviour was totally different from usual: his demands upon his mother were unlike his usual ones. It seemed that he was unable to handle any further frustration, however slight. The inability to reach the spoon seemed to Glen to be yet another indication of his lack of independence and his reliance upon his mother. Ordinarily Glen did things for himself, but his mother's absence appeared to have lessened his reservoir of emotional strength, and he simply did not have the resources to cope at that moment.

Glen's regression and apparent psychotic behaviour lessened when his mother picked him up, held him and cuddled him as if he were a much younger child. Interestingly, he pinched both her breasts in a very deliberate way and smiled at her. When she said that she did not want him to do that, Glen tried once more with one hand, and, when stopped, he settled into her lap and was calm, and the usual smile returned to his face. He began to talk, to ask questions and to tell her about his day.

Children experience psychotic moments, particularly when they feel 'deserted'. The supposed desertion may be as innocuous as being left with father or a favoured aunt or uncle. But it is the child's feeling that is important here, the child's phantasy of what has happened to the parent. Glen was hardly deserted in any real sense, and his father said that he was fine all day and that the two of them had had fun. They did enjoyable things together—perhaps too many things. It is possible that his father was 'giving Glen a good time' because he felt that he might be missing his mother and wanted to make up for her absence. However, Glen seemed to have enjoyed himself, and it was only at dinner, after his mother had been there for an hour, that he began to regress.

This regressive psychotic behaviour is not unusual for young children.

> . . . external reality is peopled in the child's imagination with objects who are expected to treat the child in precisely the same sadistic way as the child is impelled to treat the object. This relationship is really the very young child's primitive reality.
>
> In the earliest reality of the child, it is no exaggeration to say that the world is a breast and a belly that is filled with dangerous objects, dangerous because of the child's own impulse to attack them. Whilst the normal course of development for the ego is gradually to assess external objects through a reality scale of values, for the psychotic, the world—and that in practice means object—is valued at the original level; that is to say, that for the psychotic the world is still a belly peopled with dangerous objects. [Klein, 1975, p. 233]

Children regress when they feel depleted of parental affection, attention, control. Parents act as an 'external container' when they remind children what to do, and when, how, why, and where to do things. They also are an 'internal reminder'. Parents are introjected, and the introject is usually good because the external, real parents are doing good things. This good introject is used by children to maintain ego control over aggressive impulses (Klein, 1957). If the external containment somehow fails or is absent, the good introject may temporarily turn bad; the internal control gradually weakens and turns bad because aggressive impulses break through the ego controls. The impulse is then to attack, but this would result in retaliation, and so the child tries to maintain control, either by withdrawing or by being very active. Glen was very active.

When Glen was trying to reach the spoon, I think he wanted to hurt his mother; the aggressive impulse broke through the ego control and created a devastating state of affairs for him. There was a conflict for Glen. While he was angry with Mummy and really did not want to hurt her, he did seem to want to hurt her, and this was the stronger feeling. He was afraid that now she would, in turn, hurt him. So the best solution to this dilemma was a temporary psychotic state.

When his mother gathered him up and cuddled him, she seemed to replenish his ego controls. However, his aggression was not completely controlled. He pinched her, and he pinched her hard. When she said that she did not want him to do this but did not pinch or hurt him back, Glen could then regain his ego controls and smile. The anticipated retaliation had not occurred, and his Mummy in external reality could now repair his Mummy in internal phantasy. Phantasy and external reality interact in such a way as to accentuate either feelings of badness and aggressiveness or of having a good, protective, internal object. In Glen's case goodness was reinforced; he experienced this as a return of his own self-control. He was once again in charge of himself (Klein, 1940). Glen was now able to use certain 'ego-cognitive strategies or attitudes to approach, select, register, pace, compare, and cluster information, and in general to balance information from the external environment and the environment of thoughts, fantasies, motives and feelings' (Santostefano, 1979, p. 122). These 'cognitive controls' (G. S. Klein, 1954) are brought back into focus for the child by the mother's secure containment of the child.

It is, I think, very difficult for most adults to recognize that they have a very limited number of ways of thinking and rules of thumb for evaluating their beliefs, especially their beliefs about children. For example, most adults cannot tolerate the temporary psychotic episodes that all young children experience. They see them as attacks on the adults's own caretaking skills and interpret the child's behaviour as an indication that they are not good enough parents or, worse still, that they are bad parents. I think that this has something to do with their own early experiences as children. If they need to deny that their parents were at times poor parents, or that they were mistreated as children, then they have even fewer rules of thumb to use when their own child is behaving in a very difficult way. They have to deny their child's behaviour and either spank the child (which exaggerates the bad internal object) or send the child away (which frightens the child because he or she is not able to be alone with his or her phantasies). Their child reminds them of their own harsh world as children, which they need to deny; therefore, their children suffer. The consequence of this would seem to be that the child experiences weaker ego controls and has less emotional energy to invest in looking for more effective ways of expressing behaviours. In other words, sublimation as an ego defense suffers (Weininger, 1984). Thinking is affected: decisions and judgements are limited, and rigidity of thinking and action results. In such cases others cannot correct such parental bias in raising their children. No one can tell them a better way of raising or dealing with their child. The difference between what they think and what others may say is too great and triggers feelings of badness in themselves. These feelings are derived from the variance between external reality and internal phantasy (Klein, 1952; Weininger, 1984), which limits thinking and action.

Another case of a 'temporary psychotic' outburst illustrates an external anxiety that is not immediately connected with a failure in external containment but appears to emerge from the confrontation of two powerful phantasies. Two-year-old Leila was playing with some clay, holding it with one hand and passing it to the other hand. She seemed engrossed in her play, and she was calm and deliberate. She continued passing the round lump of clay from hand to hand for about five minutes and then carefully replaced the clay on the table, went over to her cuddly scarf, a woolen piece of material, squished it into a bunch against her face and started crying. At first her crying was soundless, but, as she crushed the scarf closer to her face, using it to wipe at her eyes, her crying became loud and wailing. She wanted her mother. When the adults in the room asked what was wrong, her crying intensified in loudness and tearfulness, and she continued even more vigorously to dab the scarf against her eyes. Leila became inconsolable, and talking to her seemed to make her cry all the more loudly and fiercely. Eventually she stopped asking for her mother. She then seemed to try to move towards the door to look for her mother, who was in the next room: she leaned towards the door, her eyes looked at the door, but she did not move. She was rooted to the spot and absolutely miserable.

Leila was psychotic at this moment. She was not in touch with external reality but fully taken over by the internal phantasy, and her usual effective two-year-old ego control had all but vanished. Her motor capacity was lost as she could not move. Her verbal skills had deteriorated: ordinarily a very loquacious child, now she could only say 'Mummy' in a loud wailing tone. Her need for the scarf increased, but she used it aggressively by poking at her teary eyes and dragging it over her cheeks. Her usual smiling responses when adults she knew called to her shifted to a fierce, wailing crying. Leila was immobilized, and she had deteriorated to the point where she was not approachable. When the female adult she was most familiar with in the group came towards her, she screamed loudly; the woman persisted, picked her up and held her close. Leila calmed down, irregular sobs racking her whole body. The woman carried her to her mother, and Leila fell into her mother's arms and seemed comforted.

Perhaps Leila's psychotic episode was brought on by the clay she was playing with. As she rolled the clay from one hand to the other, she may have been reminded of the pleasant experience of oral play with her tongue and the nipple, as well as the pleasant rhythmical play with her own body. I think that the body play or masturbatory experience of touching herself over and over again by running her fingers over parts of her body may have frightened her. Leila may have been afraid that providing enjoyment for herself would lead to less pleasure in nursing. That is, auto-erotic pleasure was phantasized by Leila as potentially destroying her mother, which triggered an anxiety about potential loss of oral pleasure. Thus one phantasy annihilated another. Auto-eroticism would be stronger than orality and would lead to independence and separation from her mother, which would be phantasized as losing her mother through aggression. This threat was handled by psychotic regression.

Here the symbolic equation of moving represented pleasures, both oral and urethral, and apparently led to the cognitive illusion (Tversky & Kahneman, 1974) of independence, a state that was unbearable for this two-year-old girl. Her ego's fragility did not permit her to develop other ways of eliminating or even reducing the cognitive illusion. Often decisions are made on what we call a 'cognitive illusionary' base. Some people are unable to analyse their biases or ways of evaluating their ideas. They are locked into a cognitive illusion, which is often reminiscent of Leila's psychotic episode described above. They make errors in judgement, in reasoning and in action because they cannot deal with uncertainty. They have only one set of rules with which to evaluate a situation, and they cannot go outside these parameters. To do so would create a loss of control and the possibility of suffering a psychotic state.

An interesting example has been provided by Rolf Bronner (1982). In his work, reported in *Decision Making under Time Pressure,* he notes that

> The cognitive system shields itself by rejecting inconsistent and purposive selection of consistent information and seeking information that conforms to actions and attitudes. Information contrary to the cognitive status is underrated in its relevancy, ignored, and thereby excluded from mental processing. In order to increase the cognitive value of the information the person reevaluates its source. If the existence of stress-triggering information cannot be ignored by means of these defense mechanisms alone, a process by means of selective forgetting begins, which leads to the repression of inconsistent cognitive elements. [p. 4]

People attempt to deal with stress, tension and anxiety-provoking stimuli by regression in order to regain some degree of mastery or competence in making plans or pursuing action. Bronner suggests that people attempt to master stress by a 'stabilization of the cognitive system'. He notes that the 'human being protects his cognitive status by self-censorship' (p. 5). Stress narrows judgement and reasoning skills, and, as Bronner indicates, 'clearly time pressure causes an essential limitation in almost all decision-making processes' (p. 151).

Our limits are set by early childhood experiences such as whether we have parents who offer 'safety' when our phantasies overwhelm us. When there is enough safety, the young child is not forced in phantasy into premature independence by destroying the loved object or making the loved object into a revengeful one. It is such premature independence that limits the boundaries of our thinking and decision-making power as adults.

Children have a narrow range in which they can frame their problems. When issues arise that are threatening to them—issues of dependency and independency, hostility and passivity, goodness and badness, or adaptability—they see the problem in only one basic way. Every threat is experienced as a loss of the parents, usually the mother, because the child's phantasized hostility towards her will result in her destruction and the child's aloneness (Weininger, 1984). This may lead to a psychotic episode that will further cut off the possibility of framing the issue so that different decisions, judgements or actions might occur. At the same time, the momentary regression may provide at least some hope of working through the crisis, by creating a temporary haven of safety. However, the cognitive illusion and the weakness of the ego may prevent this haven from continuing to be safe.

In making a decision, Wilensky says, we should be able 'to infer our own goals and to infer the goals of others' (1983, p. 10), but the young child is unable to do this. The child thinks about a decision or a plan usually in the same way as he or she thinks the other—in Leila's case the mother—thinks. The phantasies of revenge for taking or demanding too much from the mother, experiencing pleasure at the expense of the mother or attacking the mother in order to get more from her creates a cognitive illusion. Understanding a situation is different from solving a problem, but if understanding is limited, then solving a problem will be more complex because the capacity to imagine a solution will be paralysed. The phantasy of having done something bad to the mother obliterates the goals of needing the mother because of the anxiety of revenge, and so the child cannot move towards his or her mother when the phantasy is too powerful. A psychotic episode is a way of trying to preserve the existing fragile ego. The child decompensates in order to try to defuse the potential annihilation from a phantasized revengeful parent.

As Wilensky notes, 'The major mechanism through which problems with a plan are detected is called *projection*. As the planner formulates a plan, its execution is simulated in a hypothetical world model. Problems with proposed plans may be detected by examining these hypothetical worlds' (1983, p. 17). Thus when the child's hypothetical world becomes a hostile revengeful world, and the child *projects* to this kind of hypothetical world in order to formulate a plan or model, then he or she perceives the possibility of annihilation by such revengeful forces. The child cannot formulate other plans because projective identification has reduced the choices available and thus cannot prevent the bad thing from happening to him or herself. A psychotic episode again seems the only way out.

Similarly, adults project their plans onto a hypothetical world. If they have few solutions for figuring out their problems in their own hypothetical world framework, then their thinking skills and problem-solving capacities will be limited, and, as we have suggested, they will have problems handling their children when they are in a psychotic moment. Some parents will become very angry and threaten to punish a child who does not stop the 'bad' behaviour; others will hit the child or attempt to cajole or induce guilt by saying that the child's behaviour is 'hurting' the parent, whereas still others assume a resigned or disgusted air. Any of these attitudes will maintain the child's frightened feelings, and the psychotic episode will continue or be driven underground. If it continues, the child eventually falls into a heap on the floor, sobbing bitterly. When the regression has served its purpose of ego maintenance, the child brightens, stops crying and waits for the parents to return. In this case, the child has not had safety and containment from the parent and therefore has not felt that his or her phantasies were at variance with reality. The frame is set, and another cannot be easily developed. Thinking, goal-setting and decision-making remain narrow because nothing has countered the phantasy of badness (Weininger, 1984). Parents give stability and support to their children who are in a psychotic moment by holding them, and by avoiding arguments with them and attempts to impose logic or rationality. This allows children to revise their thinking and to turn their expectations towards more productive resolutions. They can then not only perceive new goals, but new ways of achieving them as well. They may cry and be frightened, but because the comforting, containing arms feel loving and not revengeful, they can dismiss hostility, as least for that moment, and plan other ways of achieving goals. Glen, for example, whose severe tantrum opened our chapter, left the kitchen smiling and talking to everyone there and went on to 'read' books in another room.

In order for children to understand their environment and themselves, they must gradually grasp the interaction and relationship between outer reality and inner phantasy. Gradually, phantasy must be altered to conform to reality. Through interacting with their parents, children slowly accumulate knowledge about decision-making and planning. This meta-deciding and meta-planning is gradually built up during the interactional experiences, and with it the child can learn to abandon one goal in favour of another, to express a range of plans in order to accomplish a goal, and to avoid being limited in knowledge and responding because of stress, anxiety or pressure. As Sroufe points out, 'There is something to the notion of coherence in individual adaptation. Developmental history leaves its mark. Early development and early care are important' (1981, p. 20).

If the child does not have this opportunity, either because of limited early parent–child interaction or as a result of unrelieved emotional stresses and pressures, then it seems that the child restricts the meta-deciding and meta-planning at the service of trying to maintain a fragile ego. 'Time pressure leads to an adaptive behavior in the form of a simple reduction of achievement' (Bronner, 1982, p. 32).

The method of decision-making is, as Cohen (1964) suggests, conditioned by the character of the decider:

> The act of deciding is qualitatively different from the weighing up of pros and cons which precedes the act, and it differs from the state which follows it. A decision may be regarded as a bridge between thinking and doing, the thinker being engaged in considering which of many possible bridges to cross. To be fully effective, he must first, take all the bridges into account, and second, attach 'probabilities' of success and failure to crossing at each bridge. A failure in decision-making may take place at any stage in the process: for example, in unduly prolonging the pre-decision phase; in lingering too long on the bridge, or in retreating before the bridge is fully crossed. These various failures may be due mainly to the nature of the particular decision to be taken, where the individual's *capacity* for making decisions is otherwise unimpaired, or they may be attributable to the individual's mental 'structure', which may be incapable of standing the strain of making even a trivial decision. These are people, for instance, whose powers of bridge-crossing are faulty because there are no clear dividing lines in their 'minds' between the bridge itself and the two zones on either side. Such people may fully intend to cross a bridge but because of a defective inner map they

do not know that they are still on this side of the bridge when they believe that they have crossed it. Their inner topography is insufficiently well-marked and sign-posted. [Cohen, 1964, pp. 141–142]

In the above example of impaired decision-making someone is unable to become involved in meta-planning and meta-deciding. He or she fails to think about plans or decide upon goals and lacks understanding about how he or she should act. This person's meta-thinking is rigid, and any alteration results in further anxiety or stress. This was true for Glen. Someone talking to him when he was in a psychotic moment led to further repetition of his behaviour: screaming and putting his hands over his ears. He had no other way to get out of this dilemma except to repeat his behaviour over and over again. Cohen describes an adult locked into rigid repetitive, compulsive behaviours.

Consider [says Cohen], a man of 33 burdened with four compulsions, each one as disabling and time-consuming as the rest: (i) wherever he walks, he feels compelled to clear the path, pavement or road of every small stone or scrap of paper; (ii) he is unable to close a door or remove his hand from the knob without repeatedly testing the door to make trebly sure that it is closed; (iii) he must tap his cigarette innumerable times before lighting it; and (iv) on top of this, his dread of germs makes him wash his hands countless times a day. [Cohen, 1964, p. 138]

Such behaviour will never allow for meta-planning and meta-deciding. The plan and the decision are already set, and any demand for alteration in thinking or in action will increase stress and anxiety, which will intensify the compulsions. It is never wise to try to counter behaviour and thinking with threats, demands, punishment or even, at times, an explanation of the illogicality of the decision and action. There is no way for the compulsive person to deal with these threats. However, by interpreting the origin of the compulsive action within the psychotherapeutic transference relationship, the compulsive person can think about the goal of such behaviour (Klein, 1932).

People do not necessarily learn from experience. In fact, sometimes they act in ways to preclude learning. Thus, for example, a person may decide that certain kinds of people will get angry with him if he talks about his accomplishments. Therefore, he does not talk about himself to those he considers as being more important than he is, and thereby he thinks that he will avoid their anger. He does not notice that these people do not get angry with him, nor does he differentiate them from others who do. And when others do get angry with him, he does not try to find out whether they become angry because he is talking about himself. He simply continues to assume that his judgement is accurate and behaves so that he cannot alter his actions or his thinking (Einhorn, in Kahneman, Slovic & Tversky, 1982). He is locked into a system that might be identified as 'bounded rationality' (H. Simmons, as quoted in Kahneman, 1979), which is a person's inability to figure out an optimal course of action because of self-imposed cognitive patterns that reduce the thinking potential and therefore decision-making effectiveness (Klein, 1931).

We normally assume that certain consequences will follow our actions, so that incorrect decisions will lead to disastrous effects, whereas correct decisions will lead to good outcomes, thereby providing feedback about the effectiveness of the decision so that learning can take place. However, some people are unable to learn from such feedback and thereby alter their thinking and are locked into their system. This is because their perception is limited such that they look only at what fits in with their actions and outcomes. If the outcome is bad, then it is because they did not think clearly, not because they are biased. As they have fewer and fewer good outcomes, they do not alter their thinking but either intensify their energy to make 'it work', or else make more stereotyped and rigid decisions that then allow for even fewer good outcomes. Rigidity of thinking requires expenditure of emotional energy in order to be maintained and thus less emotional energy is available for flexible thinking. It becomes more and more difficult for such people to evaluate outcomes, and repetition in thinking and action is usual. Two characteristics of a psychoneurosis, particularly a compulsive one, are a paucity of decisions and limited flexibility (Klein, 1932). This state gives further 'bounded rationality' (Kahneman, 1979), perhaps in the valiant attempt to deny the results of rigidity, but perhaps, even more, to deny uncertainty (Klein, 1930a). Uncertainty is a vacuum that cannot be tolerated, and too often such a vacuum is avoided by filling thinking processes by rigid and few thoughts. This, of course, accentuates inaccurate decisions. It also creates further difficulties in that people become even less able to assess how little they really know. Rigidity and perseverative thinking do not allow an evaluation of meta-planning and meta-decisions.

Children learn very early that strong emotional expression is generally not well tolerated, and this difficulty in holding back feelings often leads to temper tantrum outbursts. These intense expressions are but one indication that their 'rationality' has a certain limited range. The choice of action at this time seems to me to be further reduced, and their incorrect decisions as to how to behave often culminate in disastrous outcomes. The child cannot predict that the outcome may be disastrous because his ego is not sufficiently intact at this time to enable him to do so, and so he perceives most attempts to help him as attacks upon himself. Therefore, any attempts to 'reason' with children in this state or tell them what to do are met with screams, with some children throwing themselves on the floor in a tantrum, and with loud wails to 'shut up'. They cannot cope with this help, and so it is perceived as an assault. Therefore, adults need to 'lend themselves' and so become a container for the child. At such times the child is experiencing not simply a need for containment or safety, but also a drive to satisfy a basic, underlying dependency.

Thus Sroufe (1981) notes that some infants learn that other people are often not available to them when they are upset, and so they learn to avoid situations that may bring on these upsets. This may include avoiding close interpersonal relationships because they are perceived as dangerous. However, as Sroufe goes on to point out, 'because it is based in the child's biology, the underlying need for intimacy does not abate. The child's dependency needs will continue to be manifest, though perhaps in distorted ways or in restricted circumstances' (Sroufe, 1981, p. 4).

Children respond to containing, because they have basic dependency needs that are continual. These needs may alter in expression and become distorted, but in the young child, even when very upset, the need for dependency, closeness and nurturing is still prominent, and this allows the child to borrow from the ego of another and gain emotional energy and strength to recover from the stress. The child's limited flexibility and ineffective behavioural organization means that he or she is unable to figure out the best course of action. Planning, decision-making, goal setting—all parts of the ego's functions—are severely reduced, and behaviour deteriorates to a rigid expression of hostile impulses. With continued experience of stress and subsequent ego deterioration, children have a lessened capacity to 'borrow' another's stronger ego—that is, to be dependent. They see the other as attacking and resist being contained. Their biological need for dependency then becomes inner-directed, and these children begin to adapt to phantasizing that they can satisfy themselves. Withdrawal, self-stimulation and autistic behaviour come to characterize such children. No longer do they need another, for they have someone in phantasy. Attempts to contain them are met with resistance and hostility to them because such dependency feels unsafe and as an attack upon their guarded ego. Where this occurs in a child's development, thinking, planning and reasoning cannot develop because such cognitive processes are held within too tight and rigid a boundary. One cannot reason with these children or contain them to meet their dependency needs. This child will not be able to think, will have a severely debilitated ego and will be forced to guard against any intrusions (which would be phantasized as taking away some of the little ego strength function that is left). The child will attempt to preserve the ego in the face of the phantasy of possible annihilation. This is a psychosis or a psychotic process, and obviously such a child will need treatment (play psycho-therapy—Klein, 1932). However, such a process is not so different from the experience of a normal child when his ego is under pressure, as Glen's was. It is at such times that children cannot think, and it is at such times that they show psychotic moments.

CHAPTER NINE

Reparation, sublimation, learning and play with art materials

It is so very invigorating to walk into a preschool classroom and see children involved and interested in their special play projects. One morning I was introduced to a class of 12 children, three- and four-year-old boys and girls; I spent two hours with this lively group. None of the children was wandering about aimlessly or distraught; all of the children were doing something and appeared pleased with what they were doing. They talked a great deal, but the noise level was not so high as to drown out the Vivaldi record that was playing in the background. In fact, now and then, when the music became more vivid, I noticed that the children stopped to listen briefly before going on with their activities.

The activities were varied, but the number of activities available was limited. These children had been together for six months and were accustomed to the room as well as to the materials. That morning at one table there was clay and some simple utensils, a board on which to place the clay and a spray-bottle of water to dampen the clay. At another table there were cut-out letters and form-boards on which to place

135

them, and on a shelf close to this table were paper, pencils, crayons and markers. Still another table held paint in small containers, paint brushes in pots of water and a small stack of paper. Different-sized wooden blocks, books and music equipment were available at other locations in the room. In addition, a new materials centre was being tried out that morning: some carpentry tools were available, including a saw, hammer and drill, nails and wood.

The children chose where they would go and what they would make. Adults, usually two Early Childhood Education teachers, were available to the children. They walked about, staying in each area for varying lengths of time. The adults were often called by the children, and they responded by either answering the questions or going over to see the child and his or her work. No one criticized, but both adults and children alike offered suggestions, which the children usually made use of. As the children moved to various areas, it became obvious that they carried with them information that they had acquired previously. So, for example, when Lance was finally able to saw off a small piece of wood, he took it to the paint table and painted it. He had been painting pictures before he went to the wood-working centre. Joan had been mashing the clay before she went on to the letters. She had tried to make doughnuts out of the clay, and when she went to the letters she sorted them into piles: one pile of those that looked as if they 'could be doughnuts' and one of those that 'could not be doughnuts'. She sorted all the letters that had some openings in their formation such as A, B and D, and then noted how few letters looked like doughnuts. Joan said that she 'didn't get very many that way' and then sorted the letters into those that had 'sticks to them', such as P, L and T, and those that had 'no sticks to them', such as O, Q and S. Joan was at this activity for about 20 minutes.

Different materials, such as clay and letters, wood and paint, have many things in common. Children use them in an extraordinary variety of creative and interactive ways to solve new problems. Because the materials are so diverse, children learn without being limited to a closed set of formations. The materials provide the basis for transformations of a set of ideas or postulates, and new materials help new formations to develop. An idea or a way of doing something becomes more meaningful after some other ideas have been gleaned through the use of a variety of materials. In this way a new 'set' of ideas emerges, and new ways of looking at something come about. The child seems to transform the information acquired through activity with materials into a schema, a collection of action-ideas that can be drawn upon to solve problems. The child establishes ideas or concepts by finding out how materials can be used, and then these concepts become available to explore new materials.

In the creation of transformations children use a comparison of related concepts. As Lance found, paint can be put on paper and also on new material, such as a piece of wood that has been sawn off. Now having a three-dimensional object, he soon noticed that he could paint all the sides of the wood, whereas he could only 'paint one side of the paper'. He thought about this and said that he 'could turn the paper (over)'. He proceeded to look at the paper on its reverse side and remarked that the paint 'came through the paper' but 'not through the wood'. Lance had obviously thought about the materials: he used ideas that came from one set of materials and applied them to another. In so doing he was also evolving new ideas and concepts, which would be used when he worked with other materials. Transforming means transferring ideas from one material and activity to another. It is the way young children's thinking grows and expands. They start off with some structural information about an art material derived from their activity with it. When they approach another material, they often start to use it in the same way as the previous one. Soon, they either do not change their approach and leave the material or they use their previous structural information but alter it to fit with the new material. They are transforming the set of constructs and gaining new information.

As children build up knowledge through their activities with art materials, it seems an exceptional mistake to remove this opportunity to explore materials as soon as they reach the age of five or six. In effect, we remove one of the most useful ways that children have of building up knowledge. The message is loud and clear, 'Now that you are at school, we can teach you things much faster and better than you can discover for yourself.' The supporters of such an educational system need to be reminded of what Lawrence K. Frank said some 35 years ago:

> It takes a long time for a child to organize his experiences, to fit people, objects and events into categories and concepts so familiar to adults. His fumbling efforts often frustrate a child who lives in a world too big and resistant. But in play he can manipulate, organize, rapidly change and rearrange his smaller world of toys and materials, and, if given time, materials and opportunity to experience in his own way, he finds himself, rights himself when he has gone astray, and gradually learns how to get along with himself and with others in a large and complex world. [Frank, 1952, p. IX]

Children in their third year of life are very eager to try out their skills and to show their new knowledge. With the help of their teacher, they can test out their new knowledge on new materials and through their explorations discover new sets of information to be added to their reservoir of knowledge and thought. Children find the real world appealing and want to assimilate facts and ideas, but they want to do it themselves and in their own way. The growing feeling of becoming an independent person and the need to defend against the accompanying separation anxiety result in continuous attempts to 'do it myself'. When they are a little older, about four to six years old, they want information and criticism, and they look forward to some adult instruction. I think they want this because they are becoming aware of the standards and methods of evaluation we have placed on them. They are able to make plans themselves and complete an adult-planned curriculum, and so adults assume that teaching is what they want. Adults do not recognize that children's apparent readiness to be taught is an attempt to sublimate. Between the ages of four to six, children sublimate their primitive desires and try to behave according to the rules of their society. Again, it is a sad misunderstanding of children's development that we take this to mean that they want adult-directed, highly structured, information-giving classrooms. In actuality, this is the very time when activity and exploration of art materials will enable children to develop further knowledge and allow them to integrate diverse fields and systems of information, to arrive at creative solutions and to apply this to more divergent situations. Changes in ideas, re-learning and re-integration are thereby made possible, and children are highly motivated to continue to learn.

Children of this age are usually very demanding of themselves. They want to know, to be right and to please the adults who are important to them. If we set up the classroom so that they can explore materials and if we add on to these materials as we judge this to be wise and necessary, then we encourage the children to do the very thing we hope they will do—learn.

What many educators call 'lack of motivation' is often anxiety related to the learning process. The curtailment by adults of exploratory activity in the first years of school is interpreted by some children to mean, 'I can't do anything right, I am always told what to do.' These children gradually learn only to do what they are told to do. When they do what they are told, they might do it wrong and earn the anger of their teachers. They then no longer want to try anything because they do not want to anger adults.

As we have seen, children's capacities for sublimation are provided for by their desire to make reparation to phantasized damaged parents, usually mothers. If they do not have the opportunity to explore materials, which form the basis for 'making things' to give to parents as a means of reparation, then the generalization to reading and writing

C.P.—F

and arithmetic cannot be made easily. They become fixated at a psychological level that prevents sublimation. The materials acquire unconscious meaning and become symbolic of unconscious phantasies. If dramatic play and exploration with materials are not provided or encouraged at the right time, then later academic subjects will not be endowed with the symbolic equivalence of providing reparation for parents but will become associated with fear and anxieties. There will be a right and a wrong way to do reading and arithmetic, and if the child is afraid that he or she will be wrong because he or she has not had the opportunity to explore what he or she is capable of, the wrong way then becomes a way of expressing hostility towards parents. Fearing to express hostility and unable to sublimate, the child does not do anything. Thinking stops because suddenly it has become dangerous.

Many educational systems encourage the majority of their pupils to be passive non-learners. It rewards them for repeating information in a mechanical, rote way and does not inspire them to be active in their exploration and thinking. When children work with art materials, they can formulate the symbolism that is the basis of sublimation. At the lowest level the materials provide a 'safe' form of symbolic equation. Klein points out that '. . . through symbolic equation things, activities and interests become the subject of libidinal phantasies' (Klein, 1930a, p. 25). As the child gains 'the libidinal interests, it is the anxiety arising in the phase that I have described which sets going the mechanism of identification' (Klein, 1930a, p. 25). The child phantasizes destroying desired and envied objects, and then fear of retaliation ensues. In an attempt to deal with this, the child uses materials that he or she endows symbolically with anxiety. These materials can then be worked with or left by the child. It is not at all unusual to see a child rolling a piece of clay into a 'snake' or making a 'ball' suddenly get up and walk over to some new art material. Or a child who is painting and has loaded the paper with so much paint that it is beginning to drip off the page may just get up, say, 'I don't want to finish it' and wander off to a pile of blocks. One explanation for this behaviour is that materials themselves acquire the anxiety of the original objects and become terrifying in themselves. At the same time, the child is faced with exploring and formulating new interests in new art materials and coping with the experienced anxiety. These children are not told that they 'have to finish the painting' or that they must make something out of clay, and no one is telling them that they have made something right or wrong. Rather, their anxiety and their ego's capacity to bear this anxiety provide them with the opportunity of exploring a wide range of art materials and allow them to formulate the most effective methods of sublimation.

> . . . In the course of its analysis the child begins to show stronger constructive tendencies in all sorts of ways in its play and its sublimation—painting or writing or drawing things instead of smearing everything with ashes or sewing and designing where it used to cut up or tear to pieces. [Klein, 1950a, p. 274]

As Watts points out,

> . . . external causes of anxiety can abet and instigate the creative–reparative cycle at both its destructive and reconstructive junctures. These causes may be actual sources of danger, deprivation and suffering which the ego successfully negotiates and transcends through the strength of its internal objects. They may also be imaginary, stimulated by and simulated in a dream, novel or other work of art. [Watts, 1986, p. 170]

If the materials were used in academic lessons, there would be a right and a wrong way set by adults, and children would be told to 'stick with it until you are finished and have got it right.' Yet, if anxiety, because of libidinal desire and phantasized object destruction, becomes too powerful, it will prevent learning. For some children this anxiety and/or the demands of didactic instruction may result in learning problems and hyperactive behaviour.

However, in most ordinary situations, when children can use various art materials, their anxiety can be contained by their moving from one material to another until the creative capacity is set in motion by the process of symbol formation.

> Symbol formation is the outcome of a loss, it is a creative work involving the pain and the work of mourning.
> [Segal, 1973, p. 76]

Children use information about one set of art materials, apply their knowledge to other materials and develop creative and ingenious uses of materials. One three-year-old girl, for example, started her painting with poster paints, then used oil pastels through the wet painting and pressed her damp painting onto a dry piece of paper and made a monoprint. She was very pleased with her print and said she wanted to 'take it home to Mummy'.

Children learn about the world because of their need to control their internal anxieties, and if we prevent them from exploring the world and arriving at unique creative solutions, then they see the world as potentially hostile, and learning about it seems dangerous. They become certain that they will only find out that they will be hurt by something 'out there'. For example, a little boy said that he did not want the teacher to read the book she had chosen that morning because there were 'bad things in the book'. When I asked what the bad things were, he said, 'I don't want the book because the boy did bad things.' I asked him if he thought that the boy in the book was himself. He replied that 'sometimes I do bad things, but mostly I am good.' He continued saying that his mother loved him, that she said she loved him when he was good and when he was bad, but he felt that he had done some bad things that morning, and I think he did not want to risk finding out whether he was still loved. He seemed to feel that he was not loved because he had been 'too bad'. When I asked him what he wanted to do, he said 'I should make a painting of a big tree.' After making his big tree, he settled down and asked if he could now have a story.

Sometimes children have difficulty in handling anxiety, because of internal stress or external demands. Their understanding of reality will be inadequate unless they have the opportunity of handling the anxiety in ways that are effective for them. Art materials are the most successful way of helping children deal with external reality without imposing the anxiety resulting from internal phantasy. The capacity for children to tolerate anxiety is dependent upon the situation in which they have worked through this anxiety. Academic work is appropriate after children have dealt with the anxiety of libidinal desires. However, premature academic teaching will create further anxiety, with subsequent learning inhibitions.

Art materials formed the foundation for all learning in a school I set up and directed for eight years. The children in this school ranged from four to eighteen years in age, and all had been involved with mental health agencies. They were all seriously emotionally disturbed and had been diagnosed as suffering from childhood schizophrenia, autism, character disorders or psychoneuroses. Some of the children had been called delinquent and others mentally retarded, with or without brain damage. All the children were assessed as needing to be separated from their parents and placed in residential homes, because the mental health agencies had agreed that as all else had failed, this was the only remaining intervention. The school was started as a way of helping these children so that they would be able to stay with their parents.

The school was located in an old Victorian building and was deliberately made to look like a home rather than a series of classrooms. No attempt was made to 'teach' the child when he or she arrived at the school. The child was introduced to other children at the school and given a brief explanation of what would follow that day and the next one. Essentially, the child was told that there were several activities that he or she could join, but there was no pressure either to complete or to stay with one activity. The child could wander and watch, leave and return to the big sitting–meeting room where an adult was always available to talk or just to sit with. The activities included cooking, woodworking, using clay, painting, sewing, making batik, looking at magazines, using beads and string, using pencils, crayons and magic markers, cutting out pictures and pasting them onto sheets of paper. Sometimes children did nothing and watched other children involved in their projects. At other times they moved from activity to activity, either without finishing their projects, carrying them with them, or simply leaving them in an unfinished state to be returned to after experimenting with something else.

No one forced a child to remain at an activity, but the school was not unstructured in the sense that children were left on their own. It was organized in such a way that there was a limited number of activities, and an adult who had some understanding of the materials involved was present at each activity and also experimented with the materials. An adult who made a 'nice-looking painting' did not create jealousy in a child related to the painting. Rather, the child would be jealous of the internal goodness of the adult, the goodness that helped the adult to make the painting. The children needed to see that everyone was not as poor or devoid of 'good insides' as they felt they were, so that they could use the internal goodness of the adults to help them. The children's perception of reality was based upon their internal phantasies, that everything was bad and destructive out there because they had made it so in phantasy, and they therefore believed that outside forces were just ready to attack and pounce. The children were not 'jealous' of the adults' work; they said it was 'nice', admired it or said nothing. What they did express, however, was their own feelings of badness by saying, 'I can't make anything real,' 'I can't do anything right,' 'I don't know how to do things properly,' 'I'm just bad at doing anything.' We then helped them to explore other art materials in order for them to see that they were not just 'all bad'.

One day 12-year-old Giles wanted to use plaster of Paris, an available material. He already felt that he was a failure when he used clay since nothing that he made turned out as he wanted, and he said, 'I can't do anything, I bust everything.' In order to help him gain some feeling of competency, a couple of moulds were brought in. Giles noticed that the plaster became hot when he mixed it with water, but even though it seemed like an invitation to 'give' him some knowledge, no one went into any physical explanation, for that would have detracted from his efforts. The main activity was to pour the plaster into the mould, which he did. He made a plaque of a horse. When he removed the plaster horse from the mould, he was obviously pleased and smiled, but he did not say anything, nor did the staff. He wanted to paint his horse, and he painted it a brilliant green. The next day Giles announced that his father had recognized his horse; he had called it a horse, and he had also said, 'You finally made something I can recognize.' The father did not comment on the colour. The child was so pleased that he went on to make more plaster horses.

Shortly after this, he poured the plaster into a small box, and he made an imprint of his hand. He then added small bits of glazed tiles, buttons and marbles to his hand-print. Having received recognition for his horse, Giles was able to leave the highly structured mould activity for the less structured project of making his hand-prints. He later began to sculpt the plaster into volcanoes. He made the volcano with its deep crevasses and hollow interior and the lava running down the side of the mountain, and he painted it with the appropriate colours. It was during this project that he asked why plaster becomes hot when mixed with water.

Incidental teaching is one of the best ways to clarify children's thoughts and experiences for them and to generate and develop their skills and concepts. It ties right into what they are doing and learning at the moment. It is in tune with children's naturally active and concrete way of learning. These incidental teachable moments arise constantly during play periods. In fact, so many arise that educators have to be selective and make sure that the interruption of children's play is as smooth and natural as possible.

Giles's father was pleased with his project, and the boy was able to explore his volcano in an art production. He wanted his volcano to look 'real', and he asked to go to a library to get some 'good books' on volcanoes. He chose his own books, took them back to the school and after looking through them asked one of the staff to read to him 'because I can't read'. Giles was willing to talk about his 'real' deficiencies and his 'real' anxieties and was able to form a strong enough and safe enough relationship with a staff member to ask for help. It was not long before Giles was reading the books by himself, but he was always able to ask for help when he needed it.

Giles remained at the school for three years and then returned to the school system and was placed into a class at his age level. No formal 'remediation' was attempted: in our school art materials had provided the vehicle for introducing various academic subjects. Giles learned to read, to write, to do mathematics, and also to do social sciences and geography through his projects. While he attended his new school he frequently visited us to keep up relationships, to complain sometimes about his teachers and his work, and to tell us about his accomplishments. Giles had been diagnosed as a character-disordered child with homosexual, juvenile delinquent and hostile tendencies. He had been involved in treatment on several occasions, but on each occasion treatment had ended dramatically. He threatened either to kill himself or someone else or to burn down the building. The only remaining alternative was to place him in a residential setting for seriously disturbed children, away from his family, in an effort to protect him and society. However, by using art materials in a school that helped him formulate a more effective relationship with outer reality, he was able to learn, to feel 'good about himself' and to maintain himself even after he left our school.

Giles's capacity to handle anxiety had improved greatly; his essentially persecutory relationship with the world modified. His capacity to symbolize was at first very tentative because everything that he worked with, made or touched turned into a frightening persecuting object, as if it were the original object. His interest in learning was very poor; he continually failed in school and was punished for this failure by having to sit in the 'dumb seat', by having to sit outside the head's office, by not being allowed to return to school until his work was done 'perfectly' and at times by having to repeat his work over and over again. All this intensified the persecution phantasy, for everything he did produced more punishment. He stopped learning and showed very little interest in anything or in forming relationships. Everything was a potential threat and as such had to be avoided, if not destroyed. He was not able to sublimate; he could not understand how things worked because he could not try out things, and he could not try out things because they would become persecutors. His ego was not sufficiently developed to endure the anxiety created by the symbolic equations. All projections were hostile and therefore persecutory, and so he could not learn (Klein, 1930a).

Hilda came to the school when she was six years old. She had at various times been labelled autistic, psychotic, schizophrenic and depressed, and she had lasted about an hour in a state school. She was disoriented, did not speak, threw unpredictable temper tantrums, wet herself, and tried to destroy everything that crossed her path. In order to get her bearings in the school and to prevent her from being destructive, she was assigned to stay with a staff member at all times. For many weeks she followed this staff person around. Although she did not get involved in anything, she gradually began to watch what people were doing. One day, when she was seated at a table where some children were cutting pieces of coloured paper and pasting patterns on cardboard, she picked up two small pieces of paper and tentatively put them together. The adult then stapled the two pieces together, and for the first time in the school Hilda smiled. She picked up her project and stood in the middle of the room, looking at it for several minutes. Then the teacher asked if she would like to take her project with her and handed her a plastic shopping bag. Hilda smiled again and put the pieces of paper in the bag.

Within the supportive, safe and undemanding relationships with the people in the school, Hilda's delicate ego became stronger, and her capacity to tolerate anxiety increased. She made many more booklets, carrying them in her bag carefully tucked under her arm. Then one day, instead of a booklet consisting of two irregularly shaped pieces of paper and one staple, she used two staples with three pieces of regularly shaped paper. She put a colourful sticker on this special edition, and for the first time since she had come to the school she took something home to her parents. When she returned to school the following morning, she literally beamed: her attempt at reparation had been successful. She had phantasized that she had thoroughly depleted her parents and that to take more things from them—facts, bits of reality, learning—would surely bring about devastating retaliatory attacks. Therefore, she was totally immobilized; she shut herself off from the world and avoided reality. When the parents began to accept her gifts, Hilda slowly became more confident that she could repair the phantasized damage she had done to them.

The booklet that Hilda put together from the initial two pieces of paper expanded into a series of booklets, which became increasingly elaborate books with numbers and letters, paintings and drawings. The pieces of paper represented the scattered pieces of her fragile ego that kept flying off in different directions. When she began to put some of her scattered pieces together and was successful, she branched out to different materials: she glued pieces of

wood together, she started painting and making mono-
prints, and she tried her hand at ashtrays made from clay
coils. She became less compulsive in the use of these
materials. After about six months in the school, her
behaviour improved; she began to talk and interact with her
peers and to show an interest in learning to write and to
read. Gradually the obstacles that had blocked her path to
growth and learning disappeared, and Hilda was able to
make steady progress.

In a much less severe and drastic case, a young
four-year-old boy in a normal classroom had become very
anxious, was unable to relate to the teaching staff with
whom he had been for five months, was tearful and
unwilling to become involved in activities. Henry had been
fine until this time, and there had been no warning signs of
any impending problem. This behaviour continued for two
more weeks, at which time his teacher and I thought that it
would be important to meet with his parents. His mother
arrived and said that her husband just 'couldn't take the
time'. We talked with her for several minutes and asked
whether she had noticed anything different in her son's
behaviour. She had, and she said that he was 'touchier', he
cried more, and he did not seem to want to do the things that
he had done before.

I asked whether there had been anything unusual
happening in his life, or in his family's life. His teacher
noted that Henry had seemed to be such a 'good learner'
before, but now he did not pay attention, and, what seemed
worse to her, Henry seemed to have forgotten everything he
had learned in the past five months. He could no longer put
on his coat, he did not play games with the other children,
and he was not interested in piling up blocks as he had been
before. Whereas previously he had begun to paint real
things, such as people, cars, houses or dogs, now he only
painted blobs of a single colour.

Henry's mother said that a lot had happened recently,
and she did not realize that it might have affected him so
much. She had been pregnant for six months and had

recently lost the baby. Henry was well aware of her pregnancy and said that he wanted 'to see his baby brother'. Also, the family had moved two months earlier. In the past week his babysitter had become very ill and no one had told him why she was no longer there to take care of him. In addition, the woman who usually looked after him when he and his mother were at the gym was not there any more. His mother also added that her husband had become very busy lately and had not been at home much.

I suggested to her that maybe Henry felt that he was responsible for all of these calamities. He saw himself as such a wicked and bad child who caused all these problems that he was afraid to do anything any more and was attempting to return to a position where he was not as destructively powerful. I suggested that she talk with him about her own sadness at the loss of the baby, the loss of their old home, the loss of the babysitter, the loss of the woman at the gym and the 'loss' of his father. She was not sure how to do this, and we agreed that she might best handle the subject as if she were thinking about these things and trying to reminisce about them. She realized that Henry was thinking about these things but that he could not contain them by himself and that he needed her help. I also asked whether Henry liked to help her around the house; she said that he used to but had stopped. I suggested that when she cooked, she could give him some task that was obviously helpful, such as washing the potatoes or carrots, or kneading bread dough. She could also have him help her when she cleaned the house and have Henry mop the floors. She could tell him about the babysitter and visit her if possible, or telephone her so that Henry could hear her voice, and she could make sure that he saw the woman at the gym, so that he could be sure that she had another job and had not deserted him. Furthermore, she could ask her husband to telephone Henry if he was not going to be at home for dinner; perhaps she could even drive to his office so that Henry could say hello and tell him any news he wished.

This coincidental accumulation of losses had over-powered this young boy. He phantasized that he was responsible for them and felt that anything he did might result in another catastrophe, so he just stopped doing things. Although his behaviour had regressed, he was still using art materials and he was, therefore, still open to influence by his mother. Within three weeks there was a significant change in his behaviour. He was now a happily smiling, active child, involved with art materials, talking a lot and trying to play games with his peers. When I spoke with his mother, she said that at first Henry did not respond to her, but as she spoke about what had happened and how she felt, saying she was sure that he felt sad as well and that he was not responsible for these events, he became more interested in helping her do the work. In effect, Henry was able to make some reparation for what he had phantasized he had done. Gradually he became active in cleaning and in helping with food preparation, and he enjoyed his telephone conversations with his father when he could not visit with him. Henry was able to return rapidly to well-being because he had early satisfying experiences with his parents (Klein, 1929b). His relationships were sufficiently strong to permit a temporary regression without irreversible damage. However, if his mother had not intervened, I think the damage could have become more serious and limiting to his development.

Henry's behaviour was a consequence of the unconscious phantasy that he had damaged his loved objects. He felt that he had taken too much from his mother, and this meant that she did not have enough goodness inside her to sustain the new baby. His idea was that babies live in mothers' 'tummies', being fed by fathers. When I asked how babies were fed, he pointed to his penis. Henry felt that he had removed the penis from inside his mother and that she was no longer able to give enough food to her new baby. In one way Henry was pleased about this, because there would be no one to take anything from him, but in another way he saw how sad his mother and father were, and he felt that he was a bad boy to feel jealous. His father's absence was interpreted by Henry as a consequence of having lost his penis to Henry so that he was 'so mad at me that he stayed at his office so he wouldn't hit me.' Henry viewed his own behaviour as wrong and bad, and he expressed this by regressing and being sad. He unconsciously imagined that if he were a baby he would no longer do anything that could be dangerous to his parents, and his superego might be less harsh.

Children's behaviour is dominated by their imagination, thoughts and phantasies, and they understand their parents' reactions, actions and patterns on this basis. If a parent wants to reshape a child's behaviour, I do not think this is possible unless it is in line with the child's thoughts and phantasies. They need to understand their children's phantasies and thinking if they want to effect a change. For Henry, the loss of his babysitter, the woman at the gym, and the house were responses to his badness. In his mind he was a 'bad boy', and needed to achieve some reparation and effective sublimation in order to see his mother and father as 'well and undamaged'.

Henry needed to give something back to his parents, yet at the same time retain and/or regain his ego resiliency. His painting and use of art materials deteriorated when he seemed to realize that he had placed his parents in danger. Sadness and deterioration were a consequence, and no doubt he felt threatened himself—from both inside and outside objects. Doing things created anxiety because to do something meant to take something from someone else— from his mother—and so he stopped making his creations because they would be viewed as creations brought about by the penis he took from inside the mother, with the danger then of retaliatory attacks by the combined couple on himself.

The possibility of doing something or creating art work was significantly reduced (Klein, 1929a). Therefore he could not make reparations, he had nothing to give his mother and he phantasized only further badness in himself, which resulted in further sadness. As his mother was able to contain him and to provide opportunity for reparation, Henry could endure the increased phantasized anxiety, and he began to use the art materials once again. An interplay of his mother's own anxiety and Henry's unconscious phantasy had led to his psychological regression.

Excessive anxiety, a sadistic superego and a diminution of ego function lead to reduced capacity for symbol formation, with a subsequent deterioration in reparation and sublimation. Art materials are the most effective materials to use in early sublimation processes, because they provide the opportunity for children not only to express their creativity, but also to use it for reparative purposes. The acceptability of the child's reparation gifts paves the way for academic information to be used in the sublimation process. As children make things out of art materials, in unconsciously controlling their feelings and impulses, they gain a better understanding of, and control over, their thinking.

PART FIVE

Play psychotherapy: theory and practice

CHAPTER TEN

Some basic patterns
of play psychotherapy

Play is children's work, and whenever children are engaged in play they are 'doing' (Winnicott, 1968). As we have seen, play is the way children try to understand and control outside situations and events. In order to do this, they need the opportunity to play in their own way. When I asked some four- and five-year-old children what they thought 'play' was, they answered, first of all, that play was fun. Then they said that it was something that you did how and when you wanted to do it, and that you 'were happy to play' and that you could spend 'a lot of time doing it'. Essentially, they were saying that play is internally controlled, motivated and rewarded. Play also takes time, and the children pointed out that they did not like to be interrupted. They said that adults must not consider play important because they interrupted it, but they did not interrupt writing, mathematics or reading. When teachers told them to go and play, the children felt it meant that the teachers did not want to be bothered with them. They added that teachers said they liked their play, but they never asked them questions about it, whereas when it came to reading they always had a lot of questions (Weininger, 1987). Thus, although children see the vital importance of play, they recognize that most adults do not.

Play at home or play in the classroom is very different from play in the therapeutic treatment room. As Winnicott has said, play is universal, and it 'belongs to health; playing facilitates growth and therefore health; playing leads into group-relationships' (Winnicott, 1968, p. 593). Our research has shown that the playing child seems to have greater immunity to influenzas, colds, ear problems and other physical illnesses (Fitzgerald, 1983), but play is most important in the service and expression of psychic health. In psychotherapy, play is a way of restoring the growth and health of a child who is experiencing difficulties and problems. Play allows for self-expression that would otherwise be difficult or impossible; it is a medium of communication between the child's ego and the therapist. Play does, and always will, occur when no one is present, but in psychotherapy play serves as the interface or, as Winnicott suggests, occupies the 'potential space' between the child's ego and the object (usually the mother, initially) and provides children with the opportunity and time to explore the interrelationships between themselves, their phantasies, and their parents. Through this special kind of play children find out why outer reality is so anxiety-provoking and discover how their phantasies are limiting their exploration and understanding. As reality becomes less demanding and/or threatening, they gradually give up some of the omnipotent phantasies and accept some of the limitations and even frustrations of life in the world without having either to distort reality or to behave compulsively.

In play psychotherapy, the therapist is trying to help children to grow and to help them get rid of some of the mechanisms that prevent growth. The psychoanalytic framework provides an understanding of these mechanisms, but it is play that 'is itself a therapy' (Winnicott, 1968, p. 597). The therapist comes in when the play is blocked or becomes so frightening for the child that it stops. The therapist learns from the play what has frightened the child, and he or she offers an interpretation. Thus, for example, a frightening dream may be played out, but the anxiety originally provoked by the dream may be so frightening that the child stops playing. The therapist needs to understand the dream and its frightening aspects by observing the play, the child's manipulations of particular materials and toys, and the feelings with which he or she endows them.

Materials and techniques

Toys and the setting are important in our play technique. The toys used are little dolls—mothers, fathers and a variety of children—small and large cars, trains, airoplanes, domestic and wild animals, bricks, balls, a small house, fences, paper, plasticine, string, pencils, paints and crayons. The toys are usually very simple so that the child can use them 'in many different situations, actual or phantasized, according to the material coming up in his play. The fact that the child can thus simultaneously present a variety of experiences and situations also makes it possible for us to arrive at a more coherent picture of the workings of the mind' (Klein, 1964, p. 119). Each child's toys are kept in a box that is a private one for the child and is brought to each session by the therapist. No one else uses these toys, and this means that each child's objects are safe from intrusion by others. To the child this means that no one else can damage his or her objects, no one else will see what he or she does to them, and that the therapist considers these toys sufficiently important to keep them safe. Essentially, the box becomes the container for the child, the repository of his or her feelings, which will be guarded by and 'known only by the child and the therapist'.

Children are often interested in other children's boxes, and while no child's box is shown to another, discussion about why they are interested does ensue. Usually they begin to understand their curiosity about events and things that are happening around them but are too frightening for them to talk or even to think about. Their curiosity is not stifled; the therapist encourages children to explore within the safety of the relationship between the two of them and within the special room (Weininger, 1984). The room itself is simple, and the child always returns to the same room for sessions. The same room, at the same time of day, for the same length of time, has particular meaning for children. They do not just become 'attached' to the room, but, rather, it acquires the meaning of being the place where this intimate relationship between child and therapist occurs. Klein points out that the 'transference relationship can only be established and maintained if the patient can feel that the consulting room, or the playroom, indeed the whole analysis, is something separate from his ordinary home life' (Klein, 1964, p. 279). Nothing in the room should be easily breakable; the floor should be made of material that is easy to clean, the room should have a water supply, a table and at least two chairs and a small couch, and the walls should be sturdy enough to withstand some aggressive activity without being damaged.

Within the therapy room the therapist is a special adult, for he or she is not only with the child for the full session, but is also interested in whatever the child is doing. However, the therapist must also be in control of the setting and not allow the child to harm him or herself or the therapist; he or she must be able to stop some activity that is dangerous not just to the child but also to the furniture and contents of the special room. Children need to be contained, not simply because they might hurt themselves or others, but also because they may set up situations that are damaging to the materials of the room, such as furniture or walls or windows. Breaking these objects is symbolic of destroying objects that are important to children. By causing damage, the child will anticipate retaliation and will behave accordingly. The child will either become more aggressive or withdraw from a fearful reality. In either case, nothing is gained other than that the child once again believes that the world, which was dangerous before he or she entered into therapy, is still dangerous (Winnicott, 1965; Weininger, 1984).

The concept of symbolism must be understood. Melanie Klein indicates that the child gives the toys that he or she plays with

> a variety of symbolic meanings ... which are bound up with his phantasies, wishes and actual experiences. The archaic mode of expression is also the language with which we are familiar in dreams, and it was by approaching the play of the child in a way similar to Freud's interpretations of dreams that I could get access to the child's unconscious. But we have to consider each child's use of symbols in connection with his or her own particular emotions and anxieties and in relation to the whole situation that is presented in the analysis; mere generalized translations of symbols are meaningless. [Klein, 1964, p. 285].

Children endow toys with particular meaning and play out their feelings with regard to that meaning. In one therapy session, three-year-old Susan began to hit the small chair that had been holding the 'baby'. Susan said that the chair was starting to eat the baby and that if she did not kill the chair the baby would be 'very, very hurt'. She hit the chair with a paint-brush but neglected to remove the baby from the chair. I pointed this out to her and said, 'I think the baby needs to be hurt because the baby feels so angry with the mummy.' Susan looked at me and replied, 'Babies are always supposed to love their mummies and never supposed to get angry with them.' I said that the baby is being punished because the baby is so angry at the mummy. Susan stopped beating the chair and the baby and said that chairs 'don't really eat babies, but yesterday when I was sitting in Mummy's big chair I put my hand in the chair and I couldn't get out of the chair.' Susan had pushed her hand into the upholstery and had managed to push it in far enough that she felt she would lose her arm and hand. While I did not know of this incident, Susan's unconscious phantasy was that she was making too many demands upon her mother, and her mother was angry and would retaliate aggressively with an oral sadistic attack. Susan's unconscious phantasies extended to her father, who, she felt, should protect her but by doing this would also hurt her. The Oedipal phantasy of wanting what mother has so that she might be able to attract her father led her to hitting the baby and the chair with 'father's penis'. The symbols of the chair being mother, the paint-brush being father's penis were idiosyncratic to Susan; she helped me understand her anxieties by telling me that the chair will eat the baby, or that the mother will harm the baby and that the paint-brush will stop this action, or that her father will stop this. The play would not have been satisfying, nor would the episode have ended with any degree of gratification or pleasure, unless someone had been there to help her understand—that is, put her unconscious phantasies into conscious terms.

Toys represent important objects, and the child transfers feelings and thoughts to them. The toys themselves are then used in the same way as the child might want to use the original object (a form of symbolic equation). Sometimes a child will tell you, 'This piece of chalk is my mother, this piece is my father, and this is me,' and then play out some of his or her family drama, which he or she could not talk about in relation to actual people but only by using the chalk pieces as if they were actual people. It is important to find out what and/or whom the toys represent and, as Klein points out, 'who these [toy figure] people [are] meant to be, what their relation to each other is, and what they are supposed to be doing' (Klein, 1964, p. 280). The child talks about these toys as people when he or she 'comes to realize that the toys stand in his mind for people, and, therefore, the feelings he or she expresses toward the toys relate to people. . . . He or she is gaining insight into the fact that one part of his or her mind is unknown to him or her, in other words, that the unconscious exists' (Klein, 1964, p. 280). Children who suggest that the toy figures are Mummy, Daddy and siblings offer the opportunity to explore their unconscious world of phantasy through dramatic play (Weininger, 1979; 1984).

As we have seen, symbolization and symbol formation play a vital role in the development of the cognitive processes (Klein, 1930a; Segal, 1957), and without them the child's thinking and growth processes will remain infantalized. Seriously withdrawn autistic children do not evolve symbols because each symbol becomes attacking. They close themselves off and show little interest in reality, mainly occupying themselves with a sensation-dominated function such as sucking their tongues, pinching or hitting themselves, squeezing their lips, or pulling their ears in response to a stimulus in order to sustain whatever little ego functioning remains (Klein, 1932; Tustin, 1972, 1981). Thus, for example, Ralph, a severely withdrawn and non-communicative six-year-old, did not play at all but sat on the floor scratching at an imperfection in the carpet. He was so severely inhibited that he could not develop or use symbols. For him a symbol would not represent the object but would become it. It was extremely unsafe for Ralph to develop symbols because he would just have that many more objects to be afraid of. By sitting still, by not playing and thus by not developing symbols, Ralph was as safe as he could be.

In play psychotherapy, the child is free to do what he or she wishes with the toys, and the therapist then interprets the play. If a child attempts to destroy the room, the therapist not only prevents this but also interprets it.

When Johnny, a three-year-old, said he would kick the wall and knock it down, I said that I thought he was very angry with me. Johnny wanted me to bring in more toys, and I had said that I would not do that because if I did he would think that the toys we now had were not good enough. (Essentially, like the 'greedy' children of chapter two, Johnny was trying to avoid the therapeutic relationship by getting so many toys into the playroom that he would be able to flit from toy to toy and never become involved with anything—that is, never become involved in the therapeutic relationship.) Johnny's response was to look sullen, pout and lie down on the floor. When I said I thought he wanted to be a little baby again and get all the good things, he got up and began to kick the wall. Johnny needed a lot of good objects, but he could not introject them because he was afraid that the badness inside him would make good objects bad as well. Johnny saw himself as a very bad boy, and if I did not give him new toys he could get angry with me and blame me. By interpreting his need to keep things good, he was able to talk about how bad he was, how he wanted to take everything away from his little brother, even eat him up because he 'got everything from Mummy all the time.'

Interpretation is used to help reduce children's anxiety so that they can begin to talk about and play out the things that have created the problems for them. This approach entails understanding the play communication, not to try to get the child to 'warm up' to the therapist, but to rely 'on the fact that this interpretation relieves unconscious anxiety to maintain the child's interest and cooperation' (Segal, 1972, p. 405).

I was asked to see a four-year-old girl who would not go into her bedroom at night. When her bedtime came, she would start to cry and say that she was not going into that 'bad room'. When Jane arrived for her initial appointment, I came out to meet her, and she stood beside her mother giving me an occasional glance as I said to her that I had come to bring her to the playroom where she and I could play with some toys. Jane said, 'No', and clutched her mother's skirt, and I said that I knew that she was afraid to go into some rooms and I knew that she was afraid to go into her bedroom to go to sleep. Jane looked at me; I then added that perhaps she was afraid something bad would happen to her with me in the playroom as might happen to her in her bedroom. Jane seemed more interested now, and she looked at the playroom door. I said that we could all go to the room. Jane took her mother's hand, and the three of us went to the room. Once in the room, Jane just looked at the toys without touching them, and I told her that these were the toys that we would always have at every play session. Jane wandered about the room until she came to the sink; she then withdrew and went back to her mother again, standing close to her. I said to her that I thought that she was afraid of me and the room and that she was afraid that there would be so much water that she might get wet and even hurt. She clung to her mother's skirt, and I added that while she wanted mother to protect her, she was also angry with her mother for not making everything safe for her. Jane looked at me in an angry way, and I said, 'You are also very angry with me, because I have this dangerous water in the playroom.' Jane went back to the sink, turned on the tap and then walked back to her mother. This time, however, Jane did not cling to her but looked around once again.

Jane allowed her mother to leave but kept the playroom door ajar while she busied herself washing the doll family and keeping them under water for long periods of time. The water seemed to represent her overwhelming desire for oral gratification, and yet this was associated with her anxiety that she must not take too much, for it would leave her mother depleted.

Therapists should give an interpretation in language appropriate for the child and in words that are understandable. It is important, therefore, to know what the toys symbolize to the child, and what words he or she uses to talk about his or her body or others' bodies. An interpretation 'implies that the item is a disguise. Thus in the associations leading to the Oedipus interpretation to do with the biting horse, there is the presupposition that the horse is functioning on behalf of the patient's father or is a disguised version of him' (Wisdom, 1967, p. 46). In working with a child, the child may say that the horse is the pretend father horse, or the therapist may say that 'we can pretend that the horse is the father,' and then the disguise and symbolic representation are consciously known and interpretations can be made on this basis (Klein, 1929b). I have found that this verbal clarification of the symbols enhances the interpretation and also seems to strengthen the transference relationship. In writing about toys and symbolism, Klein points out that

> Often a toy is broken or, when the child is more aggressive, attacks are made with knife or scissors on the table or on pieces of wood; water or paint is splashed about, and then the room generally becomes a battlefield. It is essential to enable the child to bring out his aggressiveness, but what counts most is to understand why at this particular moment in the transference situation destructive impulses come up and to observe their consequences in the child's mind. Feelings of guilt may very soon follow after the child has broken, for instance, a little figure. Such guilt refers not only to the actual damage done, but to what the toy stands for in the child's unconscious, e.g., a little brother or sister or a parent. The interpretation has, therefore, to deal with these deeper levels as well. Sometimes, we can gather from the child's behaviour toward the psychoanalyst that not only guilt but also persecutory anxiety has been the sequel to his destructive impulses and that he is afraid of retaliation. [Klein, 1964, p. 120]

Interpretation of the phantasies helps children to reveal more of their fears and also gives them the feeling of being able to control their fears. Interpretation attempts to connect the unconscious internal objects with those in reality. The interpretation brings together what is happening in the patient's life and in the transference relationship, and also what has happened with parents and significant adults of the past. In our special school (see chapter nine) a six-year-old boy was able to draw his feeling that he was falling to pieces. Mark, a bright young boy, achieved his major developmental milestones somewhat later than average: he walked unaided at 18 months, said his first word at 21 months and was fully toilet-trained at four years.

By the time he was six, he showed no problems in either gross or fine motor movement, and his receptive and expressive language development was normal. He had no visual or auditory problems, but he did have serious emotional problems. Mark was very provocative; he teased and poked, hurt and fought, and he called other children names. He usually appeared emotionally detached and did not express the affect appropriate to a situation. He bit his knuckles and fingers until they bled, and he hurt other children or destroyed things even though an adult was working with him and then denied that he had done it. He often responded in an hallucinatory way and then became impulsive and very distractable. Mark could not stand other children looking at him and would lash out. For example, if at a restaurant another child made direct eye-to-eye contact, Mark would go berserk. He often responded to situations in an uncontrollably aggressive way.

One day Mark came into the group room where three other children were colouring, and he put a mechanical frog in one child's face. He did this repeatedly and only stopped when he was pulled away; he then sat down at another table and said, 'My father told me to kick you in the wienie,' as he tried to kick his worker. When he was restrained he became very angry, shouting and swearing, but calmed down when his behaviour was interpreted to him, 'I think you are trying to hurt everyone else so that the hurt will leave you. If you damage the other kids you may not feel as damaged and they won't be able to attack you.' He then proceeded to make a remarkable drawing, the first of a series, which revealed how he felt about himself. In his first drawing there were 'bad bits', spots of black, contained within a yellow field, which I think might have represented some aspects of goodness and hope, but with a hammer or axe-like object suspended and threatening on top of the yellow container. Gradually, in different drawings, he drew more and more black strands or 'bad bits', and he depicted the rising jail bars (his term) still with the suspended hammer or axe. His fifth drawing had two yellow spots and three bars, with the hammer suspended above, but his subsequent drawings became darker and darker, with an increasing number of bars, until in drawings eight and nine, although there was no longer a suspended object, the bars, which looked like metal window bars—like jail bars—were complete, and the black bits encompassed the entire field. Mark was trying to show how he felt: completely closed in by bars and full of badness, devoid of any goodness (yellow). Mark's drawings demonstrated that he felt that he was a bad, hostile child who was unable to control his own badness, which had become progressively worse and encompassed more of him. Perhaps the 'jail window bars' that gradually emerged represented to him the idea that he was locked in and unreachable, although they might also have been his attempt to keep his badness inside.

Play, drawings, constructions and verbalizations help the therapist to understand the internal conflicts, phantasies and problems and provide an avenue to the child's unconscious. But as we have seen, from the child's point of view drawings act also as a form of reparation. The act of creation and giving gifts to a real mother diminishes the dread of the phantasized terrifying mother. The child can imagine her repaired by his or her gift of art and existing in the 'full possession of her strength and beauty' (Klein, 1929a, p. 443). The child now introjects a good, repaired, loving object. The creative act provides the avenue for reparation and means that the mother will no longer be damaged and, therefore, will no longer want revenge. These factors—creative act, reparation, revenge and ego development—must be kept at a 'certain optimum level and in a satisfactory interplay' (Klein, 1929a, p. 443).

The transference relationship

In the transference relationship between the child and the therapist, the child projects his or her early object-representative feelings onto the therapist and reacts to the therapist as if he or she contained all these feelings. The therapist then becomes the good or bad parent—'a new edition of an old object relationship' (Winnicott, 1986, p. 75), and through the therapist's interpretive comments the child begins to understand his or her feelings toward parents and is gradually able to integrate the projections as his or her own.

In child psychotherapy the transference relationship is more complicated than that in adult psychotherapy because children are brought to therapy by a parent, guardian or relative, or possibly even a friend: they do not come on their own. This concern must be dealt with within the transference relationship as it develops. Related to the transference is how you play and how much you do with the child. A child may, for example, want me to 'fly around' the room, to eat the Plasticine, or to crawl on the floor as if I were a worm. I do not think that my doing these things, if I could, would strengthen the transference relationship. The therapist should be part of the play—i.e., participate—but not limit the phantasy expression of the child. I do not know how the child wants me to crawl, nor how he wants me to fly, and if I did these things I think I would prevent the expression that the child gives to his or her phantasies. I also think it limits the therapeutic process to answer many questions about my personal life and family; it is important that the projections of the child be unencumbered by my personal descriptions and, at times, actions. It is true I am not a *tabula rasa:* I may remind the child of certain people, feelings or thoughts, but as I am initially unaware of this, I must not limit the child's phantasies by participating too much in the play. I will say that I will pretend to fly or pretend to eat Plasticine and help a child to fill in all the descriptions about my pretending. If I participate in a more direct way, I will become involved in a form of pedagogy rather than in therapy.

The issue of children's choice in coming to sessions is also important: children are brought by adults, and it is usually the adults who are worried about the children's behaviour.

Perhaps the children are not worried or bothered, except by an anxiety that they feel, yet do not understand. However, they do not, generally, know what to do about this feeling. The parents have made the initial appointment and bring their children to meet the therapist. I have often seen young children who refuse to move out of the waiting room area, or, if they come into the consulting room, refuse to allow their parents to leave. These issues as well as other concerns complicate the transference relationship with children. For example, as children are dependent upon their parents, how can they become dependent upon their therapists? Do children have the capacity to establish a transference relationship while being so remarkably dependent for their health, welfare and nurturance upon their parents? I have found that young children are very capable of establishing a transference relationship with a therapist while at the same time exploring their relationship with their parents, particularly because they need their parents to bring them to the sessions in the first place. Often children's anxiety and dependency and the interpretations and consistencies of the therapy provide the beginning of a strong transference to the therapist.

In her first session, a four-year-old girl placed a baby doll in a cardboard box, on top of which she put a book. I said, 'Sometimes the baby makes you very angry; she takes all of Mummy's time, and makes Mummy tired.' The child looked at me and said, 'My baby sister is nasty and she makes me cry, but I don't tell Mummy.' I responded that we could talk about this at our special times when we play together. She smiled at me and said, 'Good, I want to come and play some more with you.' An eight-year-old boy told me that he could talk to me about his worries and said, 'I don't want to tell my mother and father because they worry and ask too many questions. I don't know what to tell them.' The boy asked about our sessions and then said that, 'We can talk and do stuff.'

While the child's anxiety provides a basis for the transference, the parents' anxieties are often contained within this transference relationship and must be explored by the child therapist. The child's feelings of loyalty to the parents, on the one hand, and friendship and affection for the therapist, on the other, do cause the child to experience intense conflict. Children often talk about their parents' reactions to their coming to therapy—for example, they have said how they have to tell their parents that they will be late for their appointment unless they hurry. As one child said, 'I didn't know whether to miss the appointment or get my father angry because he was going to make me late.'

One five-year-old said, 'I want to play with you, but sometimes my Mummy and Daddy say that if I am bad they will not let me come here.' Another child of the same age said, 'My Daddy told me that you will fix me up and he couldn't. Is my Daddy giving me to you?' A seven-year-old said, 'I want to come here on my own because my mother always says, "Did you have a good time with Dr. O?" and I don't want to say anything.' These comments indicate the anxieties of parents, and perhaps how they feel about having played a role in the problems of their children. Parents are afraid that they will lose their child's love or that 'he won't listen to me any more', or that he or she will 'be too independent of me' or 'won't know who his real parents are'. These are some of the statements parents have made to me. As children talk about their therapists in both loving and hating terms, parents begin to feel their transference to the therapist. Their own anxieties are stimulated, no doubt because of envy, and then they try either to control the sessions or to give their children over entirely to the therapist. One parent said to me, 'Well, as my son likes you so much, maybe he should go home with you.' No matter how much parents say that they are pleased that their child is in treatment, a time comes when their own feelings emerge and interfere with the child's transference. The parents become angry with the therapist, saying, for example, 'I didn't know it would take so long to fix him up,' or, 'We are thinking of going away for a vacation, and our child will come with us. We think it is more important to have a family holiday than for her to remain in treatment.'

All these responses at worst threaten the transference relationship and at best point to the fact that parents are uneasily aware of its development. Sometimes a child is angry with the therapist and tells the parents that he or she does not want to come to the sessions any more, and the parents telephone and cancel further appointments. What does one do about such a situation? Usually I telephone the parents and talk about adult feelings, how adults sometimes feel angry with others but they do not necessarily just stop talking to them or seeing them. I say that they may be worried about what is happening to their child and whether they still 'will have a child when treatment is over!' Parents then often repeat the child's remark, for example, 'I don't want to go there any more.' I try to help parents to bring their child back so that he or she can talk to me about this, and I try to help parents recognize their own ambivalence about bringing their child to the sessions by indicating how quickly they latched on to this one statement. The question is once again a concern of transference, and how the child is avoiding feelings towards the therapist by invoking his or her right to depend on the parents. The parents' feelings towards the sessions and their reactions to the therapist must also be considered.

What I usually do is to have a talk with the child and parents during the diagnostic period and explain the therapeutic process in terms of why the child and I will meet, feelings that might emerge and those that are present already, and the length and approximate duration of the sessions. I also say that our feelings change and that at times we might wonder whether we are doing the best for the child and ourselves. I also talk about the privacy of the conversation and how they might feel left out, how they will want to know what goes on in the room and what their child did. I stress the need for privacy except when there might be danger to the child or themselves. I try to explain the nature of therapy and to create a foundation for psychotherapy, which I know I will need to call upon as treatment proceeds. Often this is not enough, and then focal therapy for the parents to deal with this issue, with someone else if I am working with their child, is important. These are 'time-limited' appointments. Should the parents decide to enter treatment after this, then that is another issue. The main issue in the focal therapy is to clarify their feelings about their child's treatment and to help them with their role as parents.

Transference is a very powerful relationship. It has its basis in the earliest phantasy object-relationship and makes use of projection and introjection. It is as if the transference provides the opportunity for the 'reverie' (Bion, 1962) process where the parent takes in the anxious, difficult feelings of the baby, thinks about them and gives them back to the baby when the baby is strong enough to 'handle' these powerful feelings. The containing aspect of transference is the therapist's capacity to hold, to clarify and to help identify strong feelings and poorly defined thoughts and actions, to reduce the general feeling of anxiety and distress so that the child can move on to become aware of these states and then gradually 'take them back'. This is done primarily through interpretation within the transference process. The child begins to realize that the therapist is not damaged by his or her painful phantasies, and that the therapist lives on in spite of the hostility, envy and per-secutory feelings projected by the child. The therapist does not try to deny or to get rid of these feelings but, rather, provides the container and the reverie so that the child gradually takes these feelings back. The child slowly constructs his or her own effective and resilient container and gives him or herself the time to think about problems and feelings rather than impulsively projecting them and then worrying about consequences.

Children project their early phantasies onto the therapist by the means of play materials. The therapist interprets the play as the symbolic equivalent of early object-relationships along with the feelings of anger, pain, dependency and fear attached to these early objects and the relationships the child phantasizes them to be. These interpretations allow less painful, less threatening or even less powerful objects to be introjected but basically help the child to explore further through playing and also to talk through the characteristics of their early object relationships. The transference relationship helps the child to explore the close interaction of his or her inner and outer world, the interactions of phantasy and reality.

As Segal points out:

Klein sees reality and phantasy as intimately interwoven. However 'real' the event is reported, it must be considered in its interaction with the patient's phantasy life in order to show how unconscious phantasy influences and colours his experince of reality and how reality, in turn, may alter the phantasy. This makes interpretation of transference more continuous and more controlled. In Klein's view, the relationships with internal objects are reflected in and influence all activities. Therefore, the relation to the analyst, as the representative of these objects, crucially affects all the patient's relations to reality, and so the element of the transference is important in every communication. [Segal, 1979, p. 172]

The unconscious phantasy revealed in the child's play comes about and is interpreted within the transference relationship. The therapist becomes the repository for the child's earliest phantasies. How the child will respond becomes a function of the therapist's ability to accept and contain, and to interpret when appropriate, the anxiety and defense mechanisms attached to the phantasy.

Patients bring samples of their past and of their inner reality and expose them in the phantasy that belongs to their ever-changing relationship to the analyst. In this way, the unconscious can gradually be made conscious. [Winnicott, 1986, p. 103]

The transference is the object relationship, and as long as the therapist remains neutral and does not reveal secrets to the parents, or does not become so encumbered by parental wishes and anxieties for their child that he or she cannot continue to remain neutral or be an effective container, the transference goes on. 'Once the process has started up and the unconscious cooperation of the patient has been gained, there is always much to be done' (Winnicott, 1986, p. 103). This relationship contains within it love, fear, anger, anxiety, guilt, pain and all the manoeuvres the child will go through to try to undo, or destroy, or deny the unconscious object relationships. Through the transference process the child projects his or her internal object world, with its interwoven mix of inner and outer reality brought about by early experiences:

> The past object relationships which have become the structure of the internal world are relived in the transference, and in this reliving they evolve. It is this evolution in the transference which constitutes the dynamic part of the therapeutic relationship. [Segal, 1979, p. 174]

Children understand the interpretations, particularly if they are given in relationship to the play activity, clearly and in the children's words. As Klein points out, the child's 'intellectual capacities are often underrated and that, in fact, he understands more than he is credited with' (Klein, 1964, p. 284; see also 1932, 1961).

An extreme example of projection in a transference is the case of Miriam (a case reported by Mrs. Susan Rees), a nine-year-old child with cerebral palsy referred for play psychotherapy because of 'immature behaviour, temper tantrums, poor peer relationships and depression'. When Miriam started play psychotherapy, she had been removed for the tenth (or more) time from a mother who was suffering from 'borderline schizophrenia'. In the first session Miriam projected her destructive phantasies onto the therapist. She accused the therapist of being a bad mother who would give her germs and kill her by coming too close to her. Miriam would not permit the therapist to touch her or anything that belonged to her. The therapist interpreted her paranoid projective idealizations as trying to get rid of 'all her bad feelings by putting them in the therapist' and then trying to make sure that the therapist kept her distance and also by saying to the therapist, 'My Mummy hates me.' In a later session Miriam openly accused her mother of having given her poisoned milk, which had caused her cerebral palsy. For a number of sessions Miriam did not touch any of the small toys. Instead, she repeatedly sang the nursery rhyme 'There Was an Old Woman Who Lived in a Shoe.' Her play and her speech centred around themes of destroying or being destroyed, being sick and dying, giving birth to babies who died, being lost and then found, getting nothing to eat, running away and being stopped from leaving. The therapist was given the role of the bad person and was blamed for being unable or unwilling to protect Miriam.

In transference, the therapist became the recipient of all Miriam's destructive impulses and hostility. From the transference it was clear that she was very angry with her phantasized mother (although the real mother might also be someone she was angry with), for not protecting her. The therapist offered the interpretation that Miriam was afraid that she had damaged her mother by taking too much from her and that her mother's revenge was to take away her walking ability. There was a period in the therapy during which Miriam could not cope with all the badness inside her. This was interpreted as not having enough good things inside to stop the bad; Miriam felt full of badness because the phantasized mother put all her bad things inside Miriam because Miriam was so greedy and tried to take everything. In an attempt to gain some control over her persecutory anxiety, she ordered the therapist to eat her 'poo' and drink her 'pee'; Miriam repeatedly told her therapist she wanted to 'fart into' her so that she could get rid of her own 'stink'. The therapist's interpretation of

Miriam's projections created a splitting of good and bad, so that the therapist became everything bad and an aunt with whom the child was then living became all good. Miriam accepted and worked through the interpretation of her badness by showing how she would deal with her badness by making her poo and pee good, and then she could recognize how some people were good and perhaps even safe. Gradually her play had some positive outcomes; for example, the toys became safe to touch, babies lived with giving mothers, and the therapist was no longer an all-bad person. Miriam accepted and understood how good and bad can be in one person, and she could see herself doing successful things, such as being proud of her play themes: 'I liked playing going to the doctor's.' And she began to talk about her future. She decided that she wanted to learn how to walk—she had not walked until then—and even took her first unaided steps. She quickly progressed from being wheelchair-bound to using a walker and then crutches.

The therapist makes interpretations to help the child 'revise these early relations at their root and thus effectively diminish his anxieties' (Klein, 1964, p. 285). These interpretations are directed to the level at which the therapist considers the anxiety to be dominant and at which the child is primarily behaving and are always made within the transference—that is, within the object relationship.

Sometimes therapists have the reward of clear confirmation of their interpretations even outside the therapeutic setting. Thus, for example, when Kevin, a three-year-old patient, said that he was 'sad', I was able to interpret to him his concern about helping to repair and restore his mother who had recently undergone an appendectomy. Kevin made a round object out of clay, on which he made some deep impressions with his fingers. He went on to paint each indentation with a different colour, and when this was completed he said that this was a gift for his mother. When I spoke with his mother, she said that Kevin had wrapped the gift in tinfoil and presented it to her while she was still in bed. Kevin said that he made it 'special' for her, that he made sure it was clean by wrapping it in tinfoil, and she did not have to worry about him because he would 'always be a good boy'. Kevin's mother told him that he 'was a good boy', that she 'loved him' and that his gift 'made her feel much better'. She confirmed Kevin's attempts at reparation but at the same time confirmed his phantasy that he was responsible in some way for her operation. As our sessions continued, Kevin sorted out his phantasy (that he 'hurt Mummy and she needed an operation to get out the bad thing in her tummy') from her 'real' physical problem. He gradually accepted the thought that he was not responsible, but he still felt sad because his 'Mummy had to have an operation', but happy because he could make her feel 'nice' because 'I gave her a nice thing.' The sadness at her pain became reality-based and not phantasy-directed. Kevin could feel sad and yet not think he had caused his mother's problem.

This sort of confirmation is not, of course, always readily available. However, another kind of confirmation is often provided by the child's immediate reaction to an interpretation. A change in posture or facial expression, or words, or play activity may indicate the effectiveness of a particular interpretation. After I made an interpretation about his rivalry with his sibling, four-year-old Charles said, 'I don't want to talk about that any more.' When I said that he was really angry with his brother and his mother, Charles replied, 'Don't talk funny, I won't listen to you,' and he went to play in the sand box. Within ten minutes he returned to where I was sitting and said that he had had bad dreams about dogs, about a big dog biting a puppy. We talked about the dream, and I think the interpretation created the possibility for him to describe his dream even though he seemed to reject the interpretation itself.

Children become anxious and upset but do not know why, and to ask them why generally just increases their anxiety because they cannot 'do' or 'give' what is expected of them. Such questions strengthen the sadistic characteristics of children's superegos and add to their pain. The young child then has the phantasy of destructive, punishing internal objects (parents) that constitute 'a particularly savage superego with which the child's ego cannot cope' (Segal, 1979, p. 38). Anxiety, pain and symptoms become split-off bad parts with which he or she cannot cope and which are transferred to the therapist in play psychotherapy.

Termination

The termination process is part of the ongoing therapy. The therapist continues to interpret the anxieties with the play and the child's verbalizations. Transference interpretations also continue to be made, but now the therapist becomes a real person for the child, and the separation from, and loss of, this person have to be worked through. The loss does occasion the pain of grief; the experiences of successful work completed with the help of an accepting and kind person provide the basis for the impending grief at termination.

Usually the decision to terminate is made as a result of observing the child's play. Children's play themes suggest departure—as, for example, one ten-year-old boy said as he was putting his vampires into a box, 'Bye, I'm going to miss you,' or as another child said, 'Mummy and I will be going on a trip in a little while, and maybe I can send you a postcard,' or still another three-year-old, 'I think it will be fun to sit in Daddy's chair in his office.' These statements were also coincidental with a general overall well-being. The children came into their sessions easily, they talked about the 'nice', or 'good' or sometimes 'bad' things that were happening to them at school, at home or with their friends, but they were able to cope with these situations. In effect, the savageness of their superegos had abated, and their egos were functioning so that 'real' events and internal phantasies were more in line with each other: phantasy did not overrule reality nor vice versa, and the child was able to draw on internal resources to handle difficult real situations.

C.P.—G*

Children seem to know it is 'right' to terminate and deal with the difficulties of the separation and loss of the person of the therapist. Sometimes therapists do not seem to recognize this readiness to terminate, perhaps as a consequence of their own countertransference; it is so delightful to meet a 'normal healthy' child that we do not want to give up this opportunity and do not notice how effectively the child is saying or doing things. In such a situation, the child will regress, for the good internal objects and their readiness to work with reality have not been acknowledged by the therapist. It means to them that they are not good enough, and their phantasy of having too few internal good objects becomes reactivated. The therapist is not recognizing their improved functioning, and this seems to mean that it is not good enough and more is needed. The child responds to this by anger—anger derived from envy that the therapist has what is needed but does not provide it for the child. At this point it is not unusual to see a resurgence of symptoms and/or withdrawal by the child.

Other children, generally older ones, are able to make their readiness known, even if the therapist seems unable to accept it. They decide, unfortunately alone, that they do not need to come to any more sessions and either tell their parents that they do not need to attend any longer or that they have a lot of work to do and have not got the time to attend the sessions. The therapist must be able to understand the readiness to terminate and not confuse it with resistance or negative transference.

Children are ready to terminate when the following conditions are present:

1. there is an abatement of their original problems;
2. they have developed a capacity to be realistically aggressive, dependent and adaptive;
3. they can make use of their emotional energies in constructive ways that serve their growing developmental interests and curiosities;
4. they can introject and identify without becoming anxiety-ridden and/or avoidant of people or events;

5. they can accept failures as well as successes without splitting or denial;
6. they can integrate parental demands with their growing needs;
7. they can think of the future and about some of the goodness and also badness that they will encounter;
8. they can feel gratification because of their efforts, yet can rely on others for help;
9. they can gain and maintain friendships and think that they have something to offer others;
10. they can sublimate and continue symbol formation.

We look at all these factors and also recognize the child's capacity to handle the separation and loss. If the ego function is adequate and the superego no longer savage, then usually the child will work through the separation effectively (Klein, 1950b). But because the patient is a child, it is important at the end of therapy to give the child a gift, usually something that is meaningful to the child. This may be a special toy in which the child has expressed considerable interest, or it may be, for example, something like a small bracelet, which I gave a five-year-old girl on terminating. The bracelet was a plastic bangle of her favourite colour. In the same way as it is important to recognize children's birthdays (Lewis, 1974), a gift at terminating provides a transitional object to fill in the 'felt gap' between child and therapist and makes the separation less frightening (Winnicott, 1968). The gift does not become magical; rather, it furthers and helps to continue the symbol formation; it is as if the gift represents the goodness of the therapist, which the child can now take with him or her. Further ego growth requires trust, and now the child has the capacity and resiliency as well as the gift that represents goodness. The child has the good object both inside and outside him- or herself (Klein, 1958).

Usually the child and therapist agree on a date for terminating, and the therapist must help the child work through the terminating process by indicating that 'leaving someone who has been important to you is very hard; it makes us feel upset, even sad and angry that we have to do it.' The child usually feels abandoned and needs to recognize his or her internal strength, even though the child may react to terminating by symptom development, unhappiness, anxiety or dissatisfaction. Depressive anxieties are evoked once again, and the child believes he or she has done something wrong or has been bad. This is the transference within the depressive position. Interpretation relating to the desire to prolong treatment helps the child to understand that he or she is not bad and has not taken too much from the therapist, and that the therapist is not 'tired and fed up' with him or her, or sick, bored or busy with someone else. Interpretations of the depressive reactions and the symbolic gift help the child to recognize his or her own goodness and strength. The gift indicates that, 'I am giving you this so that you can think of me,' and it suggests the therapist's pleasure of witnessing the growth and development of the child. In other words, the child's success does not threaten the adult, and the thought of the child becoming psychologically healthy is pleasing. When I gave an adolescent a calendar, he said, 'Great, now I can think of you every day of the year, and that should be enough,' implying that thinking about me for a year would enable him to handle the termination and separation, but now on his own.

Termination does differ from patient to patient (van Dam, Heinicke & Shane, 1975). It is usually a difficult process, even though mutually agreed upon. The child has the problem of letting the therapist go because he or she has found the therapist to be an effective container, a good listener, a reliable person who reduces bad feelings, and a friend. The therapist has the problem of letting go because it is just so nice to work with a child who is functioning well, is so pleasant, is in control of drives and impulses, and is so responsive. I often find it difficult to end work with normal children. These children are so capable of using interpretation, so creative and eager to explore the world about them, that I often think, 'How nice to be with these children and how much less energy I have to expend!' However, termination must occur, and the transference and counter-transference must be resolved. Separation, loss and mourning must be dealt with, and this occupies the period of the termination process (Klein, 1935, 1940, 1950b). This process is 'bound to stir up painful feelings and revive early anxieties; it amounts to a state of mourning' (Klein, 1950a, p. 80). And even after the therapy has ended, the child still has 'to carry out by himself part of the work of mourning. This, I think, explains the fact that often after the termination of an analysis further progress is achieved' (Klein, 1950a, p. 80).

Once they have understood that we have to deal with termination, some children have told me that they were thinking of it and wondered how to tell me; others have been able to tell me through dreams and/or through their play. It is usually important to discuss the date of the proposed termination some weeks in advance, and with some adolescent patients even some months in advance. Young children find the concept of time difficult to grasp, and so I usually point out on a calendar the number of weeks and sessions that remain, and I generally do not make the length of time longer than four weeks. Presenting the termination phase not only starts the work of mourning with the therapist, but also 'prepares the way for him to finish the work of mourning successfully on his own' (Klein, 1950a, p. 80). In contrast to the results presented by van Dam, Heinicke and Shane (1975), many children and adolescents continue to remember their sessions and will sometimes write or draw pictures for me and mail them to my office, or even telephone me. I think this remembering for several months reflects children's work of finishing their mourning on their own, but at times needing the 'supportive reverie' of their therapist, who has become a nice person (Reich, 1950). Gradually, children can carry the therapist in their thoughts, and at the same time gain more good internal objects, making the children feel that they have 'rights to their objects' (Balint, 1950, p. 197).

In chapter eleven I trace selections of the process of play psychotherapy from the beginning through to the termination in the case of a ten-year-old boy who made use of all available resources to understand and surmount his difficulties.

The snake family: excerpts from play psychotherapy sessions with a ten-year-old boy

Background

S am was referred to a local Children's Mental Health Centre (the Centre) in a city in northern Ontario a week after his mother died. [Play psychotherapy was conducted by T. Rankin-Scholten and supervised by O. Weininger. The names and some details of the family have been changed to preserve the anonymity of those involved.] He was ten years old, the youngest by nine years in a family of five children. At the time of referral Sam was living with his 19-year-old sister, her husband and their two children— a boy aged two, and a three-month-old baby girl. Sam's sister and the school authorities were concerned about his emotional flatness. He had apparently not shown any reaction to his mother's death, and they felt that he was a 'walking time bomb'; play psychotherapy was recommended.

By the time the therapist contacted the family one month later, Sam's behaviour had become much more problematic. At home, he was now very difficult to handle; he did not listen to his sister or her husband; he was terrorizing his two-year-old nephew by attempting to smother him whenever they were alone together; and he had been caught stealing, an activity that he had been engaged in for a long time. At school, in Grade 4, he was doing poorly both behaviourally and academically; he had become a 'nuisance' and was very difficult to manage; he was moody, made inappropriate noises, lied, talked back to the teacher and was very aggressive; he was also thought to be achieving below his academic potential. No one seemed to know Sam's legal status; however, his sister was planning to apply for custody.

Sam's mother had been dying since he was three years old. She had a serious alcoholic problem, was battling lung cancer, and in the end she had died of a heart attack. Apparently she had spent a great deal of time in bed, and a social worker regarded her as unable and unfit to handle her youngest son. Reference to the Children's Aid Society records revealed that Sam had been brought to their attention many times due to lack of proper supervision and also because of many complaints of lying and stealing. Eventually, a year prior to therapy, when Sam was nine years old, he was made a Crown Ward and placed in a foster home for six months. However, he missed (pined for) his mother and was returned home on a promise 'to be good', with the Children's Aid having supervisory orders. Mother and son had spent much time in southeastern Ontario, but at this point in Sam's life they had moved north, to live with his older sister and her family. However, two months later they all returned to southeastern Ontario. When Sam's mother became increasingly ill, Sam was sent to live with his sister. A month later his mother died. Sam's father lived in southeastern Ontario as well, but he had not been with Sam since he was one year of age. Although there was occasional contact, the father was generally unavailable, either spending much time in jail or away from the town on one of his many trips to try to 'find himself'.

Course of therapy

When arrangements for psychotherapy were finally made, Sam could only be seen once a week because of the Children's Aid worker's timetable and school demands. He was seen weekly over a seven-month period, for a total of 28 sessions, by Dr. Teeya Rankin-Scholten. The first 3 sessions were held in a room at this school, the remaining sessions at a Children's Mental Health Centre. The final session was held in his own backyard. The therapist at that time was a doctoral candidate in the Department of Applied Psychology, Ontario Institute for Studies in Education, University of Toronto, and received weekly supervision.

By the final session, Sam had settled down considerably in class. Both academic and behavioural improvement was noted by the head of his school and his teacher. He was not disruptive, he accepted help, he played well with other children, he was somewhat of a leader, he made effective decisions at play and at games and he was liked by others. He 'listened better' at home and was not as aggressive or disruptive as he had been, nor was he unusually aggressive towards his nephew.

A follow-up a year later showed that he remained manageable and cooperative at home. In school, his behaviour was acceptable, and his achievement was adequate and continuing to improve. No unusual complaints were presented either at home or school at this time, and Sam was described as a happy and pleasant young boy.

In his play psychotherapy, Sam made use of a snake family to enact his anxieties, hostilities, fears, rivalries and loves. He developed snake characters that were in many ways equivalent to the people in his life. For example, while his mother was alive, his uncle would give her cigarettes, even though she had lung cancer; paralleling this reality, in the snake family, the uncle snake was portrayed as a bad person. A description of the events that took place during each session is presented in the left column. Interpretations that were actually made and additional psychodynamic comments are presented in the right column. Following the reporting of some sessions, a summary and analysis of the ongoing therapeutic process is presented.

A family tree of the snake family and their friends and enemies (Figure 1) is presented in an effort to try to make it easier to follow Sam's psychotherapy.

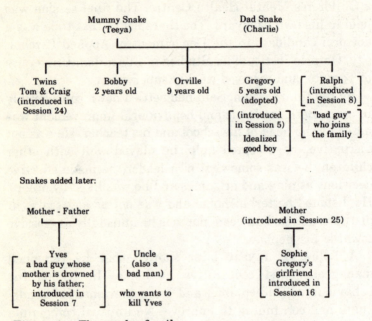

Figure 1. The snake family.

Session 1

Sam was a small, slightly stout ten-year-old boy with curly brown hair and blue eyes. He had a pale, cherub-like face and a clear complexion. After I introduced the problems of play psychotherapy, myself and the nature of the room, I suggested that we all have feelings about dying and that this was something we could talk about. He said that he was the only one who did not cry when his Mum died. In fact, he said that he didn't know how he felt about his Mum's dying.

We talked about his Mum's illness, lung cancer, how he had refused to buy her cigarettes, but that his uncle had bought them for her. The closest he came to showing any emotion was in saying and showing how he often felt like grabbing and breaking her cigarettes when she smoked.

He then told me about his belief in 'good luck' and 'bad luck' people. He had moved around a lot but always felt in 'good luck' when he was with his paternal grandmother. 'No one around her has died yet. She has a bunch of crosses. ...' He felt that he was now in 'bad luck' because of where he was living.

Sam has tried to maintain himself and his world by splitting, and this is his attempt by a kind of magical thinking and projection to maintain his own internal integrity. Sam does not feel that good and bad can co-exist together— rather, he sees all situations as good or bad, indicating an ego immaturity, a non-resolution of paranoid persecutory anxiety and an inability to resolve ambivalence towards his primal object. Bad always hurts and is bad luck, good is safe and is a good mother, who has amulets that protect. Sam has few ways of protecting himself in his sister's home, which he views as unsafe and threatening. He phantasizes the continuing influence of his dead mother, that she will destroy him for not having saved her from her heart attack. He feels depleted by her death, yet he cannot take much in from his external world, nor let much out; thus he feels that the change in balance will make him 'worse'. He phantasizes that his nephew is part of his own bad internal objects and his attempts to kill him are his attempts to destroy those parts of himself that he phantasizes as having killed his mother.

The Squiggle Game* (Winnicott, 1968) was introduced as a diagnostic technique, and he really seemed to enjoy it (Figures 2–4). Among other things, he drew a 'splat of jam'

Oral sadistic and cannibalistic impulses are seen as the major way Sam phantasizes he had taken too much from mother and had destroyed her as well.

---

*Winnicott said of the Squiggle Game:

> At a suitable moment after the arrival of the patient, usually after asking the parent to go to the waiting room, I say to the child: 'Let's play something. I know what I would like to play and I'll show you.' I have a table between the child and myself, with paper and two pencils. First I take some of the paper and tear the sheets in half, giving the impression that what we are doing is not frantically important, and then I begin to explain. I say: 'This game that I like playing has no rules. I just take my pencil and go like that ... ,' and I probably screw up my eyes and do a squiggle blind. I go on with my explanation and say: 'You show me if that looks like anything to you or if you can make it into anything, and afterwards you do the same for me and I will see if I can make something of yours.' [Winnicott, 1968, p. 100]

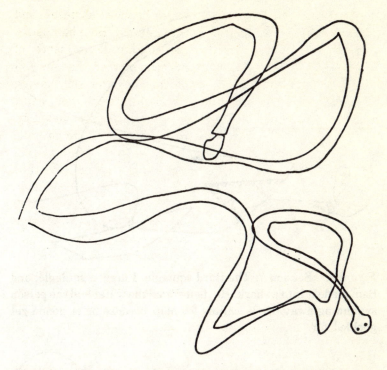

Figure 2. Session 1: The first squiggle of the therapeutic experience. I drew the squiggle, and Sam made it into a snake.

and several monsters with sharp teeth who said, 'Yum, Yum' (Figure 5) and were 'hungry for people' to eat (Figure 6). (He is creating the basis for his snake family in this session.)

When I left the room for a minute to find out the time, Sam was hiding when I returned. He said, 'Boo!' Sam asked to do an extra squiggle and was hoping I could go to his parent–teacher interview. He seemed eager to have me return next week and was

Sam is afraid his therapist has deserted him—i.e., has died; her departure is viewed as a threat, and he frightens her partly in an attempt to prevent her from being effective and finding out about him, but also to hurt her as he has been hurt.

Figure 3.   Session 1: The third squiggle. I drew a squiggle, and Sam made it into a shark. He then *added* the water and the person swimming away. He is 'calling for help' because he is 'gonna get gobbled up'.

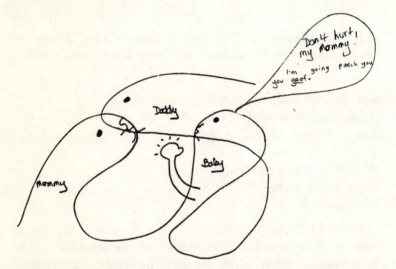

Figure 4.   Session 1: The eighth squiggle, drawn by Sam. I drew three eyes and called it a Mummy, Daddy and Baby. Sam called it a 'worm family', *added* the lips and Baby's arm and said that Baby was mad. I wrote: 'Don't hurt my Mummy!' and Sam printed in: 'I'm going to punch you, you goof!' He said that Baby wanted to have Mummy all to himself.

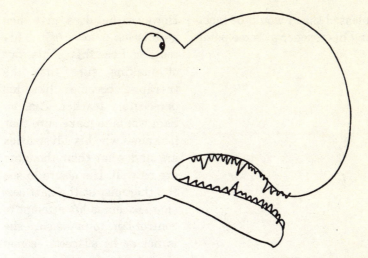

Figure 5.   Session 1: The ninth squiggle, which I drew and Sam turned into a 'hungry hippotamus' who was looking for people to eat and who said: 'yum, yum. ...'

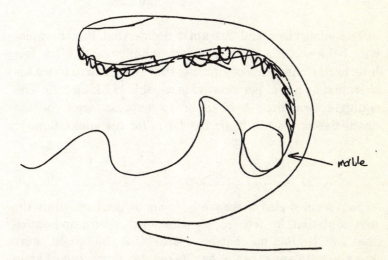

Figure 6.   Session 1: The twelfth squiggle, drawn by Sam. I made it into a hand by drawing the fingernails. Then Sam *added* the 'hair' and a marble and called the creation a 'creature' or 'hairy hand reaching up to grab somebody'. The creature was trying to eat the marble and wanted to find some people too.

pleased that I would be meeting his teacher at some point.

However he does give her permission to visit his teacher. I see this as his way of making sure that the therapist becomes like his persecutory teacher. That is, Sam wants to make sure that he knows who his adversaries are and what their thoughts are as well. His desire to see the therapist at the next session is seen as his attempt to control her, to make sure she is not as he suspects—someone who is not to be trusted and who will disappear like his mother. He needs to see the mother–therapist come back unharmed, but phantasizes that the therapist will not like him.

The supervisor and therapist decide that the therapist will behave in a matter-of-fact manner and offer few interpretations in the beginning, that is, help Sam to see his therapist as a real person who is capable of liking him. The squiggle drawings help Sam to express some of his hostilities and seem to be the basis for his snake family.

Session 2

Sam seemed glad to see me and said that he felt 'so-so' that day. He told me that he knew how to swear when he was little. He swore now too, in the schoolyard, but not at home because he wanted to be 'good'. He 'passed gas' several

Sam is anxious about the therapist's return and anticipates that he might have taken too much from her in their first session. He expresses this by anxiety about his internal objects, and attacks upon them experi-

times, burped and excused himself for these behaviours. One of his squiggles was 'pee on the floor' (see Figure 7). He seemed somewhat embarrassed by these subjects. He wanted to do more squiggles, which we did. Themes of aggression and eating up emerged again (Figure 8).

enced as hypochrondriacal fears. He feels 'so-so'. He tries to be good by not 'swearing', but his ego is not sufficiently strong to contain his hostility away from home. He does, however, show aggression at home, and while he denies this, his unconscious expression of oral and anal sadism is observed by his burping and 'passing gas'. He says that he is sorry but continues on with these attacks, adding urethral sadism as a further attack on the therapist. His need to express these feelings is seen in his desire to do more squiggles, which are oral and anal impulses against phantasized attacking external and internal objects.

Figure 7. Session 2: The first squiggle, which I drew. Sam said it was a 'P'. I asked him if it was 'pee on the floor', but he said that that 'was rude' and that we should call it the 'Letter P'.

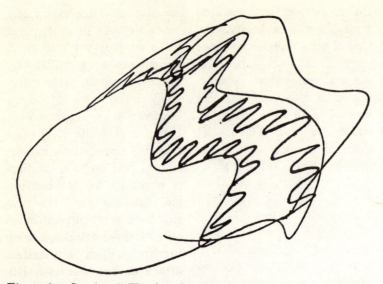

Figure 8.   Session 2: The fourth squiggle, drawn by Sam. He said it looked like a mouth, so I drew in the teeth and he called it 'Jaws—yum, yum, yum. . . .'

Sam's squiggle drawings suggest a theme of oral sadism (monsters with teeth enjoying their food). These monsters are symbolic of Sam's internal objects, which represent his internal phantasized mother who is experienced as harsh and demanding that Sam be a 'good boy'. The harsh internal mother forces Sam to deny and project his feelings. Sam also does not take in any information about reality, and this also allows him to deny his sadism and to maintain the split between his good feelings for his mother and his bad feelings towards her. Sam feels that he was not good enough to stop the monster from destroying his mother and feels that her death is his fault. His destructive internal monsters are threatening to take him over in punishment for his failure and thereby stimulate regression and further sadism. He is very reluctant to deal with his feelings of hostility towards his mother, because he is afraid he will discover he is the cause of her death—that is, his needs were so strong that he took too much from her, and, thereby, not only robbed her but mutilated her as well. His unconscious aggressive acts (i.e., burping, passing gas),

which are his attempt to destroy the external therapist—
mother for making him aware of these things, make him
feel anxious. He would like to say 'pee' and 'poop on the
floor', but he sees this as his badness. Stealing, which he
often does, is an attempt to get enough to placate his
internal monsters who need to have more than Sam feels he
has. Since he doesn't think he is good enough anyway, he
also feels that he has little to give without feeling that the
internal bad will outweigh the internal good. Although he is
very disturbed by his phantasies, he behaves in a fairly
controlled, constricted fashion in order to maintain a status
quo within himself. There is an anxiety that his internal
horrors are about to eat him up, to destroy him, as they
destroyed his mother. Therapy is directed towards dealing
with Sam's unconscious phantasy in symbolically parallel
ways, by using materials that can be symbolically manipu-
lated and interpreted and thereby give Sam the opportunity, in a direct playing way, to lessen his oral and anal
sadistic impulses and the subsequent fear of retaliation.

Session 3

At this session, the Children's Differential Diagnostic
Technique was administered.
We also did some squiggles,
and he drew a rattlesnake,
expressing dissatisfaction
with its tail (Figure 9).

His anxiety is seen in relation to the penis; he phantasizes that the penis he took
from the mother may have
made her die. His phantasized
oral cannibalistic impulses
are directed at this penis in
an attempt to chew up the bad
part; it is as if he is trying to
get rid of his bad part.

The Children's Differential Diagnostic Technique
(Weininger, 1986) indicates a severely depressed child
whose ego controls and resiliency are poor (Total Control
− 17, Differential Index + 5). This finding confirms earlier
observations of this child's responses and behaviour. The
aggressive feelings shown by Sam are his attempts to

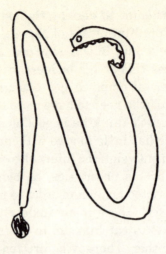

Figure 9.   Session 3: The second squiggle I drew was made into an 'Unhappy Snake', saying that he was 'mad at his tail, because he didn't like the rattle'. [The penis is seen as bad and harsh as well as an instrument that could harm. The snake drawings are continued and are expressive of his sadism.]

destroy the bad that continues to attack him. His 'bad luck' is a sort of 'rational reason' given by Sam to explain why he has to fight and steal and lie. The potential for therapeutic gain through psychotherapy is seen by the degree of emotional energy Sam has available to invest in therapy, but which is at this point 'undirected' and experienced as hostile feelings, with subsequent anxiety.

Session 4

During this first session at the Centre, the following play materials were added to the white paper and pencils used previously: two toy cars, one The marshmallows were introduced to provide symbolically the 'good inexhaustible breast', good objects that could be used by Sam.

truck, a cardboard box large enough to be a garage for the truck and a package of Plasticine. These were brought in and kept between sessions in a bag labelled, 'SAM'S SUPPLIES'. A wooden bowl filled with an abundant supply of miniature marshmallows was introduced by the therapist, who said, 'I thought you and I might be able to have these good things while we play and work.'

Sam began with a few squiggles, in which he drew a monster and snake who was about to eat a marshmallow. Sam looked worried and said, 'When we run out of marshmallows we're doomed— finished. They're gonna get mad at us!' Then he drew a 'Weird Whale' (Figure 10). This turned out to be his last squiggle.

Sam expresses his fear of annihilation when the supply of good objects is exhausted. He fears that there will be no more goodness and expresses his anxiety about persecution without ego resources. The therapist points out that the supply is always present and is replenishable.

Sam then wanted to see who could draw the scariest monster. He won the contest (Figure 11) and then he decided to make a real monster out of a strip of orange Plasticine. He gave it blue teeth, but no body. It was actually a giant mouth, which ate marshmallows. He said that someone started to throw snowballs at the monster. We drew its face on a piece of

Sam attempts to begin to look at his internal sadistic phantasies and their frightening qualities; again this monster is an oral and cannibalistic one. Sam is frightened of the monster; he does not want it to hurt himself or the therapist, so he feeds it marshmallows and then throws white snowballs at its face, presumably killing this giant. The difficulty that Sam

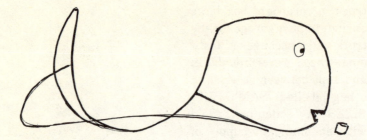

Figure 10.   Session 4: This was the fourth squiggle, which I drew. Sam *rubbed out* sections of the lines and added a mouth with teeth. He also added a marshmallow, named the squiggle 'A Weird Whale' and said: 'Now we're really finished, 'cause when we finish the marshmallows, they'll be after us. We better eat some more before they're gone'. [The therapist said, 'There are going to be a lot of marshmallows—we will have enough'. Sam phantasizes the large whale as eating everything; symbolically, his need is so great that he thinks he must be weird because he cannot ever be satisfied. Nothing seems to make him feel as if he can be satisfied and thereby trust himself.]

paper (Figure 12) and threw white Plasticine snowballs at it. In the end, the monster dies. is experiencing is that while the breast (marshmallows) is to sustain life, white Plasticine made to look like breasts (marshmallows) kills the giant. His ambivalence is seen in that he wants to be protected, but he is unsure as to whether the breast will protect, and furthermore whether he will be able to recognize the breast. Sam is also afraid that the dead monster will attack him in retaliation, and he needs some 'good luck' to protect him. His phantasy is that the good marshmallows could change into bad objects and destroy him.

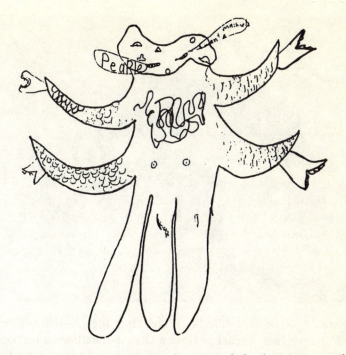

Figure 11. Session 4: Sam's drawing of the 'scariest possible monster', whom he called the 'People Eater'. He ate my monster, 'Jaws'. The monster is asking for marshmallows and some people to eat. [The monster is an oral cannibalistic one, who is trying to eat all the good objects (part objects) as well as the people (whole objects).]

Figure 12. The monster. Sam had successfully played a video game in the lobby of the Centre before the session, and now he wanted to return and play it to win. [Sam is anxious about the death of the monster, and he tries to win a game to prove to himself that he will be okay. It is almost as if winning proves to him that he can become safe and that he can fight off internal and external monsters.]

Figure 13. The snakes to be created from the Plasticine, along with the toy cars, a truck, a bowl with marshmallows, a bottle of 'healing oil', which was introduced in Session 14, and a pond of drinking water made of Plasticine.

The photograph (Figure 13) shows the number of snakes Sam will create over the sessions from the Plasticine.

Session 5

Sam offered to show me how to play the video game in the lobby the following week. He asked if I had had any 'bad luck' lately. I said, 'No', and that I would be all right. He said he had had bad luck when he fell out of bed. We had a discussion about bad luck as the feeling that he might have poisoned others, and he agreed.

There is anxiety related to the therapist and Sam's feeling is that if she and he play the game, then she might give him 'good luck'. He tries to show himself that he can win, and then maybe he will be strong enough to ward off attacks. He asks if she had 'bad luck' and expresses his own 'bad luck' (falling out of bed) in an effort to get her to help him. Because he feels that he is bad, he tries to ally himself with her as a 'good luck' mother.

I talked about feeling that sometimes we wonder whether we might be the cause of someone else's death or divorce. Sam agreed, but he said that he did not know how it really happened. I told him that sometimes parents just could not work things out between themselves, and sometimes people get sick and die of their sickness, but that this was not his fault; however, he could not accept this.

Anxiety is shown related to sickness and death, and Sam's concern is that his sadism might have killed his mother. The splitting of good and bad as represented by good and bad luck, as a defense to maintain ego functioning, is prominent. The therapist should have explored Sam's ideas further, saying, 'I wonder if you sometimes have daydreams about thinking that death and sickness is your fault.'

Sam was happy to see the marshmallows and watched me fill up the bowl. He said that he was worried that the monster might eat them. I reassured him that we would have enough marshmallows and 'stuff' for the monster.

Sam expresses his persecutory anxiety and the feeling that there is not enough goodness to make the bad internal objects become good.

Sam loaded some marshmallows into the dump truck and dumped them in a pile. This pile became a gravel pit, which we emptied by eating the marshmallows. He suggested that we should make a monster and tease it by making a border that the monster could not get over. So we made a strong border, 8 inches long, fortified by the dump truck.

Devouring of the earth-marshmallows with a border around them blocking access is his phantasy of devouring mother's difficult-to-get body.

Sam then created the monsters. They were snakes—a son and a Daddy. The son crawled over the border, but the Daddy could not. He was dumb. 'I don't like you, Dada,' said the little snake, and then he ran away. When the Daddy asked him what he had said, the little snake said, 'Nothing.' Then the son showed the Daddy how to crawl over the border in order to get the marshmallows on the other side.

Dada (as Sam calls the snake) ate the marshmallows and was sent to jail. Sam suggested we make Mum. She's mad at Dada because he got arrested. Mum and baby kissed and decided to leave Dad in jail, saying, 'He's bad.' The boy, no longer a baby, was nine years old and wanted to visit Dad in jail.

The monsters, which are like penis-like snakes, are the beginning of the snake family. In spite of the border, the son–snake eats the marshmallows; however, he anticipates revenge for his orality from his Daddy snake, attempts to defend himself by saying that the Daddy is dumb, and later triumphs over the Daddy by controlling him. The son is more capable than the father, and he expresses his contempt and aggression towards father, which is then denied and controlled. Ambivalence is expressed towards the father; Sam shows his need for internal identification; yet the fear of being destroyed by this identification is present.

The father is the 'dumb' snake who goes to jail, as he does in 'real life'. The son is smarter and more powerful than the father, but once across the border, the father is sent to jail for his stealing. In this way Sam expresses projective identification with the removal of the object in an attempt to control his own hostility. The mother's presence is to ensure a supply of sufficient marshmallows (good breast) but also to be partner to the boy who becomes a baby and then not a baby. As a baby, the phantasy is that mother would protect him from father, but once father is in jail, then protection from the angry and destructive father is not necessary, and so he becomes a boy again and can visit the father, who is locked in jail. Sam's projections are safely controlled, and he and his loving mother can form a partnership.

A baby snake was created. He was two years old and he liked Dada. The nine-year-old liked Mama.

The baby snake may be the project of the union of the mother and the boy snake who liked the father. In this way father is made to feel okay and Sam's phantasy of his father's potency is restored. Now there would not be any need for revenge by the father on the boy snake.

Dad got out of jail because Mum posted bail. Then the Bible was read to Dada so that he would become good. I was instructed to read the Bible, made of Plasticine, and to start at the beginning. I began, 'In the beginning, God created earth and heaven ...' and Sam finished it off by saying, 'then there was Noah, and Jesus died on the cross.' The family was very happy.

Mother does not view the boy as having enough for her, and so the Dad is released from jail. This also frees the boy from the phantasy of Oedipal conflicts. The Bible is the superego, and the father, who is potentially an internal persecutor, is made good and nonviolent. Mother–therapist is sufficiently strong at this moment to make the persecutor into a non-persecutor.

Figure 14. The snake family, including future members, eating marshmallows and drinking water from a pond. 'Mama' is the somewhat frail-looking snake on the left; 'Dada' is the long thick snake on the right.

At this point a little grey snake came along. He was five years old. His Mum had died, and he was lonely and jealous of the family. He was invited into the snake family and adopted by them.

Sam makes another representation of himself as a younger boy who felt alone and deserted and was not given much by his mother; he also feels lonely and jealous of the happy family. Sam attempts to gain nurturance, and the phantasy is that there is a family who will take care of him, as a younger snake boy. In this way Sam phantasizes hope.

The snakes were put carefully away in the cardboard box until the next session.

The parallels with Sam's real life are very evident here. His father has been in and out of jail, and Sam is familiar with terms such as 'posting bail'. Sam also refers to father snake by different names, Dad, Daddy or Dada. Sam is not sure what to call his father; sometimes he seems grown-up in relation to him and calls him Dad; at other times he seems infant-like and calls him Dada. Perhaps Daddy is a generic term.

Session 6

The snake saga continued. Daddy snake did bad things, while Mum and the children continued to read the Bible to him to try to make him good. Dad got bored and fell asleep. A bad guy started attacking the family and tried to take away the kids. But he, too, fell asleep while the Bible was being read.

Father's characteristics of hostility emerge in spite of attempts to make him good. Fear of revenge and retaliation are strong because of Sam's projective identification. Sam does not feel safe; he fears destruction. His anxious relationship with his therapist is interpreted at several levels. Thus, it is interpreted directly as: 'You feel there's a bad guy inside you, and that our relationship is not safe enough to protect you' and indirectly as: 'It was pretty scary when Children's Aid took you away from your Mum,' suggesting that Sam saw the Children's Aid as the bad guy attacking the family. 'You want the Bible to be good and strong, but sometimes you wonder if it can do any good' was interpreted because the therapist felt that perhaps Sam is saying: 'I wonder how the therapist will protect me.'

The family tried to destroy the bad guy, but the grey snake tried to save him. In this session the snakes were all named. Mummy snake became Teeya (the therapist's name); Dad was Charlie, and the other snakes, named in accordance with their colour,* were Bobby (blue)—the baby and the shortest, two years old; Orville (orange)—the oldest, nine years old; Gregory (grey)—the strong adopted five-year-old.

The grey snake is the five-year-old other representation of Sam as a deprived child-snake. In trying to save the 'bad guy', he is trying always to be good and never evil. He tries to save himself from his internal bad objects. An early positive transference is developing with the therapist as her name is given to Mummy snake.

A lake was made for drinking water. During this session there was a lot of feeding of marshmallows, drinking water, cuddling and kissing in the snake family. When the snakes were scared by monsters, they helped themselves feel better by eating marshmallows.

The phantasy is developed that the family has a never-ending source of supplies, of ways of defending against attacks, and of continually copulating and experiencing pleasure.

The snakes tried to feed a bad guy a marshmallow with a thumbtack in it. More direct feelings of anger and frustration with Dad were expressed.

This marshmallow also contains the hostile penis. Several phantasies are involved here; some good things are to be viewed as dangerous because they are deceptive; also, if you are bad you get something bad, and then the bad internal objects

---

*The first initial of the names of the snakes is also the first initial of the colour of Plasticine out of which they are made—an interesting aspect of Sam's play.

might outweigh the good and
make you very bad—that is,
aggressive and destructive.

The therapy sessions are held in an office containing two
desks, bookshelves and two filing cabinets. Sam often finds
items in the desk drawers such as thumbtacks, staplers and
staple removers, which he incorporates into the play.

Session 7

The snake saga continued
with the introduction of a
new yellow snake, Yves, whose
mother was drowned by Dad.

The death theme is re-
peated here, with a boy losing
his mother at the hands of
his father. Again, we have
another example of projective
identification of the boy's
unconscious greed. When the
therapist interpreted: 'Your
Dad hurt your Mummy,' Sam
did not respond. It is his own
hostility involved in having
taken so much from his
mother by 'devouring' her
that destroyed her.

Yves felt lonely and jealous
and tried to get attention by
throwing rocks at the snake
family who were eating
marshmallows, which mother
had just brought home from
the store.

The jealousy and hostility
of Yves is expressed because
there is a mother who can
feed her family. The therapist
interpreted: 'I think sometimes you may feel jealous
when you see other kids and
their families and think about
all the good stuff you imagine
they're getting.' Sam
answered, 'No, ... yeah,' at
first denying his jealousy,
then recognizing it.

Yves was accepted into the family. The grey snake continued to be good and helpful. Yves turned out to be a greedy snake who wanted the other snakes' marshmallows, even though there were plenty of them to go around. Yves wanted to drink, but did not.

The therapist interpreted: 'Do you feel that part of you has to prove you are good and helpful in order to stay?' Sam answered, 'Yeah, with my Mum.' Sam phantasizes he needs to be the good, caring boy if he is to be with his mother and help her as well. The therapist could have asked Sam to elaborate on these feelings of greed by asking, 'Do you feel you took good stuff away from Mum?'

After eating, Bobby and Gregory went to the pond (blue Plasticine) for a drink, but they thought it was poisonous and were afraid to drink it.

[The therapist could have asked why Bobby and Gregory thought that the water was poisonous—perhaps because it is where the mother was drowned.] The pond, which was safe and good, has turned bad, perhaps because of envy and greed.

Yves finally took a drink. Then the 'bad guys' in the truck started attacking the snake family. Gregory was very strong, and he took the tacks out of the family members and fixed them by putting marshmallows on their wounds; however, the attacks continued.

Yves then ignored the poisonous water quality because he is so bad that nothing can harm him any more anyway. Gregory is idealized as the very strong one, and he tries reparation in order to reduce anxiety caused by poisonous oral and anal phantasies, but his reparations do not stop the attacks. The therapist interpreted: 'It seems to me that no matter how strong the good parts are, the bad things keep hurting the good things.' Sam nodded yes.

The tacks only went a little way into Gregory since he was strong and powerful. Then a tack went into Mummy and made her sleep. Gregory took her to the water in the pond to wake her up.

Here we talked a bit about the Funeral Home and how Sam's sister wanted him to touch his mother's face. He said that she did not look like his Mum because she was so still, and he did not want to do this.

Then the 'ante was upped' and the bad guys started to use a missile (a long black pen) instead of thumbtacks. Gregory stayed out in the open while he instructed the rest of the family to hide. He took the attack upon himself.

The death theme is repeated again, with a hostile penis as the attacker. Gregory's reparation is to try to give her back her milk, but this turned out to be bad milk and did not awaken her. The pond remains poisonous and not helpful.

The therapist interpreted: 'I imagine that you might have thought Mum was sleeping when you saw her at the Funeral Home and wished you could give her a drink and wake her up.' Sam answered, 'Yeah!'

The hostile penis becomes even more dangerous, but Gregory attempts to be good and protecting. These are attempts to diminish the hostile internal object by being the target for the aggressive impulses. The therapist interpreted: 'He seems to feel guilty, like he needs to be punished.' Sam answered, 'Yeah!' Does Sam feel a need to be punished here because he has challenged his father? [A comment at this point *could* have been: 'Most of us would have been frightened by our feelings. Sometimes we don't understand how we feel. That's something we can talk about. ...']

C.P—H*

The bad guys seemed to give up, but then they told the snakes to get off their property. Gregory took the bad guys who were in the cab of the truck to jail and told them, 'And don't come back!' (Figure 15).

This is an omnipotent attempt to deny his vulnerability and, thereby, any badness. Part of the denial is the phantasy that he could not have taken anything from mother because he was adopted. Denial and projection are operating to defend against an onslaught of anxiety related to feelings of loss and persecution.

cab of truck

Greg

Figure 15.   Greg took the 'bad guys' to jail in the cab of the truck.

Then the whole family gathered around to read the Bible. Yves read it, and so did the others.

The therapist interpreted: 'The Bible is the strong part that tells the snake right from wrong.' Sam responded, 'Yeah!'

The white car came in and called the Bible 'stupid'. Gregory told Dad to come over, and they threatened to push it over the edge of the table unless he 'talked' about why he was after them, 'Tell us why or we'll push you over' (Figure 16). Apparently, his 'Boss' wanted the guy in the white car to kill Yves.

The Bible superego is very strong and needs to be toned down by a 'good car'. The white car is good, but then it turns out that the car is to kill Yves, the bad snake. This is another attempt to control destructive internal feelings and to make up for loss of mother by crushing sadism in the hope that she might return. The white car is also dangerous, as if it contains some secrets that might let Greg and Charlie be good.

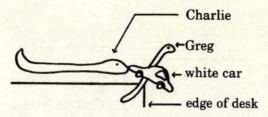

Figure 16.   Greg and Charlie, the Dad, trying to get a bad guy to 'talk'.

A new snake was made out of yellow Plasticine; he was identical to Yves (the same colour eyes, nose and mouth) but he was longer. He became Yves' uncle. He was, however, another bad guy who wanted to kill Yves, because he had joined the snake family.

Uncle thought Gregory looked weak. Gregory threw Uncle over the edge of the table. This happened quite a few times. Gregory would jump back up from the floor and knock over Uncle, who was looking down over the edge of the table (Figure 17).

Some ambivalence is shown here. The boss wants to get rid of the bad, and while the boss is a new character, it is as if the boss is functioning as some kind of primitive controlling superego. Support is needed to contain Sam's increasing anxiety and feelings of loss and guilt.

The badness seems to be increasing, and Sam is having less capacity to contain his aggressive feelings. The therapist suggested, 'Perhaps your uncle is mad because you came to live here.' Sam responded, 'No.' The uncle, made of the same colour Plasticine, tries to destroy Yves who might take him over.

Gregory has to prove his goodness and protective powers, but his power is not sufficient to control his aggressive impulses as represented in the attacks against the uncle.

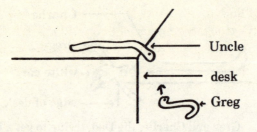

Figure 17.   Uncle looking over the edge at Greg. Then Uncle stole Mum, and Greg won her back.

Then Uncle stole Mum, and Gregory won her back.

The bad uncle stole mother, but the adopted son, Gregory, won her back, again trying to demonstrate his good internal objects. The phantasy might have been that while his Mum was taken away by death, if Sam felt that he were good or strong enough he could get her back. Sam is not strong enough or good enough to keep his mother.

When he was told there were 5 minutes remaining in the session, Sam decided on a theme for next week: *'Uncle Strikes Again.'*

Hostility is very strong, and internal goodness is still not to be counted on, but Sam uses the idea of the theme for next session as a way of containing and controlling his hostility. The theme maintains some boundaries over hostility and in this way may reduce anxiety for the in-between session times.

Sam's play reflects his perception of being 'attacked', not only due to the adversity actually experienced in the outside world, but due to his feelings that his good objects are being repeatedly attacked by his bad objects. We will need to help him restore his good parts and offer him support (ego support) against the attacks that are experienced as overwhelmingly destructive and debilitating of his resources.

At this point in therapy a regular time is set for the weekly sessions. Sam and the therapist continue to meet in the foyer of the treatment centre and proceed together to their 'special room'.

Sam's home setting is breaking down, and a foster home placement is considered. It was thought that Sam might have to be placed in a long-term arrangement and that this setting may eventually work out as an adoption placement. The 'agency' believes that Sam is 'hopeless'.

Session 8

Sam came in with candies and sunflower seeds, asking where all the spot lights were to catch the 'Friendly Burglar'.

Sam shows a strong need to try to fill up the therapist, and make sure that he and his therapist never run out of supplies. His attempts at restoration by candies and seeds are not only to restore, but also to give babies to mother. Sam feels that they should also be able to protect themselves from external persecutors (burglars). Even though Sam perceives them as if they might be friendly burglars, he also fears that they are still going to steal their supplies. This represents his phantasy that he is stealing from his mother and is anticipating retaliation.

He asked if I would be there at 4 o'clock so that his friend could come to meet me. His friend thought that it was 'neat' that Sam could get out of schoolwork and come to his session to play.

The therapist interpreted: 'I imagine that's neat for you too.' Sam responded, 'Yeah!' It is hard for Sam to maintain the therapist internally. He needs time to internalize the therapist's 'goodness' and also to make sure that the therapist/mother will not attack him for taking 'too much' and causing her death. [The therapist *should* have said, 'It's important for your friend to meet me. That's nice to hear. It's important for you to have a picture of me in your mind. I think that sometimes you worry about whether I'll be here next week. I will be here.'] Sam needs to confirm the therapist's good existence both to himself and to his friend, as well as to recognize his jealousy of mother' babies, which he will try to work through in therapy.

Sam noticed that my name was not on the telephone intercom list, so I said, 'I come here Wednesday morning for our special time together.'

Sam is expressing concern as to where his therapist belongs and whether she is there for others as well, or is she just appearing for him. Again, jealousy of other relationships is emerging.

It had been about ten days since we had seen each other, because Sam had gone skating with his class the preceding week and he had not come for the session. He had forgot-

Sam is threatened by the power of a mother object with an internal penis. He tries to maintain her goodness but at the same time make her less powerful and get rid of her

ten that Yves had been bad at our last meeting. He remembered the names of all the snakes.

Then he noticed that mother snake was the longest one and said, 'We better cut her up, she's too long.' After he had shortened mother, he re-attached the rattler part of her tail and he used the part he had taken off to make another bad snake.

badness so that she might be okay. He creates another bad snake representing another bad destroying penis, which issues from the mother. This is another indication of the badness she had in her, which Sam could not remove and so save her. The therapist interpreted: 'It seems like mother lost a bad part of her.' Sam responded, 'Yeah.' [The therapist could have added, 'and it made another snake to be scared of.' This also reflects Sam's phantasy that mother contains bad destroying objects, which might endanger him if he introjects her.]

The grey snake is sometimes called 'Power Snake' or 'Muscles Snake'. He said, 'We need to bring us some good stuff,' so the truck brought it. It was a truckload of marshmallows for the family that was 'gathered round'.

Gregory is strong, but to maintain strength he needs 'good stuff'.

I was asked to act the part of Mum, Dad and baby. The bad snake—the same colour as Mum—began shooting marshmallows and then snowballs.

Mother contains bad objects and creates the conditions to harm the good. There is potentially more bad than good, and thus internalization of any good will be turned bad or destroyed.

He wanted to 'kill that little brat, Gregory', saying, 'He's jealous because Gregory is so strong.'

He is jealous not only because Gregory is strong but also because Gregory has become a family member.

I suggested that we needed to help Gregory become stronger so the bad guys could not hurt him. Sam said, 'Like what?' I suggested making his skin really strong or making him invisible. Sam said, 'He's already made of steel.'

This attempt to create a second skin in order to reduce dependency on the mother by replacing this with a pseudo-independence indicates that Sam has already decided that nothing should be able to penetrate or harm Gregory. Gregory has a steel coating. This attempt is to help Sam create a boundary to maintain his massive anxieties. Sam verbalizes this by saying that he has a 'steel skin' for the snake.

The entire family wanted to get the bad guys, but Gregory chose Bobby. Then Bobby and Gregory went together. The bad guy shot a tack and then a missile. Gregory then attacked the bad guy and then saved him. When asked why, Sam said, 'Cause he might be able to come good again.'

The fear of retaliation is very strong. Gregory teams up with the baby snake who is good and can still gain some gratification from mother. Therefore, the bad is not destroyed, because there is hope that it could become good again. [Interpretation at this point could have referred to the therapeutic relationship and the transference process that occurs within the work, providing for the hope. The transference is phantasized as good and powerful and sustaining.]

The bad guy joined the family. Sam noticed that he was too long, so he made him the length of the other snake children and named him Ralph. Now there were five

The bad guy is not gaining any edge; he is reduced in size and joins the family as someone who is not special and not too powerful.

kids—Gregory, Ralph, Bobby, Orville, Yves—two parents—Mum and Charlie—and one uncle.

Bobby, the baby, got caught in the weapon arsenal. Ralph and Gregory went to save Bobby. Only after Gregory and Ralph had left did mother notice that Bobby was gone. Gregory said, 'Come on, Ralph, we are the only ones that are strong.'

Two snakes who are brought into the family are bad: Yves and Greg. It appears as if the baby snake may be getting too much gratification.

Gregory and Ralph are just as strong as each other, they can help each other out, but mother does not help them, she concentrates on her baby.

Gregory (adopted) is the good object and is pushed to be an adult, who is supposed to know everything. The burden on Gregory is heavy and support for him will be important.

At one point Gregory told Dad something, and Dad asked Gregory what he should do. Gregory said, 'You're the Dad, you're supposed to know!' I asked him how Gregory felt when his Dad didn't know the answer, but Sam gave no reply.

In the end, Bobby was saved by Gregory and Ralph.

In saving the baby, Sam tries to work out some of his jealousy but also tries to gain mother's love over again. The transference is positive, and Sam looks to the support that

When they brought him home, he went right to Mum, who kissed him.

Sam put the whole family into the desk drawer to protect them from attack. Gregory and Ralph closed the weapon arsenal (the desk drawer) together. Then the staple remover came out of the drawer. It had steel jaws and bit Gregory's tail, and Gregory got mad. Sam then took the stapler out of the drawer and was planning to bite the snake's tail, but I took it away so it would not get clogged with plasticine. I offered to use my hand instead of the stapler as the monster.

A battle with the monster ensued. Gregory and Ralph bit the monster and then fed him marshmallows. This strategy backfired, and the monster began to eat all their marshmallows. Gregory and Ralph attacked again and fed the monster again.

the therapist can provide. Sam plays out mother's love for baby, guaranteeing that she does have goodness.

The therapist interpreted: 'Life seems okay for Bobby, but really it is not okay enough. He keeps getting hurt. He might need to be taken care of by a loving mother.' Sam gave no response.

Gregory wants to protect the family and behave as an adult, but he begins to feel that his good internal objects are overwhelmed by bad internal objects, and he is bitten. [The therapist should not have been concerned about the stapler, but should have allowed Sam to continue with his play.]

The war between good and bad, love and hate, fear and courage continues, with good and bad guys on the same side. Sam is beginning to perceive the splitting and is attempting to integrate parts of the whole object.

Sam decided the title for next week's episode would be: *'Gregory, Ralph and Bobby bite the Monster.'* Together we packed up the snake family in the shoe box.

There are further beginnings of integration of ego functions; Sam plans his sessions, not only demonstrating this ego function, but also as a way of minimizing his anxieties.

Sam put in three marshmallows and opened his package of sunflower seeds, spilling a few on the snakes. This is how they were kept during the week.

Sam tries to make sure that the good stays good by feeding the snakes. The seeds are to provide the mother with more babies, so that she does not feel robbed or damaged.

Session 9

Sam remembered and was pleased to be on time for the session. He asked, 'How long am I going to be coming?' I replied, 'You and I will be seeing each other for several months, even to when school stops in June, and maybe we can see each other in the summer.'

This represents an expression of dependency and clarifies the transference relationship. The feeling that Sam expresses is one of pleasure at being able to be with his therapist.

During supervision, we decided to give Sam a map of how he and the therapist both get to these offices, in order to help him concretize external reality aspects, and also to help him internalize the goodness of the containing therapy environment.

I had somehow misplaced the wooden bowl into which we put the marshmallows every week. Sam was rather upset. We used a cardboard box instead. Sam became dis-

Countertransference feelings are worry on the therapist's part as to whether she will 'have enough' to carry on with Sam. This creates sufficient anxiety in Sam to make

tractible during the session, looking at the phone system, lights and my watch. At the same time, however, he actually *seemed* less burdened, happier and chattier.

him distractible and feel as if his good feelings were not good enough. The interest in the phone, lights and watch represents a turn towards mechanical things to express his feeling that things are fragile and potentially destroyable. However, the transference remained positive as Sam was able to deflect feelings onto mechanical things. The therapist interpreted: 'It seems to be a bit hard to get involved with the snake family today.' The snake family has come to represent his internal objects and their interactions with reality. His phantasies are frightening, and in order to reduce further internal stress he blocks out potential understanding. With this interpretation he begins to work with the snake family.

Sam was then able to begin with some work. He shortened Yves because he noticed that Yves was longer than Mum. Then Gregory threw Dad across the room and ran and hid himself.

The therapist interpreted: 'Gregory wants to be more powerful than Dad, but he is kind of scared.' Sam replied, 'Yeah.' The triumph and Oedipal aspects within this depressive position are very frightening to Sam. He expresses aggression and expects retaliation.

Sam noticed that Charlie, the Dad, was falling apart, so he fixed him. Everyone was sleeping. Gregory tried to get

However, Sam makes amends by repairing father. This is a somewhat indirect expression of anger by Greg-

them up by screaming, 'Time to get up! Time to see Dad.'

The family began crowding Dad, and Dad said, 'What's everyone crowding around me for?' They replied, 'We are comfortable.' Gregory took a marshmallow and said, 'Yuck, it's cold.' He then asked Mum to cook it. We made a heat source, and Sam made a Plasticine spatula for Gregory to cook the marshmallows.

Gregory screamed for the others to wake up.

ory; he has to find out and let everyone know that Dad is repaired, and not dangerous at this time. Thus the father penis will not attack him and he will also have the wall of protection of the family.

Greg, who was good, is now also showing some badness; he is feeling depleted by restoration of father who, once restored, becomes also potentially retaliative because he is so capable and he demonstrates that he has the effective penis. Gregory looks for help and assistance, and the therapist comments, 'This reminds me of when you had to cook sometimes at home.' Sam replies, 'Mum cooked *sometimes*.' [The therapist should have said, 'You sometimes wanted good stuff from your Mum, but you couldn't always get it, and this made you feel angry and sad.']

[The therapist *should* have said, 'You wish you could scream loud enough to wake up your real Mum and bring her back to life—so now you try to make her feel well and so she wouldn't die.'] He needs the mother to give him nurturance; without her, he is having considerable anxiety about containing himself and is fearful that his badness will take over unless helped.

Orville's mouth was a bit 'smushed', so Sam made him a new one. When he gave him his mouth, he noticed that Orville was happy.

The therapist asked, 'Do you think sometimes you might be feeling happy?' Sam enquired, 'Why?' [The therapist *should* have asked why Orville was happy or sad.] The therapist continued, 'I think you'd like to be happy, but the bad stuff inside you doesn't let you be happy.' Orville's happiness also indicates that oral sadism leading to internal destruction is able to be repaired.

Sam noticed that Orville was too long, so he made him smaller.

The therapist interpreted: 'Perhaps you sometimes feel you'd like to become a baby.' Sam replied, 'What? I don't want to pee in my diapers!' The therapist said, 'You might like to be taken care of ...' Sam said, 'Yeah!' Anxiety is present that urethral sadism may destroy, but if given good experiences, then his internal anxiety would be reduced.

Gregory and Ralph got caught in the weapons arsenal in the drawer. Gregory screamed, 'Open up!' and it did. Gregory was drinking Sam's apple juice, which we always got before the session began. Gregory and Ralph decided that the bad guys were still after the family, so they put Charlie into the drawer first to protect him.

Drinking apple juice is phantasized as robbing mother. Therefore, the bad guys are still after them and the family; they rationalize that they should protect father, but this protection is really an effort to protect themselves from father's revenge for the phantasy of stealing milk, which belongs to father and mother. The therapist commented: 'I don't think Charlie's very brave.' Sam replied, 'Yeah, he's a chicken. ...' By making him frightened, he becomes less powerful and potentially less destructive.

Sam noticed how skinny mother snake was and said, 'That's how skinny my Mum really was.'

The therapist asked, 'Shall we fix Mum up?' Sam replied, 'No.' Strong feelings of sadism are present, but there will be less fear of retaliation from mother if she is weak and from father if he is a coward. However, a weak mother will not be a good supplier.

When Gregory got shot with tacks, he hardly felt them. He just took them off. He did not even need a marshmallow to be rubbed on his wound in order for it to heal.

Gregory is powerful and has the steel skin again to protect against destructive external forces. The therapist interpreted: 'There is enough good stuff on Gregory for him to heal himself.' Sam replied, 'Yeah.'

The staple remover called the 'Munch Monster' got Gregory's tail. It healed by itself. Another snake surrounded the staple remover, and Sam said, 'The good power is surrounding the bad power.' Then the 'bad power' surrendered, but it had its fingers crossed and so did not have to keep its promise. It then had to be punished for three days and then for a week. So the other snake was

There is a danger from external monsters and a strong attempt to contain badness, but it is almost impossible to trust others even if you punish them and prevent pleasures. To be good adults and to be adult when you are a child is to suffer a continual loss of bits of good internal objects. The therapist interpreted: 'I think sometimes you feel that your life is the pits and you need

locked in the drawer with the stapler. Gregory found out that they were having fun together playing cards, so he took away the cards and the imaginary toys and said, 'Now it's the pits.'

When Gregory was in the arsenal, it closed, and Gregory yelled, 'Open up!' However, Gregory fell out and onto the floor when the drawer opened up. Ralph said to Gregory, 'I thought you were dead,' and Gregory said, 'Nah, never dead.'

Sam had noticed my watch a few times during the session and when the session was almost over, he said, 'Time to go.'

The next episode was set as 'Gregory Saves Mother'.

In the box, the snakes were put in the same arrangement, with everyone curling beside Pops, and mother curling around the whole group.

to be punished because you think you've been bad.' Sam gave no response but looked sad.

We wonder how long Greg can recover without supplies provided to him by a good containing mother. Sam perceives transference as containing and nourishing, but we wonder if he will be able to show growth because of his continued expressions of omnipotence.

He is afraid that he might be taking too much (of my time) from me and phantasizes that I might get angry and that he might lose me. Sam experiences a reactivation of death phantasies and loss of mother.

Sam attempts to create the loving family and the nourishing parents, but envy of the goodness that others have and receive will become a bigger issue for Sam.

Session 10

Sam came in, asking, 'Did you get a bowl?' I had found an identical bowl at home,

At this session Sam needs to know that his therapist is able to contain him, and that

and I told him that losing something important is very hard, saying, 'We know the bowl looks the same, but it is another one, and I think it will be a good bowl for the good marshmallows.' I re-arranged the desk so the telephone was not so obvious, while saying that this was not the sort of room that we might want to use, but we could make it our own special place. Sam agreed that it would be nice to have a special room. We made a sign to put up when we were there and drew a map of how each of us got to the special room.

Sam asked, 'What's your favourite album?' I gave my answer, and Sam said his was Boy George—*Church of the Poisoned Mind*.

Orville crawled over the Dad, who said, 'Get off my back!' Then Gregory and Ralph decided to follow the map that we had made. When they got to our special room, Gregory said, 'That's where I live!'

she is able to feel strong enough for him and at the same time think of him. Losing the bowl was like not having a space in her mind for Sam, and now the therapist tells Sam that although it is not the same bowl, it is a container and important to both of them and will not be forgotten or lost. To have their special room is very important and provides continuity of sessions as well as emphasis on the therapist and their room as a container. Giving a map clears up some of the confusion of emotional resistance and also provides Sam with the beginnings of being trusted to have something special for them to share. The map is also their secret way of getting to their special room.

Sam tries to form a stronger feeling of identification with his therapist but is ambivalent about his role as well as the strength of the Church. This superego is seen as a harsh destroying persecutor.

The nine-year-old Orville cannot identify with Dad, nor be supported by him. Orville is treated with hostility and has not been given the secret map to the special place—which is in phantasy mother's body.

Sam asked what the last episode was, and then he remembered that it was when mother 'got killed, almost'. Mother was then taken to the drawer by the bad guys while everyone was sleeping. Gregory was very tired. When he rolled over, he said, 'Where did Ma go?' The others said that she had probably gone to have breakfast. Gregory said, 'Something tells me she is gone ... she's been mothernapped.' Gregory decided to have a 'balanced meal' before looking for her.

Mother is in continual danger. Yves' mother was killed by her husband, and now bad guys—perhaps Yves and Ralph—attack her. Greg is feeling depleted, needs nourishment and is told that mother is trying to feed herself, but he cannot accept this and invents a word, 'mothernapped', to deny his internal hungers. The therapist interpreted: 'You want to make sure you're full of good stuff, and you might need to feed her to make her well.'

Gregory says, 'Ma, where are you? Mr. Bird [a figure on the desk], did you eat my Ma? If you did, I'll kill you.' Gregory found her and sent a message back with Bobby to Dad, 'She's unconscious and she won't wake up; get her a drink.'

In finding her unconscious, Gregory focuses on oral sadism and her possible death. Finding her unconscious, he will return her good objects and in this way repair her. At the same time, Gregory will try to reunite the married couple and provide continual aid for both.

Gregory, Bobby and Ralph took Mum back home. Gregory said to put her in her 'love bed—our family bed.' He emptied the marshmallow bag and put her in it.

The therapist interpreted: 'I imagine you wish you had been able to wake Mum up.' Sam replied, 'I wish!' Anxiety is here expressed related to Sam's inability to make mother well, but he puts her in the 'love-bed' to give her back the stolen penis and babies. The mother is considered safe in the love-bed.

When Orville was exploring, he got stuck up on a lamp that was on the desk. Gregory saved him. When exploring again, Orville got caught in the weapon arsenal. Gregory got him out. Sam said, 'Orville and Bobby are going to grow up and be strong like Gregory some day.'

Bobby was cut in half by a paper clip. He needed three marshmallows to make him better quickly.

Bobby was put with Mum in the family bed. Gregory said, 'Now let's have something to eat.' Gregory made a stove and cooked six marshmallows, three at a time.

When Mum groaned, Gregory asked if she was all right. Mum came out of bed and said that she was starved. Then the shed, which was also referred to as the weapon arsenal, caught fire, and Gregory said, 'Get water!' Gregory and Ralph and Bobby put out the fire together. Sam then said, 'So the good destroyed the bad.'

Orville is still unable to be effective. He always gets into trouble, and Gregory always has to save him. Gregory continues to be the ideal son. However, hope is present and integration of feelings is possible. The therapist interpreted, 'Sometimes when we are exploring and searching for things, we find things out there that we'd rather not know; it can be pretty scary; we can talk about these things sometime.'

The therapist interpreted, 'You might even feel that part of you will be destroyed, but we will have enough good stuff to make you feel well and strong.'

The two-year-old snake Bobby is threatened with death, but the goodness of Gregory who is the idealized good part of Sam is successful in helping Bobby.

Mother is depleted, but her starvation is too frightening to deal with and the hostility is expressed by the fire, which is quenched by the three brothers together. The therapist interpreted the internal situation for Sam, 'Sometimes you feel that the good inside of you is destroying the bad.' The therapeutic relationship is helping to contain and destroy the bad, but the danger is that there is not enough good, because mother is starved (depleted). The three snakes join to put out the fire, which threatened to blow them up. Their combined strength saves them. The idealized good in Gregory is sufficiently strong to overcome internal badness.

Then Sam asked what time it was and said, 'Darn, almost time to go.' The next week was spring break, and Sam asked if his friend could come.

The therapist interpreted: 'It seems pretty important for your friend to meet me. I think sometimes it's difficult for you to have a picture of me in your mind when we're not together. As we spend time together, you will be able to remember me and carry the idea with you even when we're apart.' Sam smiled and then said, 'Yeah, but can he come?' Perhaps his friend is seen as possessing qualities that he phantasizes might make him more acceptable to the therapist. It's almost like one of the snake brothers.

Sam had eaten a lot of marshmallows during the session and was concerned that I eat marshmallows too.

Sam is concerned that he might be robbing the therapist. He doesn't want to rob her because he is afraid that she might leave him, die or go to sleep, and it would be hard for her to wake up. The theme of depletion of mother–therapist is prominent, with internal persecution possible unless the mother–therapist also eats and fills up.

Session 11

Sam was waiting for me. He had remembered his session because it had been a few weeks since our last meeting. He told me that his science project was returned to him. It seemed that he still needed some material for it. He asked me what we had done at our last session, and I talked about our last meeting in a reflective manner, helping Sam to remember and have a kind of 'reverie'. He asked me to make up a theme for today.

Sam has missed some weeks, and, worried about the therapist, he needs her to talk about their relationship and how she is able to hold the bad objects and bad feelings without being harmed. Sam is concerned about his science project and wonders whether the therapist will be annoyed with him because he has not got enough 'stuff'. However, Sam is exploring reality and is becoming more aware of what is needed without resorting to destructiveness. The therapist interpreted: 'It seems important for you for me to decide what we should do today.' She told him that this was their special time for him to work out some of the things going on in his life. She gave him the example of the mother snake sleeping and Sam wanting to wake her up, and she told him that that was really like feelings he had about his real mother. Sam seemed to understand. Sam is also asking the therapist to demonstrate some of the good objects. [She should have said, 'Let me feed you as we are thinking about what we want to do.'] This reverie furthers the mutual relationship and the genuineness of the interest that the therapist has in Sam.

Everyone was eating marshmallows. There were eight altogether, and each snake got one. Charlie then disappeared into the drawer. Gregory made a bell and tried to wake everyone up. Three search parties were formed, each with their own walkie-talkie. When Charlie returned home, Bobby and Yves got caught in the drawer and were given sleeping gas. They were then saved by Gregory and Ralph. Orville was the 'fetcher' in this session. The bad guys came back in the white racing car. When Gregory, Ralph and Orville discovered where the bad guys were, Orville was sent back to spy on them; they were in a cave smoking and drinking and counting their money.

Again, Gregory is the good idealized introject who saves and is aware of feelings and needs. The bad Yves and baby Bobby are punished for possible aggression towards Charlie (father). But then even Sam's hostility is too dangerous for the family and so is split off into the bad guys. They use the white car, perhaps because the good mother is depleted; they do bad things in a cave, that is, within the mother's body, but they seem to have money, which Sam sees as valuable and good. It is hard for Sam to integrate good and bad feelings and he vacillates between persecutory and manic feelings. The mother's interior is robbed. It has some good objects in it (money) but also bad things—smoking and drinking.

Gregory asked for a torch for Orville so that he would be able to see.

This sequence shows the curiosity about the insides of mother and again Sam's desire to explore and find out, representing the process of further symbol formation. The unconscious needs are new and may later be seen as

The bad guys began to chase the snakes, with Gregory saying, 'I can take the pain.' Then Gregory, Ralph and Orville surrounded the bad guys and threw them into the drawer. Gregory told Orville to call the cops to take the two criminals away in a big truck. The police told Gregory and Orville that they could keep the money that the bad guys had stolen, so they decided to buy a huge supply of marshmallows with it.

Time was spent in the session with Ralph driving a racing car and Gregory driving a tractor trailer around. Orville started to drive the car but had an accident.

Ralph showed Orville how to drive. Gregory and Ralph showed off in their car and truck. They went 'joy-riding' while Mum and Dad 'smooched'.

being increasingly expressed through the taking-in of information.

Gregory is powerful, he is knowledgeable and brave, and he punishes badness and is rewarded by the mother's good objects. Gregory will use money for restoration and reparation of mother's insides. He is becoming the 'man' of the family. The therapist interpreted: 'There will be enough stuff for everyone.'

Ralph is taking risks, Gregory is being productive, and Orville is hurt and not able to work with reality. The therapist interpreted: 'It looks like Orville gets into trouble when he tries to act like a grown-up.' Orville also needs help from some of the bigger guys. Orville is the growing but immature, and yet older, brother—an image Sam has of himself as inadequate. The danger still exists that he could become bad like Ralph, wanting continual pleasure as in driving a racing car. This represents the feeling of a need to 'show off' in a homosexual display to counter hostility felt towards the copulating couple.

Then Gregory fell into the fire, which was in a waste-paper basket, but he was unharmed and got out. He stopped the others, Ralph and the truck, from falling into the fire.

Mum needs Dad to feel a bit better, and Sam allows father and mother to repair each other orally, but the subsequent anxiety that Gregory will not have enough because father is taking what he may need leads Gregory to fall into a fire—perhaps to be punished—and in doing so he is still idealized because he saves the others.

There is a demonstration of power. Interpretations are made at this point about Gregory being strong and powerful. He can sometimes save others. Gregory is so good that no one could think he has a bad 'bone in his body'. Sam is not sure that everything is always good. He wonders aloud about badness and how he contains it so that it does not overpower him.

Comments were also related to Sam, such as, 'the car went through a lot but is still surviving.' He smiled.

The therapist is helping Sam reinforce his identification with the good Gregory, and to begin to understand that while taking 'stuff' from mother (marshmallows) that this did not cause her death.

Sam noticed when it was time to go. Before, he had wanted to put the snakes into the box himself and give them marshmallows. This time he left the materials for me to clean up, and he went back to school. Often he stayed to

Sam maintains the strength of the family and gives the mother–therapist supplies. He is the benefactor but continues with his feelings of ambivalence. He leaves the therapist to clean up and does not want to see or

play a video game, but this time he did not.

hear her clean up his mess. He behaves as if he is afraid.

The cars and trucks are more involved in this session, and the 'bad guys' are fairly easily overpowered. Sam seems to be a bit more comfortable in relating to me. There is more interaction and talking about reality (like the science project), and more playing-out of phantasy.

Session 12

Sam came in and asked me what we had decided this episode would be about. When informed that we had not made that decision, he asked me to think of something.

The therapist's remarks are ignored by Sam, who then develops the theme. The therapist interpreted: 'It's pretty scary trying to think of what to do.' Sam replied, 'Yeah.' Sam is afraid that he will discover the destruction he phantasized he did to his mother. He is also expressing the greed and envy for the good objects of mother–therapist and tries to make them less important in order to reduce his hostility.

The monster returned in the form of a staple remover, and competition ensued between 'the good' and 'the bad'. The good forces were strengthened by marshmallows and became equal in power to the bad. Gregory and the monster then had a competition to find out whether the wind caused by the swish of Gregory's tail was able to blow over the lamp on the table.

The play with good and bad forces enables him to feel that he has recovered the strength to overcome bad objects. The penis, which could be hostile, becomes helpful. In the ensuing battle, the retaliation for oral sadism could destroy but is compensated for by her pretend death—a punishment but not a death punishment. Oral sadism of Sam is phantasized as killing his mother by depleting her of

C.P.—I

her strength, but if he does a good deed, he might bring her back. Ralph, who is bad, is lost. Hostility is phantasized as resulting in death, annihilation and loss. The idealized snake could become angry, and Sam has yet to recognize that getting angry does not necessarily mean annihilation.

Gregory, Bobby and Ralph battled with the monster. The monster was poisonous and bit Gregory and Ralph, who pretended to die. Then Gregory returned to life, but Ralph could not be found. They thought he was dead. Sam said, 'Watch it! Greg is getting angry.

The therapist interpreted: 'You are mad at the bad forces that hurt your Mum.' Sam said, 'Yeah!' The therapist continued: 'You also think that because you can't see your Mum, she might still be around and be able to come back, especially if you were strong or powerful enough.' Sam replied, 'Yeah, I often think that.'

Then the monster got 'good blood' on his teeth when biting the snake.

The good blood is something powerful enough to stave off the bad qualities. The good blood is the good milk from mother and could stave off badness and, if strong enough, could also change the quality of life.

The monster thought about repenting and joining the good side, but he never did and was finally killed. In his attacks, he had also eaten through Sam's styrofoam cup with juice in it. The family

Perhaps the good milk (blood) is not enough (ambivalence) or Sam once again feels that in taking the goodness, he destroys the mother. The monster is Sam's own internal monsters, which he can-then got better eating marsh-mallows.

An identical staple remover then came out. He was the brother of the bad one, but this one was good and visited Gregory and Bobby and told his mother, who is the black stapler, that it was good that his brother had died.

Then everyone decided to have a rest.

Sam was told of an impending meeting at the school between myself, his teacher, his head teacher and his sister. It was presented in such a way that all of the people who cared about him were going to meet with each other.

not change and so has to kill, but there is a price attached to this, and he loses his container.

This demonstrates the splitting of good and bad, with the bad (stapler) destroyed. The difficulty Sam has in making decisions about what to do is seen now as a fear that he might do bad things. Further integration of parts has not occurred, and experienced hostility creates regression in order to try to overcome anxiety.

We noticed that the snakes were beginning to dry out a bit. They were cracking. The school conference revealed that Sam was beginning to listen better at home, but he was still really very rough with his two-year-old nephew (which might be represented by the baby snake, Bobby). The parents had been sending the young child away to be cared for by someone else when Sam was at home. They were advised to discontinue this practice, and, if Sam was found hurting the young child, then he should stay with a parent as a 'time-in' (to help him contain his hostility).

Session 13

I was waiting for Sam today. It was a thirsty, hungry day for him. He asked me why I was meeting 'Sissy [his sister] today', and I told him again that the people who cared about him were meeting to talk about how he was feeling.

I did not mention that the Social Worker who was seeing his sister and her husband had not been able to come to the meeting, but he asked about her immediately, found her name on the intercom list and asked where her office was. I told him and he wanted to go exploring to find her. He thought that her office would be nice and big and comfortable.

Sam imagines that the social worker may be able to help his sister and her husband, as her room is big and comfortable.

Sam had noticed that the snakes were cracking and decided that we should remake them soon. He had the idea of bringing in some 'magical healing oil'. He asked if we had written down an episode theme, and as we had not, I reminded him of the staple remover and he immediately began to play.

Sam has difficulty starting and looks to the therapist to remind him that she is capable of containing him and his strong feelings, that she thinks of him and continues to think of him.

Sam had turned on the light over the desk as well as those overhead. He checked the drawer and found the bad guy in his grave/jail. The guy was represented by a mug in the drawer. Then he saw the

This is an enactment of punishment of the bad by death and of the good as being with mother. Interestingly, the mother does forgive the Dad who is to die, perhaps for the bad guy's badness as well

bad guy's Dad. He was a black stapler who was about to be electrocuted. The mother stapler and the good son came to say good-bye to them. Even though the Dad had punched Mum, she said that she did not care and she cried when she said goodbye and kissed and hugged her husband.

All the snakes were watching the electrocution. There were 16 minutes left in the session; however, when Gregory saw that the mother and son still loved the bad guys, he decided to try and save them. He knocked all the policemen over with his tail, but he could not get through the bars. Then the staple remover (who was the good son) bit through the bars, and the father and bad son were just about to escape when the guards overpowered them (Figure 18).

as his own hostility. The splitting of good (mother and son) and bad (father and son) is powerful, and bad is destroyed but with some forgiveness and perhaps the feeling of some reconciliation.

Greg is again to do a seemingly good deed, but he has to knock down his superego to do so, and he needs help—idealization does not appear sufficiently strong and is less than required. The assistance by others is important. However, escape is not yet possible from one's own badness, even though there is such powerful support. The transference relationship is strong, but the concern that it is not sufficient is present.

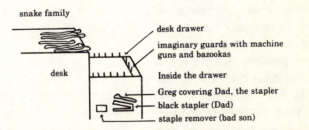

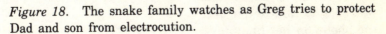

Figure 18. The snake family watches as Greg tries to protect Dad and son from electrocution.

There were repeated attempts to rescue the father and son. The next attempt consisted of Bobby being instructed to pull out the plug of the cord. This electrocution then failed, but the guards plugged the cord in again. Gregory then lay on Dad to protect him while the guard fired at him with shotguns. All the snakes watched what was going on and cheered. Throughout it all Gregory stayed okay. The guards then took their bazookas and fired. When the air cleared, Gregory did not move. Ralph went down to see how he was, but Gregory pretended to be dead. It turned out that Dad and son had really died but not Gregory. There ensued a long drama of the whole family mourning Gregory's loss, especially because there was nobody left to protect them. There was a great deal of weeping and wailing and drinking from the pond of water. Each snake took turns going into the drawer and saying goodbye to Gregory. I asked if Sam had said goodbye to his own mother. He said that he had not been allowed into the hospital but was able 'to talk to her over the phone' in her final days. However, he felt that he 'never said goodbye'.

Idealization, denial and omnipotence are not sufficient. The phantasy of being great is interacting slowly with the reality of mortality. Manic defences are giving way to further development. Gregory pretends to die, and his death is so difficult for the family that they try to bring him back magically; they also try to protect themselves from disaster. The death of Sam's mother is at the foundation of these expressions of hostility and attempted savings and feelings of great loss. Sam is trying to work out a way of being able to say goodbye to his dead mother. The therapist reflected: 'I imagine you were pretty mad that you weren't allowed in the hospital.' Sam replied, 'Yeah!'

We talked about his Mum and her illness, and Sam definitely appeared sad.

As everyone's misery increased, Gregory realized that the drama had gone on too long, so he returned home to the snake family who was drinking at the pond. The snakes were all glad to see him, but Dad was very angry at his trick of pretending to be dead. So he sent Gregory to his room. Gregory did not go to his room but went somewhere else and fell off a cliff and then returned home and slammed his bedroom door. Bobby is sent to Gregory as a mediator. Charlie, the Dad, then came over to apologize because Gregory thought from his reaction that he had not been glad to see him alive. The next episode was called, 'Knock, knock: Charlie has a conversation with Greg.'

Sam is experiencing his feeling of loss.

Interestingly, Gregory does not want his family to suffer any longer. He feels the guilt of his pretence, and as the idealized object he cannot do this without being punished for this misdemeanour. He seeks out his own punishment, and falling down is almost like 'falling from grace'. Then he can be punished by his mortal father, who does not always behave well himself. The baby Bobby tries to intervene. Sam imagines that no one cares for him, that all they see is his anger and do not realize how desperately he needs to be told that he is loved, wanted and in fact needed by his family. He has such little confidence in himself.

Session 14

Sam seemed to be worried about not having enough marshmallows, and he was glad to see that I had brought another bag. 'Magical Healing Oil' was introduced, and we re-rolled all the snake bodies. Sam mentioned that he would be going south on

Anxiety about supplies and concern about sufficient good objects is expressed. The magic healing oil might be the good milk, good blood from the mother–therapist. She provides this 'stuff' to keep everyone well and safe. Sam feels that the loss of his

Easter weekend with his sister and her husband and her husband's Dad, whose name is Charlie (!). Sam's father and his grandmother would be there too. As we worked on the snakes, Sam remarked, 'Gregory never came apart.'

We fixed all the snakes and let them dry on a paper towel. We discussed feelings of ambivalence towards Charlie. He was a worthless 'fruitcake', but he looked after the kids, Sam stated.

mother has made him think he might not be able to keep himself together, that his internal badness would destroy him, and the object he took from his mother would start to attack him internally. He feels as if he is falling to bits, and the overt hostility he shows is to fight off the internal dangers by destroying the external objects. When Sam commented that Gregory never came apart, the therapist said, 'I know somebody else who never came apart.' Sam said, 'Me? ... crumble, crumble ...' The therapist said, 'It may not look like you came apart, but inside you may feel like you did.' Sam replied, 'Yeah!'

Reparation is made to the snakes, and feelings of anger and love are expressed toward the father with some integration. The therapist interpreted this ambivalence: 'You love your Dad but at the same time you're angry at him.' Sam asked, 'For what?' The therapist said, 'For disappointing you. For not being there when you needed him because he was in prison. Sometimes when you feel angry at him it makes you feel scared.' Sam said, 'I'm not

We spent some time shooting at Charlie with elastics and with tacks. I had to intervene at this point and suggest that we use only elastics or if we used tacks that we place them carefully because tacks are dangerous, and tacks were flying around the room. Sam decided to do both and said, 'He got it right between the eyes.' We were shooting at Charlie because he was being punished for being bad; he had spanked Bobby too hard. At this point, Gregory intervened to protect his Dad.

scared, he's a crazy fruitcake.' Sam tries to hold his rage by making father into a 'crazy fruitcake', and, thereby, less valuable. However, the ambivalence is strong.

Sam's hostility is beginning to 'take over' and is becoming dangerous. The therapist, by presenting limits on his actions, acts to prevent Sam from feeling that he has lost control. He would then feel he had damaged too much and would have to anticipate revenge from the damaged object, the father. This would then result in Sam becoming even more hostile to try to stop father's revenge. A cycle of danger and anxiety and hostility is present, and is Sam's usual response. As the therapist can limit and contain Sam's anxieties, Sam may feel more secure and less attacked. She interprets: 'Part of you loves your Dad and wants to protect him.' Ambivalence is present, but the split is maintained as part of the ego function to maintain an ego coherence. Gregory is still a powerful object, and perhaps his presence now indicates a need for Sam to acknowledge his internal hostility towards his father.

Gregory then shot a tack at Sam. I had to intervene, as Gregory started to shoot elastics at me as well. We brought in the truck and car instead to shoot elastics at them.

Gregory got the car and shot elastics at it. They then escaped and were brought back by Gregory, Bobby and Orville.

[The therapist *should* have said, 'Sometimes you feel all bad, and want to destroy those whom you feel are hurting you or even making you think about what is happening to you.'] There are negative transference aspects present with hostility expressed against good objects, the therapist, and the good parts of Sam. Interestingly, it is the good Gregory who is shooting tacks; the idealized has now attacked, and in phantasy it may be that Sam has not felt he has been able to defend himself against his greed and envy.

The shoebox that we had been using for the snakes had no top, and I decided to find another more solid one that will protect the snakes and prevent them from drying out. The snake family now intrude directly into some of Sam's reality. They talk to him as if they are people. Sam is having trouble coping with the anxiety generated by his hostility and his negative transference.

Session 15

Sam wasn't there when I arrived. I called the school, and apparently he had asked the teacher to telephone to see if he was still supposed to come. I had him come over.

Sam talked again about going down south for Easter. We talked about his being

Again, there is the expression of negative transference and hostility towards the therapist. He is afraid this hostility will harm the therapist and destroy her as he phantasizes it destroyed his mother. He wants to protect her from his anger, but also to

excited about the trip but also having feelings of sadness and maybe some anger that his Mum would not be there. We talked about the long ride and that it might be difficult at times. I gave him the key-chain that holds the key to our room to hold on to when he was away and upset. He liked the idea, but he did not put the key-chain into his pocket right away. He had to be reminded to take it at the end of this session. We did not seem to be able to get much farther in discussion, and Sam began acting out Gregory's part, saying, 'I don't want to go. ...'

Then Gregory woke up the family, who decided to help themselves to marshmallows. Gregory told Bobby to 'Get out of there.' There was a very easy flow between play-acting with snakes and Sam's acknowledgement of interpretations.

protect himself from suffering another loss and mounting feelings of anger that could also destroy himself. His hostility to his therapist could also occasion retaliation from her. The therapist attempts to give Sam a reminder of their special therapy room—the key-chain for the room key—but Sam is afraid to take it. He may be afraid that he might lose it, and then he would lose his special room and therapist. He is not sure that he can trust himself and does not have sufficient confidence in himself. Sam is also indicating that he is unsure as to whether he wants to go away and leave his therapist. She interpreted this, saying: 'Part of you doesn't want to go, it's pretty scary.' It is scary because he will be leaving the source of hope and gratification and thereby the belief in himself as a good person. He takes the key-chain when reminded.

The therapist interpreted: 'You're afraid there won't be enough good stuff left for you.' Sam replied, 'Yeah.' He will lose the supplies. He might be so bad without his therapist that she would never want to see him again, and then he would surely be destroyed by his new loss.

Charlie turned into a rattlesnake. He had become poisonous. Gregory tapped Charlie on the head, and when he did Charlie fell over. The same thing happened with Ralph. Gregory was upset. He had not meant to hurt them.

Sam then asked me to become Ralph, who was strong. All the snakes then came on top of Gregory in an effort to control and contain his strong emotion.

Then mother got 'snake-napped' again and was put into the left-hand drawer of the desk. Gregory and I went looking and found her while Ralph brought her up onto the top of the desk. She woke up. At once the bad guys started to spray more sleeping gas, and everyone fell asleep except Gregory and Ralph. They blew the gas back in the bad guys' faces and threw their truck around.

Sam then noticed that there was no one in the trucks. Then Gregory went away. He told Bobby and Ralph to 'get lost', but Bobby and Ralph followed in fear.

Father once again 'shows his true venomous colours', and when Gregory does 'accidentally' hurt the bad father and Ralph, he is upset because he is supposed to be only good and does not realize his anger. The therapist interpreted: 'You're afraid if you express your anger, it will destroy others.' Sam replied, 'Yeah!'

The therapist interpreted: 'You need to feel that I am strong enough to contain your powerful emotions and make sure that no one gets hurt.' Sam replied, 'Yeah!'

The sleeping gas seems like anal attacks on the mother that damage her by expelling anal gas. However, Gregory, now teamed with the goodness of the therapist as well as with Ralph, controls the badness. The therapist interpreted: 'You feel angry at the bad forces that took away your Mum. You're afraid that they will take away the rest of your family, and it feels pretty scary to think about that.' Sam replied, 'Yeah!'

The mother's death is such a powerful event that it invades all of Sam's play and is prominent in his thoughts. He would like to control and stop himself from hurting as

Gregory went along the desk and up into the window-sill, on his way to the filing cabinet. However, along the window-sill were several gates, for which Gregory knew the secret code words. These words were 'jelly beans' and 'peanut butter'. Lastly, one's name had to be given to the 'computer centre', which was now located on top of the filing cabinet.

Ralph and Bobby had overheard the code word, and they found Gregory. They alternated between chasing Gregory and running away from him. They decided to go back home to the family and enlist their help in getting Gregory back. However, they told Dad to stay home. He got captured. The bad guys then stole some marshmallows with which to fill up Dad before they killed him. Sam decided the next episode would be: *'Dad gets snake-napped and then rescued.'*

much as he does. The therapist interpreted: 'Part of you is scared of hurting and wants to be left alone and not talk about it. Another part of you wants to express it.' Sam responded, 'Yeah!'

Oral satisfaction and anal ordering appear to be able to provide Sam with a feeling of control and perhaps some further ego integration. The voyage to the 'computer centre' reminded the therapist of a long, difficult passage, almost as if Sam is attempting to become a new person and be good and kind. The feeling that the therapist gets is of a kind of re-birth process, with Sam having a long journey.

This play sequence demonstrates the themes of losing 'goodness' and the ideal object of bad fighting good, and bad capturing good supplies. Yet in this session he gives supplies to Dad before the bad guys kill him—suggesting that goodness needs to be accompanied by something else, perhaps that phantasy needs to interact with reality. Sam needs to acknowledge what has happened in his real world so that the internal phantasies may gradually alter.

I brought in a new cardboard box today with a lid that was supposed to protect the snakes more effectively. Unfortunately it was a 'wildcat'* box used to pack children's shoes and Sam asked me a lot of questions about where I got the box and whether I had any children and how many. At the beginning of the session he had also said to me, 'You look tall.' Perhaps he is beginning to feel as if he is not the only important person in his therapist's life and is jealous of the relationships others have with her. He tries to trust reality but finds it dangerous; she is tall, perhaps distant from him, not as available as he needs her to be. He is aware of other relationships that she has, and perhaps he is becoming more aware that he shares his therapist with others. Jealousy is present, but the theme of the next session is suggestive that he will provide a father for the mother so that she may 'feel better'.

Session 16

I asked how Sam's weekend had gone, and he said it had been wonderful. He told me they had had a flat tire coming back. I asked later about his Dad, if he had been thinking about him, and Sam said that he had been hit by a car.

The wonderful trip is not marred by a flat tire, Sam is able to feel good and continues to feel safe. The therapist interpreted: 'Sometimes when kids are feeling angry at their parents and bad things happen to them, they feel as though it might be their fault. ...' Sam answered in a forceful way, 'I'm not angry!' Aggression is denied, nor did he mention how Dad was hit by a car.

Sam then asked me how far away I lived and on what street.

Sam wants to know if the therapist lives close to him and whether they will continue to be close. She interpreted: 'Sometimes you worry

---

*A trade name on the box.

Several times there were interruptions in this session. Sam needed to go to the washroom, and then he asked about how much time we had in this session and talked about what was going on in school that day. I asked him if he still felt okay about coming here and missing some things like gym. He said that he liked coming here and did not miss that much because the next day was usually his best day as he got gym and art.

Sam remembered the title of this episode from last week. Gregory was supposed to rescue Charlie. In this session the mother appeared to be a much stronger personality. Sam talked to her for the first time. Prior to this, I always had to give mother's lines. Mother organized a search party for Bobby, the second-smartest snake, who was missing. She also spent time in this session kissing the other snakes. Parentification of Gregory is shown when mother cried on his shoulder when Bobby was lost and

and you want to make sure I'll be here when you need me.' Sam replied, 'Yeah.'

The attachment is strong but worrisome to Sam. The negative feelings have been denied by talking about the goodness of the therapist, but the disguise is thin, as shown by his questions. He wants to know whether he has more time with her, whether she has other children, and whether she might disappoint him and not turn up for a session because she lives too far away. Anxiety is present, and he often has to go to the toilet to urinate—that is, to get rid of the bad stuff in him that might damage his therapist.

Sam recalls the theme for himself, which is a change for him, an ego development in fact, for now he can talk about the mother; she is stronger, not as depleted and wants to rescue or protect her children. But she has weaknesses, and Gregory is the idealized strength for her and her family. Bobby the baby is lost, and the mother's foundation is shaky; at times, Bobby takes too much from her; he needs too much, but he is still wanted and without him she is sad. Sam feels the loss of love when it is given to his

later when she worried about Bobby and was walking back and forth so much that she wore a hole in the floor. Gregory offered to take over the pacing for his mother.

Gregory finally managed to find Bobby, who was then taken to the hospital in an ambulance. But he wouldn't wake up. Gregory was finally able to arouse him by threatening to go out with his girlfriend. At this point a new snake was created out of white Plasticine. She was named Sophie. Gregory said, 'Is she cute?' Eventually he began to go out with her. While they smooched, the other snakes spied on them. Bobby was still in the hospital at this point.

siblings and not himself. The therapist interpreted: 'Sometimes you had to assume a lot of responsibility when your Mum was still alive, and you had to act more grown-up than you really were.' Sam would take over the mother's worries, so that she might not become exhausted and depleted. This is his attempt to do something for her in return for what she has done for him; this is a reparative drive.

Gregory does succeed, but only by threatening to take over a 'girlfriend', which must be the mother, because Bobby is two years old. If the mother figure, Sophie, is lost to the baby, then the baby might die. Jealousy is used to evoke a feeling of well-being in the baby, and in this sense it is a positive feeling. The new snake, Sophie, is an image of mother and therapist who could become a satisfying girlfriend, but who might have to be shared with others. The jealousy is then Sam's. Sam is suspicious of what his jealousy will evoke, as he takes supplies from mother, and as he grows up and is challenging father. It seems like somebody wants to get rid of Bobby. He seems to be getting in the way because he is such a needy baby. The baby demands a lot and seems to deprive Sam, but Sam places him in a potentially safe place, the hospital, where he can get all his needs met. It is almost as if Sam needed to be in a hospital or a 'safe place' when he was a child so that he would feel satisfied and gratified and then feel more confident about himself as someone who could give something to others. As he places the baby in the hospital for 'safety', where presumably his needs will be met, he does not need the mother at this point.

The Mum and Dad started smooching when all the snakes went out. They returned and began to spy on their parents, but they fell asleep. After a while, they went back into the house one by one and found their mother and father 'only kissing'. Each one said 'Whoops!' and went back out of the house again.

The mother and father can help each other and in fact repair each other, without fear of interruption at first; but when the children wanted to spy, their anxiety put them to sleep. The private affair between parents is not to be watched for fear of parental sadistic attacks. The combined internal parent is now present for Sam, splitting is not as strong, and while acting-out will still occur, ego integration is taking place.

But the mother got mad at each of them for spying and sent them to their respective rooms. Uncle came in and

Mother feels wronged by her family and punishes them. However, the bad uncle makes it possible for the

defended the snakes, and they returned to where the mother and father snake were. Mother snake apologized to the little snakes for being in a bad mood. Meanwhile, Gregory and Sophie had been out on a date. Gregory walked Sophie home, and during this time jumped in the air with happiness. However, Gregory became mean and nasty to the other snakes when he returned home.

The snakes said, 'Since Gregory met that girl, he hasn't been the same.' Gregory and Sophie then decided to go to the computer centre on top of the filing cabinet. Mother followed with Ralph, got through the secret gate and told Gregory to 'get home'. Then Sophie and Mum went back home together. They seemed to get along just fine and had a tea party with the other snakes. At the same time Gregory and Ralph got into a fight and began to throw each other across the room. The title for the next episode becomes: *'Ralph versus Greg: Ralph gets his head booted in. ...'*

family to become voyeurs, which threatens to make for parental sadistic attacks on the children. The fear of retaliation is present, but is dealt with by having the mother apologize because of her bad mood. The father snake seems to have been able to give something good to the mother snake, representing reparative aspects to the mother. Sam is threatened by the sexual aspect of a relationship, but it is the phantasy of the sexual Oedipal aspects with the mother that made Sam mean and nasty, as if anticipating attacks.

Sam is not sure whether he will be punished for voyeurism and sexual pleasures. Sophie is described as the stimulus for Gregory's idealized goodness. Sam phantasizes that if he liked a girl, his therapist would be angry with him and see him as not good any more. Her jealousy would be such as to make him bad, and she would attack him. He sees the therapist as containing both good and bad (Sophie and mother together). With mother and Sophie getting along, Gregory can show some of his aggressive, competitive feelings towards Ralph, who is at times bad and who might harm the mother snake.

Session 17

Sam 'forgot' about our session today. I called the school, and he came over. When he came in he asked if we could use the other desk (there were two desks in the room). I told him that he could do whatever he wanted in this room. He also wanted to use the chair that I had been sitting in. This was a black swivel chair. Before we started playing with the snakes, I told him that I had been thinking about what we were talking about and the questions that he had asked me about other children and how far away I lived.

At this point he changed the subject to the theme for this episode, and I interpreted his wanting to change the subject as being a sign that some of the material we were talking about was hard to deal with. We then talked about why Sam had forgotten about today.

The anxiety of the last session concerning the fight of love versus anger and the possible loss of good objects— that is the loss of mother– therapist—was too strong for Sam, and so he forgot his session. The therapist interpreted: 'I thought it was because you were thinking that maybe we are close and you weren't sure if someone else would come and take me away from you.' Sam replied, 'Sort of. ...' It is difficult for Sam to acknowledge his love for the therapist, and although he wants to be inside her (using her chair), he also feels very anxious when talking about this.

The therapist interpreted: 'Maybe you are a bit mad at me.' Sam replied, 'No.' The therapist continued: 'I think you like being with me just as I like being with you, but you are afraid that if you really get used to coming here and meeting me that you might lose me and then be disappointed and feel very hurt. You might be afraid that something bad might happen to take me away.' Sam said, 'So and so. Yeah.'

At this point he said, 'Darn, I forgot my candies.' Apparently he was going to give me a piece of licorice.

Again, Sam shows his desire to show affection as well as his fear of doing so. Sam is also afraid that he is taking a lot from me and he wants to make sure that I maintain enough internal good stuff too. The candies are seen as an attempt at reparation.

The snake saga started with Ralph and Gregory continuing to fight. Dad tried to stop them, then Ralph and Dad fought, and Gregory went away. When Gregory returned, Ralph hurt him and thought that Gregory was dead. Ralph felt so badly that he decided to go to the computer centre to jump off the top of the filing cabinet in order to commit suicide. Instead, Ralph happened to drop into a rubbish bin that was beside the cabinet, and he was not hurt badly. He felt very guilty as if everything was his fault. I asked Sam if it were really Ralph's fault, and he said that Ralph only thought it was.

The theme of internal fighting is continued, and Sam shows graphically how he feels inside and the pain that he is experiencing in trying to integrate his feelings. Sam tries to acknowledge sadness and the feelings of desperation that bring on feelings of suicide. The depressive elements of having harmed and done damage to love objects create feelings of guilt and suicide. He tries to destroy himself so that he cannot do any more damage. Ralph is a bad snake, but he seems to be atoning for his hostility and for the badness he has inside himself. Sam seems to be acknowledging his phantasy and trying to take into account reality at the same time.

Ralph then went again to the computer centre. This time when he jumped he landed on the floor and died. Everyone began crying and began to feed him marshmal-

Death is reversible. Those who seem to die can return to life, but you need to know what to do to make them live again. Mother's supplies given to others can create life.

lows, but he didn't eat them. They began to think that Ralph might be trying to trick them, and when they turned away Ralph quickly ate a marshmallow. That gave him strength and he jumped and ran away, but the whole family stopped him by jumping on him.

An episode then ensued around the rubbish bin in which Gregory had landed. Sam began to describe it as a volcano. It was hot, and there was fire inside it. Lava was leaking out of the volcano. Everyone was afraid that Gregory had died, that he was 'gone'. But then they remembered that he was 'strong enough'.

In this instance phantasy overtakes reality and is no doubt Sam's phantasy of how he would have liked to bring his mother back to life. The family stops him from running away because it seems better to know what the dangers are than always to anticipate them. Sam feels that he should run away, and he wants his family to contain him and make it safe for him. The therapist interpreted: 'Sometimes you feel so badly that you even think of killing yourself.' Sam looked at me sadly and nodded his head, yes.

The therapist interpreted: 'Sometimes your insides feel like a volcano ready to explode.' Sam nodded, yes. It is hard for him to contain feelings that are so explosive and volatile. Anal sadism (explosions), combined with urethral sadism (lava), might destroy even the omnipotent ideal. The therapist interpreted: 'Our time together helps you to feel good and strong enough to fight the pressures inside.' Sam replied, 'So and so. Yeah.' Sam sometimes says 'so and so' as if he is trying to say 'something more is going on in my head but I can't say it, I haven't words to put to these feelings.'

Then Gregory asked for a fan with an extension cord while he was still inside the volcano. Charlie got it for him. Gregory was able to cool himself off. Sam said, 'It's fun in there.' Then the snake family returned home. The bad guys came to steal more marshmallows and told the family that if they wanted the marshmallows back, they would have to give up Gregory.

The family didn't want to give up Gregory. They wondered, '. . . but who will protect us?' Gregory was now no longer strong. He could not lift up his mother. Everyone then decided to rest. While they were all asleep, mother got up and got a handful of marshmallows and put them out for the family to have when they woke up. Gregory woke up and ate some and got strong again. However, the bad guys came and took him away to the desk drawer.

Sam seems more willing to look at his anger and to try to cool it internally. He seems to be saying that it is fun to be in the volcano of angry feelings as long as you are in control of the feelings. The need for supplies, the rivalry over these supplies and the bargaining over who gets what are still strong. Sam seems to wonder whether he can get mother back with more effective bargaining, and/or by having returned more of her supplies, or by being a more ideal son.

Without the continued feeling of internal good objects, a continued belief in the self as very powerful is not possible. The idealized object needs the environment to supply it with nurturance, and the mother seems to be able to give the snake boy what he needs. Yet even with his strength regained, he can still be captured by the 'bad guys'.

It is interesting to note that Sam had 'forgotten about today's session'. He is afraid that he may be taking too much from the therapist and that she may not last. *He needs to know that she is a strong person and that they can be strong together.* Sam feels that he is bad and that his badness killed his mother. The process of therapy continues as Sam grieves for the loss of his mother and mourns her absence. He needs to decathect from his mother (which he cannot do as long as he feels angry) and to reinvest his emotional energy in another person. The transference relationship becomes very important during this kind of transition. This was a very important session for Sam.

Session 18

Sam was waiting for me today. He had not ridden his bike over to the Centre because the bike was 'grounded'. He did not want to talk about this at all. In this session there was much more positive feeling. Sam continued to work at the new desk today. He began with the healing oil. Pop and Gregory got fixed, and Ma's tail was re-rolled. Sam asked what had gone on in the last session, and I reminded him of Gregory being kidnapped. Orville and Bobby went to find Gregory. When they found him, they realized his memory had gone. He had amnesia and needed to be hit on the head again to remember.

Perhaps as a consequence of his punishment for having been 'bad', Sam works at reparation, of both Pop and Gregory, although Gregory is basically good. However, the positive feelings to the therapist have been developing, though associated at times with negative feelings, and Sam is able to feel safe and contained in his sessions. He can explore his reparative capacities, and the healing oil given by the therapist can now be used symbolically as mother's goodness to help father (symbolic of reparative coitus) and also to ensure Gregory's goodness; the hit on the head brings Gregory back his memories—memories of his phantasized destructiveness of the internal mother, which are changing to the external mother. The hitting on his head is both sadistic and reparative, as if to get better you must suffer a bit.

The therapist interpreted: 'Sometimes you feel like you're being punished by people who care for you and you wonder whether you can ever be good enough.' Sam responded with 'Yeah.'

Orville was made shorter—'the real baby'. Sam asked, 'How old are these babies?'

The therapist interpreted: 'We've been meeting for 18 sessions, so I guess they're 18.' Sam said, 'But we didn't make the snakes at first.' The therapist said, 'You're right. I think you are wondering about our times together.'

The session basically consisted of Gregory and Ralph still fighting with each other and eating marshmallows to get better and be strong. Ralph then asked Sam to open the door of the therapy room so he could throw Gregory out. Sam opened the door, but Gregory threw Ralph out instead. Orville tried to prevent Gregory and Ralph from fighting. Gregory and Ralph stood up to each other, and it struck both Sam and me as looking really funny.

Sam appeared to suggest that he is beginning to feel as if he has some internal resources; while the snakes were not made at the first few sessions, the sessions became meaningful after the snake family was created. Ralph, the bad, and Gregory, the good, are still fighting; love and hate are difficult to reconcile, and Sam says that he will throw Gregory out, but he throws Ralph out. Good objects are overcoming bad internal objects, but it appears as if the two snakes have to fight it out to make sure that goodness succeeds. The ability that Sam now shows to see humour in aggressive and difficult situations certainly appears as a sign of more effective ego functioning and resiliency.

During this confrontation between Gregory and Ralph, Orville had tried to get some marshmallows. He did not want anyone else to have the marshmallows that his uncle had brought.

Orville, the nine-year-old, tries to gain some goodness, perhaps for himself, and this may be true of Sam. It is interesting that the bad uncle brought in the marshmallows; Orville may not see them as good, and he may be preventing others from getting badness. The therapist interpreted: 'This reminds me a bit of your home now, where your brother-in-law has control of the good stuff. Your nephew is given all the good stuff, and you are afraid that none might be left for you.'

Gregory then knocked Orville off the desk, into the rubbish bin.

The therapist interpreted: 'I bet you would like to do that to your nephew.' Sam smiled and said, 'Yes, I'd like to dump him.' Gregory, the ideal good snake, does have some bad in him, which is expressed when he is threatened or denied. Sam is more aware of his aggressiveness towards his nephew.

Mum tried to stand up to Gregory for what he had done to Orville. She was mad at him and began to 'stomp', but as she did so her tail stuck to the desk. This looked rather funny, and we both laughed and decided to make a 're-take of the scene'.

The muscular sadism of mother (the stomping) is a projection of hostility. The scene is funny, and Sam laughs at the hostility. He looks at the phantasy and can see the humour, as well as ways of reparation.

Several times during the session the snakes stopped to talk to Sam or myself, asking our opinion about something or stopping to view a commercial about puppy-chow. Several healing episodes were also needed and carried out. When Sam was trying to decide about what our next episode would be, he said, 'I wonder what we can do tomorrow—I mean, next week.'

More interaction between phantasy and reality is played out, with more opportunities to adjust phantasy, not only directly but also indirectly to effect a friendly reality through reparation. The therapist interpreted: 'You would like to come every day.' Sam said, 'Yeah.' Sam would like to attend every day, but circumstances prevent this. Sam has been able to adjust to once a week, but expresses a sadness about this and a feeling of loss. Quite possibly he feels some rejection at once-a-week sessions as well as some difficulty holding the sessions in his mind.

As Sam got up to go, he accidentally stepped on Orville who had been thrown on the floor, and squashed his face. He decided to *remake* Orville. He got some new orange Plasticine but took Orville's 'soul out of his old body' and put it in his new body. Healing oil was used to make Orville as well. Sam looked at Orville's mouth and said that you could tell from his smile that he was happy. We had made a sign for our room and decided that we should colour it. He promised to bring his own crayons next week.

With his stepping on Orville (himself perhaps) and remaking him, we see further ego integration as well as the development of an ego coherence. He is now full of 'good stuff'. Orville is remade, and remade as a happy snake.

Sam noticed the desk that we had worked on and was worried about marks that the oil and Plasticine had made. I showed that the marks came off easily with a paper towel.

Sam fears revenge from the owners of the desk, but with the therapist's demonstration of possible restoration he feels well. His ego capacity now encompasses the ability to recognize his destructiveness and, at the same time, not to fear annihilation as a result of this but rather accept the way in which restoration can be accomplished.

Sam's aggression towards his nephew is a way of trying to get rid of an influence that might drain Sam's sister and destroy her. He wants to make sure she is not depleted, and that there is enough for everyone, including himself, as well as for the mother. The reality situation he created parallels his phantasy of himself, his mother and other babies she had. He wants to get rid of any of these babies so that his mother might live and be able to supply him with the goodness that he might restore his belief in himself. This belief in himself and his reparative capacities is developing, and Sam does trust himself more now than ever before.

Session 19

Sam had missed the previous week because he was sick. When he came in, he immediately said he had not brought his pencil crayons because his were all broken. He suggested asking the Centre's receptionist if she had any. She did have some crayons. (Sam had remembered that two weeks ago we were going to colour our sign).

Sam's illness may have left him feeling depleted but also as if his objects were not good enough. The illness may have been experienced as an attack on his developing goodness. Forgetting the crayons and asking for those from the receptionist make it clear that he thinks his therapist should be able to keep him well. His feeling of well-being

We worked on the sign together. In the past, Sam had sat to my right, a little off-centre of the desk. Today, he sat at the centre of the desk. We spent a lot of time colouring the sign and deciding how to fill in the letters. We filled each letter of the word 'room' with tiny drawings of marshmallows. On one part of the paper was a marshmallow hiding in a corner while another marshmallow looked for him.

fluctuates at these times, and he expresses annoyance at the therapist by not using her crayons (her pencils) but getting them from a substitute. Of course he may also be trying to spare the therapist. Sam continues to need the Centre to provide him with strength, and he wants to identify this place very clearly. Sam participates in a cognitive task very well, as if it is a reparative task, but now on a symbolic level, where he is able to point out his special room with its good objects (marshmallow breasts) clearly. The therapist interpreted: 'This reminds me a bit of how you felt at the beginning. ... You couldn't figure out how you felt, and we found out together.' Sam replied, 'Yeah, we met in the school and did the scribble game, and then we came to our special room.'

Sam wanted to put our sign on the door so the other people who shared the office wouldn't come in and disturb us.

Sam and his therapist have a special relationship, and he points out that he is unwilling to share her with anyone right now. She acknowledges this: 'You wish this was just our room. You don't want anyone else in.' Sam replies emphatically, 'Yeah, that's right.'

After colouring in the sign, Sam drew a face on a marshmallow, and I suggested putting it on our sign. He liked that idea. He drew another monster and made a marshmallow with a face on it, which had tears. This marshmallow was just about to be eaten.

Sam had also drawn a couple of monsters on our sign. I coloured the one on the left with blue curlicues. Sam said, 'I am glad you made that monster look funny; otherwise he would eat everyone up.' Then Sam took another marshmallow and drew a vampire face on it. He said that it was going to bite the monster on the neck. He then drew another vampire monster and asked me to draw the wings (Figure 19). We then tried to stick these vampire marshmallows and the ones

The face and the smile on it point out the goodness of the special room for its occupants; however, Sam also points out that everything is not completely well, for he makes a bad monster—but with a tear. The tear is his sadness and feelings of depression as a consequence of his aggression. Oral incorporation of the monster and the sadness seem to mean potential recognition of his sad and bad parts and what he may be taking from others. The therapist interpreted: 'Sometimes you worry about your sister looking after you, that you might be hurting her. ...' Sam looked at his therapist but did not say anything.

Humour may be Sam's way of dealing with his anxiety and aggression. If he can see humour in situations, he can then not only defuse his internal hostility but he can also continue on to explore more of his phantasies. It is as if he recognizes an ego control that will not desert him in the face of greater hostility. Sam needs to protect his room and to have others see how dangerous it can be for him if they intrude on him without asking his permission, which makes him feel a loss of ego

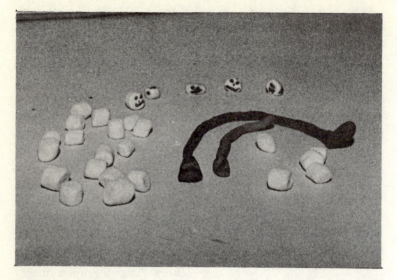

Figure 19.   Mother and Greg, with ordinary marshmallows and some others upon which faces were drawn in Session 19.

with ears on the actual sign, but they would not stick to the sign. We tried the glue stick, cellophane tape and masking tape. Finally I suggested that we try to make some marshmallows out of paper that we could stick to the sign. Sam thought that was a good idea. He began to pick some of the glue off the sign and said that it was becoming messy. He then put some on me and said, 'This is fun.'

control. The vampire sucking blood is the phantasy of the son emptying the mother of her goodness and leaving holes in her neck (damaged). He does accept the therapist's help, and together they make symbolic paper breasts (marshmallows). Now he will not have to take the mother's good objects but can substitute others. He finds the 'messy' glue interesting, and in putting some on his therapist it is as if he is putting something good on her, fixing her up, giving her babies, because he smiles as he does this. 'You want to mess me up,' the therapist said. She should have said, 'I think

you'd like to give me something in a nice way.' The
white glue seems to represent
semen, restoring the mother–
therapist by good intercourse.

We made and pasted six
marshmallows on our sign:
two vampires, one crying, one
sad and one normal-looking.
Throughout the session Sam
had checked the time twice
and said, 'Oh good, lots of
time left.'

Sam keeps his feelings
separate, yet there is some
integration because these
feelings are all on the one
sign. The therapist suggested:
'You are worried that we
won't have enough time.'
When he noticed that it was
time to go, he said, 'Oh darn.
Oh well, I don't care.' The
therapist said, 'You care but
you don't want to. ...' Sam
said, 'I'm just not going.' The
therapist said, 'You want to
stay here forever, just you and
me.' Sam said, 'Yeah.'

As we had almost finished
making the sign, I said that
we had time for two more
glues and then we would be
finished for today. Sam left
quite amiably, smiling as he
went.

Sam has a strong affectionate relationship with his
therapist. He now knows that
searching through his phantasies and working with them
will not damage the therapist,
and he feels at ease in showing his strong dependency
feelings.

Session 20

Sam had noticed a picture
of the Children's Centre Staff
in the foyer. He was con-
cerned because I was not in it.
I reminded him that I came
here on Wednesday mornings

Sam needs to know that his
therapist is real and belongs
somewhere, just as he needs
to know his feelings are real
and he belongs to a family.
The   therapist   interprets

to be with him for our special time in our special room. Sam had brought in a bag with some candies in it.

Sam asked if we had finished our sign. We took it out and he decided that we had finished it and we could hang it up. After we had taped it to the door, I tossed the tape back into the drawer, and Sam remarked on my action and he did the same thing with the tape. He remembered that we had put something away during the last session, but he could not remember what it was. It was the marshmallows that we had drawn faces on (Figure 19). Sam took them out, looked at them and laughed at one that he said had a 'squished' face. He then carefully wrapped them up again.

Sam then took out the snakes. The female snake, Sophie, came out first. Sam asked, 'How long have these guys been around?' The snakes were anxious to 'get going'. Sam got out the healing oil, and while trying to

Sam's bringing her candies: 'You'd like to give me some good stuff too.' Sam does this to make sure that the therapist (mother-in-phantasy) is now being effectively restored with all her goodness and that she will not feel damaged and Sam will not experience attacks from her.

Sam sees the therapist's 'throwing' as an aggressive act and is able to repeat it. Aggression is not always bad, and Sam seems to be allowing himself to be aggressive without fearing some retaliation. Humour is used more frequently, and it appears to be very appropriate. Reality and phantasy interact, and gradually Sam seems more capable of accepting and owning his own feelings. The therapist interpreted: 'These marshmallows remind me of real people who sometimes do some bad things but are generally good inside.' Sam answered, 'I sometimes feel good now and sometimes angry.'

Sam continues his reparative trends, but, interestingly, when the oil spills on himself, it becomes dangerous. It is as if he might be killed by the healing oil. We think that it is not the idea that the oil touches him, but rather that

open the top he spilled some on his shirt and trousers. Sam said, 'Yikes, get this stuff off, it's going to kill me.' He washed off his top, trousers and hands and then asked, 'We spilled the oil before, first on the table, now on me and *next on you!*' He laughed, and I did also. Sam then remade Orville once again and saved his soul.

he is wasteful with the oil. If he wastes the precious liquid, then he is not a good person, and he phantasizes that he would be punished. However, if he puts some on his therapist, whom he has endowed with such powers that she would not be killed, then maybe he would be forgiven for this 'accident'. Sam has 'accidentally' tested the reliability of the goodness of both his therapist and himself. He adds, 'Now you're healed too.' The first phantasy of being destroyed for spilling is followed by the phantasy of reparation, healing and laughter. Humour again prevents a potential disaster. The therapist interpreted: 'We can change the way we think or behave but some still stay the same.' [The therapist might have focused on the issue that if part of mother's soul is in Sam, then Sam can remember her goodness and recognize that his anger did not kill her. Her soul survives.]

Sam said, 'Look at Mum, doesn't she look innocent?'

Sam needs to have a 'good, innocent' mother, not one who hates. He needs to see his mother as having more good than hate; she may have been an angry mother at times, but there were some good experiences.

Sam then wanted to give power to Bobby. Ralph and Bobby trade powers through a power exchanger. The power exchanger is a light that shines on the snakes when they are held up to it in a paper bag; but Bobby became mean. He fought with Gregory and cried, 'I'll mertelize you. I'll make you eat your tail.' However, Gregory was still stronger. Father was now much stronger still. Mother tried to mediate the conflict between Gregory and Bobby. Dad came in and sent both Bobby and Gregory to their room. They then decided to hold 'a snake court'. All the snakes gathered around to determine who was guilty.

Sam asked me to operate the power exchanger. We both thought of using the empty juice and coffee cup instead of the paper bag to put the snakes in for the power exchange. Sophie came out to watch Gregory and Ralph at a standoff. Then Ralph got his power back from Bobby and became mean. We then had to figure out some way to get 'the meanness out'. Gregory, Ralph and Mum all decided to go to the computer centre. Here Ralph got 'the bad zapped out' and returned with

The baby snake, Bobby, becomes bad by 'light'; perhaps bad feelings are coming to light and fighting the ideal objects. An interesting word—mertelize—is used, which is actually 'mortalize'. Sam is afraid that getting well may mean some form of castration, some loss, but while his strength is still present and father is stronger, he does not need to envy someone else's power and strength. Power and strength are now to be determined democratically, perhaps to be seen as qualities that can be shared by several members of the family.

Sam tries to find out if somebody did something bad or if it just happened. Again, bad and mean qualities are to be looked at and then 'zapped out' and taken up in pretense by mother. Sam as a baby needed his mother to contain feelings that he could not hold on to, and he now thinks that she pretended to be zapped by his bad feelings, but she was not in reality hurt by them and actually is a loving mother. He seems to be incorporating a good image of his mother. Her 'soul' is good and

Gregory and Mum. Mum took a short-cut home and pretended that the badness had gone into her. However, she stopped pretending, and they kissed and made up.

not threatening. The therapist interpreted: 'It seems like you might want to get rid of some parts that you feel are bad inside you.' Sam is also exploring the feelings of being sad.

His hate and grief begin to resolve as he sees that he did not damage his mother.

Sam decided that the next episode would be to make someone else bad: 'Orv Goes Bananas'. Sam spent some time in this session talking about the eclipse of the sun.

Sam plans, as he has been doing for a little while now, to explore the themes of aggression, protection and insanity.

We used symbolic material to help Sam with his uncertainty and poor acceptance of his feelings. It is very difficult, we think, for Sam to acknowledge his anger towards his mother consciously, but he is using the snake family and the play materials to help with some understanding and perhaps some resolution. Then further changes in ego functioning might occur, along with some consolidation and integration of his feelings.

Session 21

I asked Sam what had happened with the oil on his clothes. Apparently his sister had not noticed it. We had removed the oil. Sam began looking for a pen, saying, 'scribble ... scribble', while pretending to scribble on me. He went back to the power

[The therapist should probably not have asked Sam to tell her about the oil stain problem. Sam seems to have resolved this in the last session and does not carry any residue.] The therapist's body (and the mother's body) is not frightening; he can explore it,

chamber again and began to zap Gregory and Ralph. Gregory became bad, so Sam put him in the power chamber (which was a styrofoam cup) with a marshmallow. The marshmallow, however, became bad. This bad marshmallow was the vampire-faced marshmallow that we had made in Session 19. Sam said, 'People say there is no such thing as a vampire that sucks blood out. Is there?'

The vampire began sucking blood. He turned Sophie and Orville into zombies. Sam drew blood on Sophie and Orville with a red marker. Sam did not want to use red Plasticine for blood because he was planning to heal the snakes. The Plasticine would have been incorporated into the snakes, whereas the red pen marks would rub off. The vampire then tried to attack Mum, and Sam smashed it away.

The vampire then goes after Sam and spits in my face too. This reminded Sam of the movie, 'Indiana Jones'. He

and he can express interest in it without fear. He expresses an ambivalence about good and bad, and Sam needs to have the therapist tell him that we all have feelings that are sometimes good and sometimes bad, that we gradually understand how we feel, but others often do not know what we think or even how we feel until we let them know. The therapist interpreted: 'People may say there is no such thing as vampires, yet it really seems there are some bad things. The vampire could be a sort of bad feeling we might have at times.'

Sam explores how his oral sadism might have destroyed others, but now he can imagine how he could make three people become well again. The situation reaches the point where Mum is attacked, but now Sam does not allow this to happen. He protects and saves his mother. The therapist interpreted: 'You wish you could have saved your own mother.' Sam looked at the therapist.

The therapist interpreted: 'The badness can sometimes attack you and me, but you know how to make things

told me about several scenes where someone's heart gets ripped out and they turn into a zombie. We then acted out me being bitten by the vampire instead of drinking a potion (as they did in the movie) and turning into a zombie and Sam rescued me with a torch, as they did in the movie. When Sam was bitten by the vampire, he did not turn into a zombie. When the session ended, Sam said, 'I'll leave this mess for you to clean up.'

The next episode will be 'Zombies Galore'. We played the video game *Frogger* after the session, and Sam beat me by eight points. When I returned to clean up, I discovered that Sam had left his baseball hat in the room.

better now.' Sam adapts the movie plot to his own needs and works through some of his internal bad feelings. Sam is powerful enough to prevent my death and have sufficient good for himself so that he can maintain his goodness. His mess can be cleaned by the therapist who is now seen as not depleted because she has been given goodness by Sam. He can now make some demands without fear of being attacked. In a therapeutic relationship Sam knows that the therapist will be able to clean his mess without being messed herself. He is testing her and his own demands as well; the risk is that she might be damaged and die. However, he feels sufficiently safe with the feeling that she is not going to die and his mess is not a 'bad mess'.

Sam will explore overwhelming odds against goodness in his next session. He does not want to leave the room and the therapist; he leaves his hat for her to keep safe. Next week she will say to him: 'I kept your hat and it was safe with me. I wondered if you had thought about it.'

We consider termination of his play psychotherapy sessions, because the school term is coming to an end and we do not think that Sam will be brought to play psychotherapy by anyone. Furthermore, he may have to go on a vacation with his family, or he may move to another district. Sam has been able to explore his feelings and work some of them out, he is able to think more effectively and is also able to defuse potentially damaging feelings by humour. We will have several more sessions and talk about termination. We will also give him a gift. The gift we shall give him is an *Adidas* bag, symbolizing the containing, carrying mother who is strong, big enough and safe. (We usually give a child a gift upon termination, partly as a transitional aspect. The child will have this gift and be able to recall—contain—the therapist, and this is also a gift to mark a significant event in the child's life.)

Session 22

I was late coming to meet Sam in the foyer of the Centre, and he had the receptionist call me through the telephone intercom.

Perhaps the therapist is upset about the coming termination and arrives late for the session. She interpreted: 'Were you worried that I wouldn't be here?' Sam said, 'Yeah!' She told him, 'I will be here.' Sam was worried that she had disappeared, that she, like his mother, had deserted him and that when he begins to feel good, he will not be on guard sufficiently to keep sadness out and that things will go bad again.

I then showed Sam his hat.

The therapist said, 'I kept your hat, it was safe with me. ... I wondered if you had thought about it?' Sam said,

'No ... I knew it was okay with you.'

Sam said that he remembered the title for this week's session, 'Zombies Galore'. He brought a pen and a large piece of graph paper, which was folded. We got set up for our session, the black chair for him, our sign and marshmallows, and then Sam took out the 'Map to Our Special Room.' He wanted to write on it the actual street name. During the spelling of one of the street names, he misspelled a letter, and I 'whited' it out; he immediately left the map and opened up the folded paper he had brought. This was a floor-plan of an 'ideal school' that his previous teacher had had the class draw (Figure 20).

Order and structure are important and make explorations possible. These safety qualities permit exploration of feelings that are still dangerous. Cognitive aspects make their appearance as an indication that Sam can look at things and not be afraid that what he will find is a mother damaged by himself, but, rather, he will recognize that she damaged herself. Her death is gradually seen as not being his fault. He is able to see that he tried to help her, but that he was not powerful enough, and while he blames himself, he alternates between the idea that he was good and that he was bad. His floor-plan is an aspect of real-

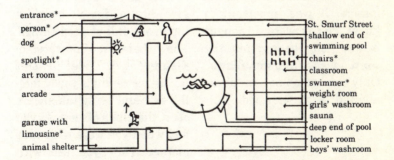

Figure 20. Sam's floor plan of his 'ideal school'. The items marked with an asterisk were added during the therapy sessions, along with other features (not shown).

This was done at the beginning of Grade 4, during the time when his mother was very ill. We spent the rest of the session 'peopling' his school and making adjustments and additions to the floor-plan. I made some interpretations about Sam being the powerful guy in the weight room. There was also a NO SWEARING sign.

There was also a portable STOP sign.

There was a giant swimming pool, and a lifeguard who saved someone who was drowning.

Then Sam decided that the person could save himself. He drew a giant limousine in the garage. It was important to know the password. I thought it was 'jelly beans', but the word was 'marshmallows'. Only one person at a time was allowed to go for a ride.

ity that he can bring into the session. He can discuss reality now and can also recognize some of its restrictions. [The therapist might have interpreted this as 'something to stop yourself from doing bad things', as a superego sign.]

[The therapist might have said: 'You are making your own stop sign to help you say things that are okay to say.'] He can now impose controls on himself, and this is seen as ego growth.

'I am the lifeguard,' Sam says, and he sees himself as helpful and saving, and not as bad and weak.

Sam recognizes that his mother had a responsibility to herself, and he does, however, give her a fancy 'body', a limousine full of good things. The therapist interpreted: 'Going for a ride in this limousine reminds you of feeling safe and being taken care of . . . the kinds of feelings you had when you were with your mother. Now you are with people who want to care for you.' Sam replied, 'Yeah.'

Then Sam immediately drew racing stripes on the car. It became a car that went fast. Someone else got the idea to go for a ride. He broke into the garage but was spotted by a hidden camera and was gunned down by a bazooka machinegun. ...

The therapist interpreted: 'You don't want anyone else to intrude on the good stuff. It's a bit like D [his nephew] ... you'd like to get rid of him so he doesn't take away all the good stuff from your sister. You are afraid that there'll be nothing left for you.' Sam replied, 'Yeah, that's it.'

Then Sam drew spotlights in the hallways of his school, to make sure the way was always bright.

Sam deals with reality situations in an imaginative manner and is capable of effective responses. The therapist interpreted this: 'This is like therapy, in the beginning you didn't know how you felt about your mother ... now through play and our talking you can understand how you feel.'

There ensued a little Oedipal drama, with a little boy sneaking into the girls' washroom. He changed his mind. Then a little girl peeked at the boy urinating— ('going pee wee'). Then Sam drew the girl on the toilet and wrote the word 'plop'.

This is an Oedipal drama, with a little boy and his penis resulting in the phantasy of intercourse with the girl and making babies with her. The therapist interpreted: 'She gets to see that his penis is okay and that it does things well.' Sam can now explore some of the things he has been thinking about for a while. He wants to have his mother–therapist acknowledge his growing maleness and sense of strength. The girl has a baby through anal birth.

Another little girl was washing her hands, and said, 'Pee-you.'

Perhaps this is a denigration remark expressing contempt in order to deny envy. The 'pee-you' could be an expression indicating badness and contempt and a concern about Sam's growing sexual interest.

Then Sam began to act a little silly and was giggling.

The therapist interpreted: 'We laugh sometimes when we are a bit nervous. Ten-year-olds are pretty curious about girls and babies, and we don't always understand how things work, but we want to know.'

Sam then asked me to draw a dog. I asked him whether I should draw a poodle or a german shepherd and he said to draw a doberman who was escaping from the animal room and chasing a female dog. The female dog was making little 'woof-woofs', and she was running with her mouth open.

Sam wants a strong animal who can escape from the room and find a female. Sexual exploration is safer when in the realm of animals. The little 'woof-woof' may be sounds of enticement.

The therapist interpreted: 'Do you think that they make babies by mouth?' Sam replied, 'No, but she's chasing this guy and he's burning rubber to get away from her.' This sexual scene reflects his imagination of a man giving the woman babies through her mouth, but as well of a woman eating up men. Sam expresses his fear of castration and Oedipal anxieties in this way.

There were only a few minutes left, so Sam asked that we leave the play and that I keep the floor-plan for next week. I said that it would be safe with me. He also asked me to keep his hat once again.

The hat and the floor-plan are important objects for Sam. The therapist is directly acknowledged as the container for his thoughts, ideas and plans, as well as for his good and bad feelings.

After the session, we played a game of *Frogger,* and Sam beat me.

His strength is expressed, and Sam is not afraid of retaliation.

I checked with the social worker who was working with Sam's sister to find out about the family's summer plans, so that we could arrange for termination of the sessions.

Sam can now express his concern when the therapist is late, he can explore his feelings about mother's death and the loss it was to him. He can explore some of the things he has been thinking about—for example, oral–sadistic phantasy about sex. In sex do men lose their penis, which is devoured by the women—women must, therefore, have a lot of penises inside. To be sexual, one has to be aggressive, yet this can be threatening because of the fear of castration as well as of retaliation.

Session 23

Sam came to me as I drove into the Centre in my car. I had just been given a rose by someone in the driveway, and I handed it to him.

Sam is obviously eager to be with the therapist and have the safety of her car (her body) to see it as undamaged and containing. Sam said 'Ouch.' She told him, 'Hold the rose where it doesn't hurt.' Sam said, 'I'd like to prick you.' An interesting interchange! Sam is hurt when given the flower; the therapist responds as she might to a normal, healthy child, and Sam retorts with aggression, which he can now feel and yet not imagine as destructive. However, he has to explore this theme some more.

Today we resumed play with the snakes. Sam announced the 'Zombies Galore' title. Before beginning, he asked me about his hat and maps.

Sam asked, 'Do you still have my hat?' The therapist interpreted: 'Yes, I'm keeping it safe. Shall I keep your maps too?' Sam said, 'Yes.' He said this smiling and calmly, obviously pleased with the therapist's willingness to hold his objects.

Two snakes had been turned into zombies, and during the rest of the session all the other snakes and a bunch of marshmallows were also turned into zombies. One of the little marshmallows thought it all very boring. During this procedure I was 'bitten' twice. The first time I was bitten, I pretended to be a zombie, and Sam said that I should 'cut it out'. The second, aggressive time the vampire bit me on the nose and sucked 'snot' out and then

While Sam is expressing a certain sense of boredom about his play, he nevertheless becomes intensely interested in the aggressive play that he can now indulge in and do so in a very elaborate way. The therapist might have said, 'I know I am not going to be really hurt.' Obviously Sam did not want the therapist to be hurt or damaged. She is good and strong. A bite on her nose seems to represent the removal of bad stuff from her

spat it out. One zombie sucked 'red slime' out of another zombie, and he spat it out. This landed on the Dad's face, who wiped it off with a tissue. I was asked to do the wiping. Then the zombie spat over the side of the desk on Sam's trousers where the oil had fallen before—on his left thigh—and he pretended to wipe it off and put it on my clothes.

A tiny marshmallow, which had been very happy, began to cry, 'I'm going to get bitten, I'm going to get bitten.' He was jumping up and down, and after being bitten he said the same thing again. However, the marshmallow was able to stay happy throughout.

A sad marshmallow didn't want to be a zombie, and in the end he booted the other marshmallows away.

and is spat out so that any of the badness she might have ingested from Sam is now removed. Zombies or lifeless creatures seem to be able to explore the bodies of others without evoking the phantasized dangers. Sam explores his own aggressiveness and control. He can explore his father's aggressiveness, his own damage, and his approach to the therapist. While he might be hurt or bitten, he nevertheless has sufficient reserves to remain 'happy'.

The good might be harmed, but some remains. There is more goodness than badness.

Then those that bit are booted away, and the danger is gone for now. The therapist interpreted: 'I bet you'd like to do that to the bad things in your life.' This also symbolizes to us that 'We have both good and bad inside of us, but mostly we're good.' Sam looked very pleased when his therapist said this.

Gregory and Ralph were still okay. Then Sam made a new marshmallow with a nose and mouth and told me to give the marshmallow eyes.

Then the new marshmallow and Gregory got into a fight. They hit each other back and forth across the room repeatedly. We had to clear away all the other marshmallows for the fight. Sam put the vampires into the box, saying, 'Bye, I'm going to miss you.' After the fight, the soul of the crying, sad marshmallow was discovered to be in the new marshmallow. So, Gregory punched it across the room, and the soul came out and re-entered the sad marshmallow.

The sad marshmallow didn't need to be sad any more. Sam wondered what we would do in the next session, and after thinking for a moment he announced the title, 'A New Member Comes to the Family'. It will be a tiny snake, even smaller than Bobby.

The therapist interpreted: 'It's like what happens when you come here, you begin to see things more clearly.' Sam said softly, 'Yeah. ...'

Gregory was the ideal at one point, and could 'see' everything; however, his idealization was challenged, and perhaps a less ideal object will now be able to 'see' reality more clearly. It is as if Sam is saying that what might happen to him is not just because he was bad, but because he is human. We think that Sam is ready to work through aspects of the separation from the therapist now. He is preparing himself for separation, and while he might be angry, he does not have to regress to oral cannibalism. This soul seems to be the soul of his mother. After death, he is left with her goodness. Sam can now maintain a feeling of goodness of his mother inside himself.

A new baby, perhaps indicating that good parental coitus was successful and that the mother did get something good from father.

Session 24

This session was held on the first day of the summer vacation. Twenty minutes into the session Sam had not arrived, so I telephoned him at home, and he said that he was coming. His brother-in-law dropped him off. When he came in, he noticed some cars and trucks in another room and asked if we could use them. I said that we could and that we would bring them back after our session. I added that they would not be here next week, but that if he wanted to use them now, it was okay. He chose three cars and one large red truck/van. He remembered that the title of the session was that a baby was going to come into the family and asked what colour we should make it. He chose green, saying it was 'snot', and then added 'I'm just kidding.'

Anxiety about the session is shown by his lateness, about his developing strength and whether it will remain. His use of the cars and trucks may be his way to alleviate anxiety and avoid playing with the snake family. However, he does remember the theme of the session and expresses aggression towards the new baby, yet counters it with humour. His use of snot may be symbolic of semen and may be his expression of the anxiety involved in having mother and father make a baby. The therapist commented, 'It's something that the body produces.' [She might have said: 'It's interesting to think about, something like that might be used to make babies.']

He rolled out the piece of green Plasticine until it was very long and then cut it in half. I suggested that we make twins, and he agreed wholeheartedly and immediately made the snakes while I was getting the right colours for the eyes, nose and mouth. Without these parts they moved around, but they were blind and were not able

Perhaps the therapist suggested twins so that Sam might imagine that there was always going to be enough good stuff. The twins might indicate that the mother has enough internal good objects to make twins. The therapist helps Sam to gain a means of understanding his environment by giving eyes, nose and mouth and perhaps, thereby, to smell or talk. Sam filled the delivery van with marshmallows and dumped them out again. Then he put the babies in the van. Once they had been formed, they were put into the truck (the delivery van) and delivered.

Then Gregory was put in the van, and it delivered him by throwing him out of there!

The delivery van then loaded the babies again and drove them to the top of the filing-cabinet. The babies were then driven to the snake family. On the trip the van pushed through the rocking chair. It had previously been a gate where a password was needed. A password was no longer needed here. When the babies were delivered from the van, Mum and Dad 'took them over' and paid attention to them while ignoring the rest of the snakes. Gregory and the rest of the snakes decided to ignore their parents.

The snake children took off in the red van. They couldn't give the babies back, so they tried to figure out what to do.

to gain more access to understanding reality. The mother truck is filled with babies and good supplies. The therapist commented, 'It's just like a uterus.' Sam asked, 'What is a uterus?' The therapist said, 'It's where the mother gives birth to babies.' Sam responded, 'Oh, yeah.'

The therapist asked, 'Do you feel you were born that way?' Sam gave no response. Gregory wants to explore the mother's insides, but it is still difficult to do.

The babies are delivered without any problems and accepted by the parents, but the parents cannot attend to the rest of the snake children. The parents are ignored in an attempt to deny the children's greed, yet express irritation over being ignored. The therapist interpreted: 'The snake family is afraid that the little snakes will take all the good stuff and there will be nothing left for them.' Sam said, 'Yeah!'

The therapist reflected: 'Sometimes you feel like taking off.' It is difficult to wonder about such difficult things, like greed and rivalry, but Sam seems to be trying. She continued: 'You are trying to figure out what to do too. The snakes feel pretty mad at the parents and also at the babies.' Sam said, 'Yeah.'

Gregory and the rest of the snakes returned home. They found mother and the babies were playing hide-'n-seek. Sam asked what the babies' names should be. I suggested the names of his niece and nephew, but he said 'No!' He named them Craig and Tom. During the game mother found one of the babies under Sam's hat. While everyone was sleeping, Tom went over to Gregory, who said, 'Get lost.' Tom said to Gregory, 'Don't you like me, Gregory?' Gregory then decided to mellow and became nicer to Tom. They went out together to eat marshmallows. Then Gregory took Tom for a ride in the van. The other snakes woke up and still felt jealous of the babies, so Gregory punched them out. One by one he convinced all the others to be nice to the babies. Then Gregory took both babies and Orville for a ride back to the computer centre.

The snake children return home, and Sam plays out his feelings of separation-loss and reattachment to reassure himself of his mother's goodness. Sam did not want the baby twins to have too close a relation to reality and so named them imaginary names. It is interesting that Sam's hat plays an important role, for even though he is rivalrous, he offers his hat as protection to a twin. Tom contains Gregory's projections, but gradually the rivalry is reduced. Aggression lessens, and with less fear of his own aggressiveness and the anxiety that this creates, love and jealousy merge, and the hostile projections are reduced. Sam's ego shows greater capacity for integration and for being able to synthesize objects. This would mean that Sam would also now be able to think about his imagined damage and harm he thinks he has done to his loved object, yet without self-destructive regression. The computer centre symbolizes the 'good place', perhaps the 'fixing place', and contains the workings for a good relation of others to parents as well as with each other. With parents pleased, their combined aggression is not directed against their children, but rather directed to help their children.

Mum and Dad were worried that Gregory was going to hurt the babies. On their way to the computer centre they tried to get through the gate by 'booting it away'. Once they had arrived, they tried to jump over to the desk where Sam and I worked. It was about five feet away. They jumped and landed first in the rubbish bin next to the desk.

The mother and father seem to be working together, and their combined force is to help the children, even though it may be dangerous for them. The therapist interpreted: 'Part of you wants to be friends and help the babies, and part of you still wants to get rid of them.' Sam smiled in agreement and continued to play out his theme.

The babies finally made it in a jump from the centre to the desk. Then Gregory and Orville tried to do the same. They landed on the floor instead.

The therapist interpreted, 'Gregory is becoming a little more human; he doesn't need to be as all-powerful.' Sam said 'No, he made it farther than the babies.' Gregory is still powerful and helps to allay anxiety, and Sam sees Gregory as somewhat more than human but not superhuman.

This was the end of the session. We had only had 45 minutes. Sam asked if he could stay longer, and I told

Sam may not have felt that he was able to resolve some of his feelings and needed to be able to 'get' more from the

him that we did not have more time today, but we would be meeting again soon. We discussed when he would have to leave the house next week to get here to his session on time. Sam decided that the next episode would be, 'A New Member Comes to the Family. Part II: Gregory and the Twins'.

therapist. Time was not available to carry on, and this could have been interpreted as some attempt to get more, with subsequent fear of retaliation. Sam will continue to explore his capacity for ego integration and the goodness and badness he is experiencing.

We decided to talk to Sam about terminating his sessions during the next therapy hour. This will be introduced at a point when he and the therapist are talking about missing somebody, with this concept woven into the next few sessions. 'You and I can talk about the time we spend together and also how much longer we will be seeing each other. I think you might have been thinking about this. . . .' If he asks how many more days he and the therapist will be working together, the therapist will circle the dates that they will meet on the calendar for him to have. She will tell him that she will think about and remember the work they have done during their time together, that she has been able to 'see' his goodness as well as his worries and that he has been able to keep his therapist inside himself, that she has become a good part of him, and although they will not be seeing each other every week, she will think about him and remember him and he will be able to think about her. This planning for termination is considered important in terms of helping the child to recognize that the container is maintained, but now in the mind of the child.

Session 25

Sam came to meet me at the car. He had been waiting at the Children's Centre since

Perhaps Sam is already aware of the discussion about termination, is anxious about

9.00 a.m. (15 minutes before the therapy session began). He was visibly cheerful and friendly when he saw me. We looked for apple juice. Sam was very thirsty today. Once in the therapy room, Sam noticed some Plasticine marks that had dried on the desk.

meeting with his therapist and does not want to be late. He wants to make sure that she is well and strong and still giving and that no harm has come to her. Sam drinks a lot, as if orally filling up, but he does not express any anxiety about this. He does not feel as if he is taking too much from the therapist. The therapist showed him that the marks could be wiped off easily, and Sam did not become upset about this. He accepted her help without concern.

Sam remembered the title of the session as 'Part II: Gregory and the Twins', but then he noticed Sophie and said that she was going to die. We set Sophie up where we left off last week with Gregory and the twins jumping off the filing cabinet. Sam said, 'They're happy.' Mum and Dad thought Gregory, and now Orville, had been hurting the twins, so Mum spanked Gregory and Orville and told them to go to their rooms, but they went to the window-sill instead. This seemed to be a place of comfort for them. The babies were scared by their mother's anger, and they ran away to their bedroom, which was a tissue box. The twins

Sophie, Gregory's girl-friend, is a part projection of Sam's ambivalent feelings toward the death of his mother. This theme comes up now and again. Sophie is loved and is 'going to die', but the theme changes to play with siblings and misrecognition of feelings by parents. Sam is trying to work out why his phantasized parents did not give him the love he felt he needed from them. There is a real camaraderie between Gregory and the babies, a closeness and feeling of help-fulness.

then told Mum and Dad that they liked Gregory and that he wasn't trying to hurt them, so Mum and Dad apologized to Gregory.

The babies showed themselves to be strong and powerful, just like Gregory when he was little. Gregory showed them he was still more powerful and began to race around, but he couldn't stop. One twin stopped him by tripping him. His face got squished, so then Gregory was remade.

Gregory and Orville and the babies began to fight with the other set of snakes. The other team did not like babies, but 'they got outpowered'. The fighting occurred on the window-sill. While Sam was standing at the window, he noticed one of his friends going by. His name was Craig (interestingly, the name of one of the twins). This seemed to be an opening to introduce the termination.

There is also identification between these snake siblings, but Gregory is still the 'older and stronger' brother who can protect. At times he is overcome by his need to demonstrate himself, and as a result he loses some ego control. Gregory is not as idealized, he is strong but not perfect. The therapist interpreted: 'Even though he changes, he has his basic goodness inside, which stays the same.'

The snakes fight the badness and overpower it, and now Sam is able to look out the window and see his friend, Craig—someone with whom he plays in reality and about whom he might have been thinking by having a baby twin snake called Craig. The therapist begins to interpret the termination process: 'The snakes have been doing interesting things, feeling pretty good ... just like we've been doing. Sometimes you want to do something with some of your friends. ...' Sam, however, did not seem ready to discuss this.

Sam accidentally stepped on Bobby, and he said, 'He's dead.' Bobby was brought back to life with marshmallows. Bobby had been knocked onto the floor by the twins, and everyone (the whole snake family) came to see him on the floor. At this point Sam smelled my feet and said, 'Phew!'

Perhaps the therapist's remarks are felt as attacks and as if they were killing the baby Bobby (the baby in Sam), but life is restored by the goodness of the marshmallow breast. Fighting and hostility result in anxiety and the feared death of the loved object. Sam seems to work with this but at the same time expresses some aggression towards the therapist. He seems to devalue the therapist and see her as not perfect. If she were perfect (idealized) and he lost her, how terrible it would be for him. He might not be able to cope with the real world. As he does not seem to idealize her now, the therapist continued: 'These snakes are wondering how much longer they will be playing, just like I think you wonder how much longer we'll be seeing each other.' Sam said, 'No ... how much longer will it be?' The therapist answered, 'I'll bring a calendar next week and show you.' Sam said, 'Show me on this one.' The therapist explained, 'We will have three sessions in July,' but by then Sam had lifted up the calendar page for August. She replied, 'Our last session is in July.' Sam responded with 'Aah' (a pained groan). The therapist said, 'You wish we could go on meeting forever.' Sam said, 'Yeah.' The therapist interpreted: 'Even though we won't always be meeting, I will always think about you. And I know you will also think of me.' Sam said, 'Yeah.'

All the snakes went home. Then Sophie arrived. Sam said she would have a heart attack. She hadn't been feeling well. Sophie said, 'Hi, boys.' She said that she was okay, but the twins knew differently. When the therapist suggested that she's an older snake, Sam corrected her and said that she was only 19 (this was the age of Sam's sister).

Sam is now playing out his mother's heart attack as the termination of his play therapy. His need to understand this sad event as not being his fault is very important. The therapist commented: 'Sometimes you worry about your sister dying. ...' Sam said, 'No—she'll be around for a while. ...'

The bad guys tried to get Sophie, but the twins protected her; then she had a heart attack, but no one wanted to go and tell Sophie's Mum. We then created a new snake, the same colour as Sophie, to be her mother. She was very sad. The babies went to get Sophie's Mum and Ma (Gregory's Mum); they came over to have a mother-to-mother talk with her. She said, 'Sophie is dead.' Then the mother cried, 'No!' and ran away. She tried to jump off the window-sill, but the twins saved her by giving her

Sam enacts Sophie's death caused by a heart attack and begins to resolve some of his sadness and guilt by bringing Sophie's mother into his family. The sad part of Sam is given sympathy and care. The therapist said, 'Even though she's not here any longer, the snakes will always think about her and remember her goodness.'

something to land upon (on them). The whole family went over and talked to Sophie's Mum. They invited her to join their family. She agreed and became happy. Sam asked what we should do with Sophie, and I suggested that we better have a funeral. He agreed.

Sam put Sophie on the marshmallow bed.

The therapist interpreted: 'Her soul is going to heaven. She looked happy and peaceful on the marshmallow ... just like your mother's soul.' Sam said, 'I wondered about that, and that's right.'

Sam seems to be moving away from his therapy. He sees his friend, and he works out his mother's heart attack but is still obviously involved in the work of therapy. Next week his therapist will bring a calendar to show him the three remaining sessions of therapy. She will also bring in a camera to take a picture of the members of the snake family. This will be introduced by telling Sam that our work has been very important and that she would like to take a photograph of our important work so that we could have it for a long time. The therapist telephoned to inform Sam's sister of the termination and promised to phone in late September to see how the summer had gone. Termination, while somewhat premature, was necessary to be set at this time because of plans that were made for Sam that were beyond our control, and rather than have the therapy sessions terminated by an outside source and without warning, we set our own timetable.

Session 26

I called Sam about 15 minutes after our therapy session should have started. He was not out of bed yet. There had been a misunderstanding, and his brother-in-law had gone to work and had not awakened Sam as he said he would. He arrived in about ten minutes, and we went together to buy some polaroid film and a flash. We spent the remaining part of the session taking pictures of the snakes.

We think that both Sam and his brother-in-law colluded to create this lateness. Sam is anxious about the termination, and certainly the brother-in-law knew of these final appointments and their times, and together they avoided the appointment. Perhaps the brother-in-law was anxious that Sam might become bad again, and by not awakening him, the brother-in-law was expressing his own anger at the termination. The therapist commented: 'Sometimes people sleep in when things are happening that are unpleasant that they'd rather not face.' Sam said, 'Are you crazy?' while looking at the therapist with a funny smile on his face.

Sam wore his 'Hostess Munchie' hat home today.

He takes his important hat home today. He seems to be collecting the important parts of therapy into himself. It does look like Sam's own developmental energies are not available for him to use. The therapist, verbalizing Sam's development, appears to help Sam's ego. Sam's ego is sufficiently strong to terminate in this short a time-period. Separation is difficult to tolerate, and as children have difficulty in expressing their feelings, the therapist tries to put into words the child's feelings. This supports the ego during this stressful time. As termination is a separation and a loss (transference loss), as already experienced by Sam because of the death of his mother, a gift will be given to him to help him feel contained.

Session 27

It was a cool day and Sam wore his winter jacket and kept it on during the entire therapy session. We took a few more pictures with another camera.

Sam seems to be keeping the warmth of the therapist inside so he will not have to worry.

Sam said, 'We don't have a title for today.' The therapist responded that we could have 'Sophie's Funeral'. Sam said, 'Forget that.' The therapist said, 'What do you want to do with her?' Sam said he wanted to throw her away.

Termination has created angry feelings in Sam. He wants to be at the session, but he is irritated.

But, instead of throwing her away, Sam decided to roll her up and put her back in the Plasticine supply. As we rolled her up, she began to look like a marshmallow, but a bit of green Plasticine still showed. It looked a bit like her mouth, and depending

Sam said, 'She looks happy.' He does regain his ego strength and he is able to see an integration of feelings in the same person.

upon which way you turned her she could look happy or sad.

Sam wanted to take the snake family on an adventure through the building.

The therapist commented, 'I think the snakes want to leave the room because it's difficult for them to face their sad feelings about soon not being in this room any more.' Sam said, 'They'll be with me.' The therapist said, 'They'll be with both of us in spirit.' Sam said, 'What do you mean?' The therapist interpreted: 'Just like the souls we talked about stay with us when people die, and we remember people after they die, I will always remember the snake family and you and the work we did together; I will have those memories inside me and you will also have them and the good stuff we did inside you.'

I suggested we take the snakes on an adventure in the therapy room. Sam agreed. He had been planning to go to an amusement park at the end of August, so he pretended to take the snakes to this amusement park. The snakes noticed his birthday on the calendar. We made a 'devil's drop' out of a tissue box and a 'roller-coaster ride' out of a closed envelope. The twins, Gregory and Ralph, went on the rides. The twins

Sam tests out his new-found independence and his ability to face adventure. Sam has introjected the good objects effectively, and while there may be danger, he nevertheless has the ego capacity to deal with this. He has become his own container. He can recognize that people can have strengths whereas others may have some weaknesses, but this does not make them bad people.

were very brave, but Gregory
and Ralph got a bit dizzy. The
vampire marshmallows came
out of their box and bit the
guys who operated the 'devil's
drop' ride. This is what they
did instead of paying for the
ride.

The therapist is planning to send him a birthday card on
his birthday a few months hence and will write on the
birthday card: 'I wanted to send you happy birthday
greetings. I have thought a lot about you and wanted you to
have a happy time.'

At the termination interview, we decided that the
therapist should let Sam make the first move as far as a hug
or handshake is concerned. The termination present has
been purchased—an *Adidas* bag—and it will be introduced
the following way: 'I have done a lot of thinking about the
work that you and I have done and I'd like you to have some
of the supplies that we have worked with. I thought that
this bag is a good thing to hold these supplies.' During this
last session, the therapist also plans to say something like:
'Sometimes you might be worried that you might not be able
to keep the warmth of the good feelings inside you—some
days will go okay and others might be difficult. When things
are not so okay, you can think about me and you in this
room where we did a lot of important work.'

The session should end whenever it seems appropriate to
do so, and the therapist plans to walk out of the room with
him and say goodbye to him.

Session 28

TERMINATION

On Wednesday, on which   A difficult situation arose
our final session had been   for Sam; he had to go on the
scheduled, Sam did not come. camping trip. (This situation

He had gone camping with his relatives and had not been brought back for his appointment. I called a couple of days later when he was back, and he wanted to meet me then. It was 7:30 at night, and he seemed very eager to hear from me and to see me. I told him that I wanted to see him the following Monday morning at 10:00. When I called his home that morning, he had apparently gone out looking for his bicycle. He had forgotten our 'good-bye time'. I asked his sister if she would ask him to stay at home if he returned within the next half-hour. He returned about half an hour later. When I called back, he was at home, but he had not found his bicycle yet. As my time was limited, I went to his house. As I pulled up in the car, he immediately noticed the *Adidas* bag and asked whose it was. I said it was for him, but I left it in the car at this time. He was delighted. He was at home with a friend.

We sat down at the picnic table, and then I gave him the snakes and the bag of Plasticine, the map to the Children's Centre, the sign to our room and his floor plan of his ideal school. He wanted me to

all too often happens to children in therapy. Parents and guardians sometimes just do not understand either the importance of treatment, or the strength of children's feelings.)

Sam is having difficulty saying goodbye. He is afraid he might be so angry with the therapist that he might be avoiding this last session. The bicycle is also of great importance to him—it represents his independence and power.

The last session has been scheduled, and the therapist was then to go off on her vacation. We felt that this was a way to end the therapy and, while quite different than planned, would still be appropriate.

Sam wanted the therapist to have something of the sessions, and interestingly he gave her the map—so she would never be lost? The therapist interpreted: 'You may be worried that you

keep the map. I told him that I had done a lot of thinking about the work he had done, and these are the things I wanted him to have from the work. He looked at the floor plan and he looked as if he was going to give it to me. But I encouraged him to keep it, saying: "We've done a lot of work together ... now you are able to see and deal with your feelings.' Sam, looking at the plan, said, 'Yeah, you helped me figure this all out.'

Because it was rather windy and Sam's friend was hovering in the distance, it was a bit of an awkward scene at first. We went through all the pictures we had taken, and Sam chose the pictures he wanted. We made sure I had copies of the pictures. Then we went over to my car and I got out the *Adidas* bag, telling him that this was something that would be good to hold the things from our work together. He was very excited as he eagerly put the box, snakes, map and picture into the bag. We then went into his house, and I explained to his sister that I would call the family around the end of September. As I left, Sam was in the living room with his nephew and friend. I said

won't be able to keep the good feelings inside you. Some days will go okay, but others might be hard. When things are not okay, you can think about you and me and our room where we did lots of things together.'

Sam said goodbye to the therapist and looked as if he felt that he had worked out some of his own sad feelings and did not want them reactivated. Perhaps he is avoiding his sadness, but the last few sessions were devoted to the termination of the therapy, and Sam seems to have been able to work through his feelings. Perhaps the beginnings of forgetting the therapist had also set in. Sam does not need to continue, at this time, with his snake family play, uncovering deeper phantasies. He now plays well with friends, and his play is the ordinary play of young children.

goodbye, and he continued to
play but looked at me. I felt
sad as I said good-bye, but
Sam seemed content and was
now playing quietly and
appropriately with his friend.

'The more integrated ego becomes capable of experiencing
guilt and feelings of responsibility, which it was unable to
face in infancy; object synthesis, and therefore a mitiga-
tion of hate by love, come about, and greed and envy,
which are corollaries of destructive impulses, lose in
power.' [Klein, 1957, p. 91]

REFERENCES

Balint, M. (1950). 'On the termination of analysis'. *International Journal of Psycho-Analysis, 31,* 196–199.

Bick, E. (1968). 'The experience of skin in early object relations'. *International Journal of Psycho-Analysis, 49,* 484–486.

Bion, W. R. (1962). *Learning from Experience.* New York: Basic Books.

Bronner, R. (1982). *Decision Making under Time Pressure. An Experimental Study of Stress Behavior in Business Management.* Toronto: Lexington Books, D. C. Heath and Company.

Cohen, J. (1964). *Behaviour in Uncertainty.* London: George Allen & Unwin.

Einhorn, H. J. (1982). 'Learning from experience and suboptimal rules in decision making'. In D. Kahneman, P. Slovic & A. Tversky (Eds.), *Judgement under Uncertainty: Heuristics and Bases* (pp. 268–83). Cambridge: Cambridge University Press.

Fitzgerald, D. (1983). 'Play and incidence of illness in four- and five-year-old children'. Unpublished Master's thesis. Toronto, Ontario: University of Toronto.

Freud, S. (1911b). 'Formulations on the two principles of mental functioning'. *Standard Edition, 12.*

Frank, L. K. (1952). *Understanding Children's Play.* New York: Columbia University Press.

Isaacs, S. (1948). 'The nature and function of phantasy'. *International Journal of Psycho-Analysis, 27,* 73–97.

Kahneman, D. (1979). *The Psychology of Irrationality.* Lecture at the Vancouver Institute, Vancouver, Canada, October 27.

Kahneman, D., Slovic, P. & Tversky, A. (Eds.) (1982). *Judgment under Uncertainty: Heuristics and Biases.* Cambridge: Cambridge University Press.

Kincaid, J. (1984). 'The long rain'. *The New Yorker,* July 30, pp. 28–36.

Klein, G. S. (1954). 'Need and regulation'. In M. R. Jones (Ed.), *Nebraska Symposium on Motivation.* Lincoln, Nebraska: University of Nebraska Press.

Klein, M. (1928). 'Early stages of Oedipus Conflict'. *International Journal of Psycho-Analysis, 9,* 167–180.

———. (1929a). 'Infantile anxiety-situations reflected in a work of art and the creative impulse'. *International Journal of Psycho-Analysis, 10,* 436–443.

———. (1929b). 'Personification in the play of children'. *International Journal of Psycho-Analysis, 10,* 193–204.

———. (1930). 'The importance of symbol-formation in the development of the ego'. *International Journal of Psycho-Analysis, 11,* 24–39.

——— (1931). 'A contribution to the theory of intellectual inhibition'. *International Journal of Psycho-Analysis, 12,* 206–218.

———. (1932). *The Psycho-analysis of Children.* London: Hogarth.

———. (1935). 'A contribution to the psychogenesis of manic-depressive states'. *International Journal of Psycho-Analysis, 16,* 145–174.

———. (1940). 'Mourning and its relation to manic-depressive states'. *International Journal of Psycho-Analysis, 21,* 125–153.

———. (1946). 'Notes on some schizoid mechanisms'. *International Journal of Psycho-Analysis, 27,* 99–110.

———. (1950a). *Contributions to Psycho-analysis.* London: Hogarth.

———. (1950b). 'On the criteria for the termination of an analysis'. *International Journal of Psycho-Analysis, 31,* 204.

———. (1952). 'The mutual influences in the development of ego and id'. *Psychoanalytic Study of the Child, 7,* 51–68.

————. (1957). *Envy and Gratitude: A Study of Unconscious Sources*. London: Tavistock.

————. (1958). 'On the development of mental functioning'. *International Journal of Psycho-Analysis, 39*, 84–90.

————. (1961). *Narrative of a Child Analysis: The Conduct of the Psycho-analysis of Children as Seen in the Treatment of a Ten-year-old Boy*. London: Hogarth.

————. (1964). 'The psychoanalytic play technique'. In M. R. Haworth (Ed.), *Child Psychotherapy, Practice and Theory* (pp. 119–121; 277–286). New York: Basic Books.

————. (1975). *Love, Guilt and Reparation and Other Works*. London: Hogarth and the Institute of Psycho-Analysis.

Klein, M., & Riviere, J. (1953). *Love, Hate and Reparation*. London: Hogarth and the Institute of Psycho-Analysis.

Lewis, M. (1974). 'Interpretation in child analysis'. *Journal of the American Academy of Child Psychiatry, 13*, 32–53.

Money-Kyrle, R. (1971). 'The aim of psychoanalysis'. *International Journal of Psycho-Analysis, 52*, 103–106.

Piaget, J. & Inhelder, B. (1958). *The Growth of Logical Thinking: From Childhood to Adolescence*. New York: Basic Books.

Reich, A. (1950). 'On the termination of analysis'. *International Journal of Psycho-Analysis, 31*, 179–183.

Santostefano, S. (1979). 'Cognition in personality and the treatment process: A psychoanalytic view'. *McLean Hospital Journal, 4*(3), 116–139.

Segal, H. (1957). 'Notes on symbol formation'. *International Journal of Psycho-Analysis, 38*, 391–397.

————. (1964). *Introduction to the Work of Melanie Klein*. London: Heinemann.

————. (1972). 'Melanie Klein's technique of child analysis'. In B. B. Wolman (Ed.), *Handbook of Child Psycho-analysis*. Toronto: Van Nostrand.

————. (1973). *Introduction to the Work of Melanie Klein*. London: Hogarth.

————. (1979). *Klein*. Sussex: Harvester.

Sheleff, L. S. (1981). *Generations Apart: Adult Hostility to Youth*. New York: McGraw-Hill.

Sroufe, L. A. (1981). 'Infant–caregiver attachment and patterns of adaptation in pre-school: The roots of maladaptation and competence'. Paper presented at the Minnesota Symposium, Minneapolis, Minnesota, October 22.

Tustin, F. (1972). *Autism and Childhood Psychosis*. London: Hogarth.

————. (1981). 'Autistic objects'. *International Review of Psycho-Analysis, 7,* 27–40.

Tversky, A., & Kahneman, D. (1974). 'Judgement under uncertainty: Heuristic and biases'. *Science, 185,* 1124–1131.

Van Dam, H., Heinicke, C. M., & Shane, M. (1975). 'On termination in child analysis'. *Psychoanalytic Study of the Child, 30,* 443–474.

Verburg, S. (1985). 'Melanie Klein's psycho-analytic theory applied to adolescence'. Unpublished paper. Toronto, Ontario: Ontario Institute for Studies in Education.

Watts, D. W. (1986). 'Creativity and catharsis: The psychoanalytic perspective of Melanie Klein'. Unpublished Master's thesis. Edmonton, Alberta: The University of Alberta.

Weininger, O. (1979). *Play and Education: The Basic Tool for Early Childhood Learning*. Springfield, Ill.: Charles C Thomas.

————. (1982). *Out of the Minds of Babes: The Strength of Children's Feelings*. Springfield, Ill.: Charles C Thomas.

————. (1984). *The Clinical Psychology of Melanie Klein*. Springfield, Ill.: Charles C Thomas.

————. (1987). 'But what is play, anyway?' *Teacher Education,* April, 30, 32–42.

Winnicott, D. W. (1965). *The Maturational Processes and the Facilitating Environment: Studies in the Theory of Emotional Development*. London: Hogarth.

————. (1968). 'The squiggle game'. *Voices: The Art and Science of Psychotherapy, 4*(1), 98–112.

————. (1968). 'Playing: Its theoretical status in the clinical situation'. *International Journal of Psycho-Analysis, 49,* 591–599.

————. (1975). *Through Paediatrics to Psycho-analysis*. London: Hogarth and the Institute of Psycho-Analysis.

————. (1986). *Home Is Where We Start From: Essays by a Psychoanalyst*. New York: Norton.

Wisdom, J. (1967). 'Testing an interpretation within a session'. *International Journal of Psycho-Analysis, 48,* 44–52.